GREAT ILLUSTRATED CLASSICS

Benjamin Franklin, 1783, by Joseph Siffred Duplessis

The Autobiography
and Other Writings of
BENJAMIN FRANKLIN

With selections from Poor Richard's Almanac
and papers relating to the Junto,
together with sixteen pages of
illustrations and commentary
by Frank Donovan

NEW YORK·DODD, MEAD & COMPANY

Contents

Illustrations

Chronological Table

1706. Benjamin Franklin born in Boston, January 17 (January 6, 1705, O. S.).

1714–16. After a year in Boston Grammar School is sent to learn writing and arithmetic in school kept by George Brownell, from which, after a year, he is taken to assist his father, Josiah, a candlemaker.

1717. James Franklin returns from England, following apprenticeship as printer.

1718. Benjamin is apprenticed to brother James.

1718–23. Period of assiduous reading in Anthony Collins, Shaftesbury, Locke, Addison and Steele, Cotton Mather, Bunyan, Defoe, etc.

1719. Writes and hawks ballads of the "Grub-Street" style, "The Lighthouse Tragedy" and "The Taking of Teach the Pirate."

1721–23. Aids brother in publishing the *New England Courant*. During 1722–23 in charge of paper after James is declared objectionable by the authorities.

1722. His *Dogood Papers* printed anonymously in the *New England Courant*.

1723. Breaks his indentures and leaves for New York; eventually arrives in Philadelphia.

1723–24. Employed by Samuel Keimer, a printer in Philadelphia.

1724. Visits Cotton Mather and Governor Burnet (New York). Meets James Ralph, Grub-Street pamphleteer, historian, and poet in the Thomson tradition. Patronized by Governor Keith. Leaves for London in November on the

London-Hope to buy type, etc., for printing shop to be
set up in his behalf by Keith. Upon arrival he and Ralph
take lodgings in Little Britain.

1725–26. Employed in Palmer's and Watts's printing houses.

1725. Publishes *A Dissertation on Liberty and Necessity, Pleas-
ure and Pain*. One result of this is acquaintance with
Lyons, author of *The Infallibility of Human Judgement*.
Through him Franklin meets Bernard Mandeville and
Dr. Henry Pemberton, who is preparing a third edition
of Sir Isaac Newton's *Principia*. Is received by Sir Hans
Sloane in Bloomsbury Square. Conceives of setting up
a swimming school in London.

1726. On July 21, with Mr. Denham, merchant and Quaker,
leaves for Philadelphia on the *Berkshire*. Between July 22
and October 11 writes *Journal of a Voyage from London
to Philadelphia*. Employed by Denham until latter's
death in 1727.

1727. Ill of pleurisy and composes his epitaph. After recovery
returns to Keimer's printing house. Forms his Junto club.
Employed in Burlington, New Jersey, on a job of printing paper money.

1728. Forms partnership with Hugh Meredith. Writes *Articles
of Belief and Acts of Religion*, and *Rules for a Club*—his
Junto club "Constitution."

1729. Buys Keimer's *The Universal Instructor in all Arts and
Sciences: and Pennsylvania Gazette* (begun December 24,
1728). Changes name to *Pennsylvania Gazette*, first issue,
XL, September 25–October 2, 1729. (Published by Franklin until 1748; by Franklin and David Hall from 1748
to 1766, after which Hall, until his death, and others
publish it until 1815.) Contributes to *American Weekly
Mercury* six papers of *The Busy-Body*, February 4, 1729–
March 27, 1729. Writes and prints *A Modest Enquiry
into the Nature and Necessity of a Paper Currency*.

1730. Appointed Public Printer by Pennsylvania Assembly (incumbent until 1764). Partnership with Meredith dis-

solved. Marries Deborah Read (Mrs. Rogers). Prints in *Pennsylvania Gazette* his *Dialogues between Philocles and Horatio.*

1731. First public venture: founds the Philadelphia Library Company, first subscription library in America. Begins partnership with Thomas Whitemarsh, Charleston, S. C. (1732, publishes *South Carolina Gazette.*) Begins Masonic affiliations: enters St. John's Lodge in February. William Franklin born.

1732. Begins *Poor Richard's Almanac* (for 1733). His son Francis Folger Franklin born (dies of smallpox in 1736). Elected junior grand warden of St. John's Lodge.

1733. Begins to study languages, French, Italian, Spanish, and continues Latin.

1734. Elected grand master of Masons of Pennsylvania for 1734–35. Reprints Anderson's *Constitutions,* first Masonic book printed in America.

1735. Writes and prints three pamphlets in defense of Rev. Mr. Hemphill. Prints, in the *Pennsylvania Gazette, Protection of Towns from Fire.* Secretary of St. John's Lodge until 1738. Writes introduction for and prints Logan's *Cato's Moral Distiches,* first classic translated and printed in the colonies.

1736. Establishes the Union Fire Company, the first in Philadelphia. Chosen clerk of the Pennsylvania General Assembly.

1737. Appointed postmaster of Philadelphia (incumbent until 1753); also justice of the peace.

1739. Beginning of friendship with the Reverend George Whitefield.

1740. Announces (November 13) *The General Magazine and Historical Chronicle.*

1741. Six issues (January–June) of this magazine (the first planned and the second issued in the colonies). With J. Parker establishes a printing house in New York.

1742. Invents Franklin open stove.

1743. *A Proposal for Promoting Useful Knowledge among the British Plantations in America* (circular letter sent to his friends).

1744. Establishes the American Philosophical Society and becomes its first secretary. Daughter Sarah born. *An Account of the New Invented Pennsylvania Fire-places.* Writes preface to and prints Logan's translation of Cicero's *Cato Major.* Reprints Richardson's *Pamela.* Father dies.

1746. *Reflections on Courtship and Marriage,* first of his writings reprinted in Europe. Peter Collinson sends a Leyden vial as gift to Library Company of Philadelphia. Having witnessed Dr. Spence's experiments, Franklin now begins his study of electricity.

1747. *Plain Truth: or, Serious Considerations on the Present State of the City of Philadelphia, and Province of Pennsylvania.*

1748. Withdraws from active service in his printing and bookselling house (Franklin and Hall). *Advice to a Young Tradesman.* Chosen member of the Council of Philadelphia.

1749. Appointed provincial grand master of colonial Masons (through 1750). *Proposals Relating to the Education of Youth in Pensilvania.* Founds academy which later develops into University of Pennsylvania. Reprints Bolingbroke's *On the Spirit of Patriotism.*

1750. Appointed as one of the commissioners to make treaty with the Indians at Carlisle.

1751. *Experiments and Observations on Electricity, made at Philadelphia in America, By Mr. Benjamin Franklin, and Communicated in several Letters to Mr. P. Collinson, of London, F. R. S.* (London.) *Idea of the English School, Sketch'd out for the Consideration of the Trustees of the Philadelphia Academy.* Member of Assembly from Philadelphia (incumbent until 1764). *Observations Concern-*

ing the Increase of Mankind, Peopling of Countries, Etc. Aids Dr. Bond to establish Pennsylvania hospital.

1752. Collinson edition of Franklin's works translated into French. Alleged kite experiment proves identity of lightning and electricity. Invents lightning rod; in September raises one over his own house. Mother dies. Aids in establishing the first fire insurance company in the colonies.

1753. Appointed (jointly with William Hunter) deputy postmaster general of North America Post, a position he held until 1774. Makes ten-weeks' survey of roads and post offices in northern colonies. Abbé Nollet attacks Franklin in *Lettres sur l'électricité* (Paris). Beccaria defends Franklin's electrical theories against Abbé Nollet. Receives M. A. from Harvard and from Yale. Receives Sir Godfrey Copley medal from the Royal Society.

1754. Proposes Albany Plan of Union. Second edition of *Experiments and Observations on Electricity*.

1755. *An Act for the Better Ordering and Regulating such as are Willing and Desirous to be United for Military Purposes within the Province of Pennsylvania. A Dialogue Between X, Y, & Z, concerning the Present State of Affairs in Pennsylvania.* Aids General Braddock in getting supplies and transportation.

1756. Supervises construction of forts in province of Pennsylvania (a task begun in 1755). Chosen Fellow of the Royal Society of London. Chosen a member of the London Society of Arts. *Plan for Settling the Western Colonies in North America, with Reasons for the Plan.* M. D'Alibard's edition of Franklin's electrical experiments (French translation). Receives M. A. from William and Mary College.

1757. Appointed colonial agent for Province of Pennsylvania (arrives in London July 26). *The Way to Wealth* (for 1758). (In 1889 Ford noted: "Seventy editions of it have been printed in English, fifty-six in French, eleven in

German, and nine in Italian. It has been translated into Spanish, Danish, Swedish, Welsh, Polish, Gaelic, Russian, Bohemian, Dutch, Catalan, Chinese, Modern Greek and Phonetic writing. It has been printed at least four hundred times, and is today as popular as ever.")

1759. Receives Doctor of Laws degree from University of St. Andrews. September 5, made burgess and guild-brother of Edinburgh. *An Historical Review of the Constitution and Government of Pennsylvania.* (See Ford, pp. 110–111, where he suggests that this "must still be treated as from Franklin's pen.") *Parable against Persecution.* Meets Adam Smith, Hume, Lord Kames, etc., in home of Dr. Robertson at Edinburgh. Makes many electrical experiments. Chosen honorary member of Philosophical Society of Edinburgh.

1760. Provincial grand master of Pennsylvania Masons. *The Interest of Great Britain Considered with Regard to Her Colonies.* Elected to society of Dr. Bray's Associates. (Corresponding member until 1790.) Successful close of his issue with the proprietaries.

1761. Tour of Holland and Belgium.

1762. Receives degree of Doctor of Civil Law from Oxford. Leaves England in August, arrives in America in October.

1763. Travels through colonies to inspect and regulate post offices.

1764. Appointed agent for Province of Pennsylvania to petition king for change from proprietary to royal government. Leaves for London in November. *Cool Thoughts on the Present Situation of Our Public Affairs. A Narrative of the Late Massacres in Lancaster County. Preface to the Speech of Joseph Galloway, Esq.*

1765. Presents Grenville with resolution of Pennsylvania Assembly against Stamp Act.

1766. Examined in House of Commons relative to repeal of the Stamp Act. *Physical and Meteorological Observations.* With Sir John Pringle visits Germany and Holland

(June–August). Chosen foreign member of the Royal Society of Sciences, Göttingen.

1767. With Sir John Pringle visits France (August 28–October 8). Meets French Physiocrats. *Remarks and Facts Concerning American Paper Money.*

1768. Preface to *Letters from a Farmer in Pennsylvania* (J. Dickinson). *A Scheme for a New Alphabet and Reformed Mode of Spelling. Causes of the American Discontents before 1768. Art of Swimming.* Appointed London agent for colony of Georgia.

1769. Visits France (July–August). Appointed New Jersey agent in London. Elected first president of the American Philosophical Society.

1770. Appointed London agent for Massachusetts Assembly.

1771. Begins *Autobiography* (from 1706 to 1731) while visiting the Bishop of St. Asaph at Twyford. Three-months' tour of Ireland and Scotland. Entertained by Hume and Lord Kames. Chosen corresponding member of Learned Society of Sciences, Rotterdam.

1772. Chosen foreign member of Royal Academy of Sciences of Paris.

1773. *Abridgement of the Book of Common Prayer* (with Sir Francis Dashwood). *Rules by Which a Great Empire May Be Reduced to a Small One.* M. Barbeu Dubourg's edition of *Œuvres de M. Franklin.* Sends Hutchinson-Oliver letters to Massachusetts.

1774. Examined by Wedderburn before the Privy Council (January 29) in regard to the Hutchinson-Oliver correspondence. Contributes notes to George Whately's second edition of *Principles of Trade.* Dismissed as deputy postmaster general of North America. Deborah Franklin dies December 19.

1775. First postmaster general under Confederation. Returns to America in May. Member of Philadelphia Committee of Safety. Chosen a delegate to second Continental Congress. *An Account of Negotiations in London for Effect-*

ing a Reconciliation between Great Britain and the American Colonies. Appointed member of Committee of Secret Correspondence.

1776. A commissioner to Canada. Presides over Constitutional Convention of Pennsylvania. Appointed one of committee to frame Declaration of Independence. In September appointed one of three commissioners from Congress to the French court. Leaves Philadelphia October 27; reaches Paris December 21.

1777. Elected member of Loge des Neuf Sœurs. Chosen associate member of Royal Medical Society of Paris.

1778. Assists at initiation of Voltaire in Loge des Neuf Sœurs. Officiates at Masonic funeral service of Voltaire. Signs commercial treaty and alliance for mutual defense with France. *The Ephemera.* Altercation with Arthur Lee.

1779. Minister plenipotentiary to French court. *The Whistle. Morals of Chess.* B. Vaughan edits Franklin's *Political, Miscellaneous, and Philosophical Pieces.*

1780. *Dialogue between Franklin and the Gout.*

1781. Chosen Fellow of American Academy of Arts and Sciences: elected foreign member of Academy of Sciences, Letters, and Arts of Padua, for work in natural philosophy and politics. Appointed one of the peace commissioners to negotiate treaty of peace between England and United States.

1782. Elected Venerable of Loge des Neuf Sœurs.

1783. Signs treaty with Sweden. Prints *Constitutions of the United States.* Elected Honorary Fellow of the Royal Society of Edinburgh. Interest in balloons. Signs the Treaty of Paris with John Jay and John Adams.

1784. With Le Roy, Bailly, Guillotin, Lavoisier, and others, investigates Mesmer's animal magnetism (results in numerous pamphlet reports). *Remarks Concerning the Savages of North America. Advice to Such as Would Remove to America.* Chosen member of Royal Academy of History, Madrid. At Passy resumes work on *Autobiography*, beyond 1731.

1785. *Maritime Observations. On the Causes and Cure of Smoky Chimneys.* Signs treaty of amity and commerce with Prussia. Resigns as minister to French Court, and returns to Philadelphia. President of Council of Pennsylvania (incumbent for three years). Associate member of Academy of Sciences, Literature, and Arts of Lyons. Councillor for Philadelphia until 1788. Member of Philadelphia Society for the Promotion of Agriculture, and Royal Society of Physics, National History and Arts of Orleans, and honorary member of Manchester Literary and Philosophical Society.

1786. Chosen corresponding member of Society of Agriculture of Milan.

1787. President of the Pennsylvania Society for the Abolition of Slavery (incumbent until death). Pennsylvania delegate to Constitutional Convention. Chosen honorary member of Medical Society of London. Aids in establishing the Society for Political Enquiry; elected its first president.

1788. At Philadelphia works on *Autobiography*, from 1731–1757.

1789. *Observations Relative to the Intentions of the Original Founders of the Academy in Philadelphia* and several papers in behalf of abolition of slavery. At Philadelphia resumes *Autobiography*, from 1757 to 1759. Chosen member of Imperial Academy of Sciences of St. Petersburg.

1790. Paper on the slave trade, *To the Editor of the Federal Gazette*, March 23. Dies, April 17, in Philadelphia.

I. COMMENTARY ON THE

Autobiography

OF BENJAMIN FRANKLIN

IN THE early days of August, 1771, sixty-five-year-old Benjamin Franklin was taking one of his rare vacations from smoky London at the country home of Bishop Jonathon Shipley. The surroundings were delightful and the Bishop's five daughters, aged eleven to twenty-three, pampered and petted the old man, whom they adored. But, holiday or no, Franklin could not be idle. In what the girls forever after called "Franklin's room" he started to write his memoirs; addressing them to his son so that his posterity might know of the means by which he had achieved success and perhaps find these means "suitable to their own situations, and therefore fit to be imitated."

When he left the Shipleys he took eighty-six closely written sheets back to London. They told the story of the first twenty-four years of his life; from his birth in Boston in 1706 as the son of a "poor but honest" candlemaker; through his childhood struggles to overcome the lack of a formal education; his adventures as a friendless and penniless youth in Philadelphia and London; the establishment of his printing business; the beginning of his financial success; and the start of his newspaper.

Thirteen years elapsed before Franklin had leisure to continue the story. Much had happened in the interim. He had returned to America to help draft a Declaration of Independence; he had journeyed to France to negotiate a treaty to gain the

1

wherewithal to fight a revolution; he had remained there to draft the peace treaty that ended the war. Then in 1784, at the urging of two friends, he returned to his memoirs. But they were no longer addressed to his son William. Father and son were not now speaking to each other, for William had taken the side of the King in the War of Independence. From this point on his memoirs were "intended for the public."

This brief second section, written at Passy in suburban Paris, told of his leadership in establishing the first public library in America and of his system to achieve moral perfection through a thirteen-week practice course, to be repeated four times a year. With this section his purpose changed. He was frankly giving advice on how to achieve a successful and useful life. Particularly he was writing to instruct young people in general rather than to present a private message to his son for use in the family.

When he left France in 1785 he wrote to a friend: "I propose on my voyage, to write the remaining notes of my life." But he did not get around to it. Instead he made further experiments in connection with charting the Gulf Stream—a subject in which he was the first scientist to take an interest—and, since he was at sea, he wrote his *Marine Observations,* a great catch-all of nautical information and conjectures. Arriving in Philadelphia, he was called back to public life as Governor of Pennsylvania. And he had to help draft a Constitution for the new United States.

So it was not until 1788 that he started on the final section of the memoirs. He hoped he would finish it that summer, but he was still at it the following year when he wrote, a few months before his death, that he was not "able to bear sitting to write" and had started to dictate to his grandson, which he wished he had done sooner. The final section takes the story to the year 1759. The *Autobiography* is not the full story of Franklin's life. It terminates abruptly in his fifty-third year, before he had become America's greatest diplomat.

The third section, written by a very old man, is even more moralistic than the second. It covers many of his public service projects; the development of *Poor Richard's Almanac;* some of his inventions; his retirement from business at the age of forty; the experiments through which he laid the foundation for the science of electricity; his brief expedition against the Indians as "General" Franklin; and takes him back to London as the agent for his colony.

This is the brief story of the only book that Benjamin Franklin wrote—the unfinished book that has been called "one of the great autobiographies of all literature and the first great American literary classic." Many erudite critics do not agree that the *Autobiography* should be classed with great literature. Perhaps, in terms of *belles-lettres,* they are right. But it is still fascinating successive generations of Americans almost two centuries after the old sage started to write it.

Certainly at the time it was written it was a new departure in eighteenth century prose. Franklin's clear, concise, simple style blew away the fog of verbosity and redundance that shrouded the meaning of much writing of that era. Franklin was, essentially, a journalist from the time he wrote his first editorials for his brother's newspaper at the age of sixteen. He believed that the most important quality of writing was clarity. Of his scientific writings he said, "If my hypothesis is not the truth itself, it is at least as naked for I have not, with some of our learned moderns, disguised my nonsense in Greek, clothed it in algebra and adorned it with fluxions."

And certainly Franklin—together with Rousseau, who wrote his life story at about the same time—established the essential form which every subsequent successful autobiography has followed. It was, then, a new literary format.

As a journalist, as a scientist, as a statesman, Franklin had the rare ability to view any subject with detachment, to consider it objectively. In the *Autobiography* he applied this ability to telling his own story. It may not be great literature but it is a great story and Franklin was a great storyteller. It is the first and biggest "success story" in the American tradition.

The manuscript of the *Autobiography* had a rather adventurous career before it got into print. Franklin brought the first section back to Philadelphia in 1775. When he went to France in 1776 he left it for safe-keeping, together with other papers, with his friend Joseph Galloway. The depository turned out to be not so safe. Galloway became a Tory, his house was ransacked by patriots and Franklin's papers dispersed. Apparently, Mrs. Galloway saved the manuscript of the *Autobiography* for it turned up ten years later in the possession of her executor, Abel James, who wrote to Franklin in Passy urging him to continue the memoirs and enclosing three pages of outline notes which Franklin had made before he started to write. These notes are reproduced in this volume ahead of the *Autobiography*.

Franklin asked the advice of another friend, Benjamin Vaughn, who wrote him also strongly urging that he continue. Franklin included these two letters between the first and second sections of his memoirs, possibly to justify his addressing the continuation to the public at large.

In 1789, seven pages before he had reached the end of the manuscript, he told his grandson, Benjamin Bache, who was acting as his secretary, to make two fair copies. He sent one of these to Vaughn in London and the other to Louis Le Veillard in Paris, asking their criticism and advice as to whether the work should be published. Before such criticism could reach him he was dead at the age of ninety.

His other grandson, William Temple Franklin, inherited his papers, including the original manuscript of the *Autobiography*. Temple was supposed to edit an edition of his grandfather's papers, but he was much more interested in land speculation than in his literary legacy. At some later time, on a visit to Paris, he saw the fair copy that had been sent to Le Veillard. The original, with its many changes, was difficult to read. Incredibly, Temple traded the original in his grandfather's hand for the copy. Finally, in 1818, Temple published the *Autobiography* in conjunction with the first edition of Franklin's works. It did not, of course, contain the last seven pages. Also, there were several minor differences between the original and the copy—

whether ordered by Franklin or made by Benjamin Bache is not known.

It was not until 1867 that John Bigelow, American Minister to France, tracked down the original manuscript and published it in 1868. The entire *Autobiography* was first printed in English seventy-eight years after Franklin's death. The original manuscript was subsequently acquired by Dodd, Mead & Company, the publishers of this book. From there it went to the library of E. Dwight Church and from there passed into the collection of Henry E. Huntington. It now reposes in the Huntington Library in San Marino, California.

The text used in this volume is generally the Bigelow text taken from the original, except that spelling, punctuation and capitalizing have been modernized for easier reading.

Franklin's Draft Scheme

of the *Autobiography*

MY WRITING. Mrs. Dogood's letters. Differences arise between my Brother and me (his temper and mine); their cause in general. His Newspaper. The Prosecution he suffered. My Examination. Vote of Assembly. His manner of evading it. Whereby I became free. My attempt to get employ with other Printers. He prevents me. Our frequent pleadings before our Father. The final Breach. My Inducements to quit Boston. Manner of coming to a Resolution. My leaving him and going to New York (return to eating flesh); thence to Pennsylvania. The journey, and its events on the Bay, at Amboy. The road. Meet with Dr. Brown. His character. His great work. At Burlington. The Good Woman. On the River. My Arrival at Philadelphia. First Meal and first Sleep. Money left. Employment. Lodging. First acquaintance with my afterward Wife. With J. Ralph. With Keimer. Their characters. Osborne. Watson. The Governor takes notice of me. The Occasion and Manner. His character. Offers to set me up. My return to Boston. Voyage and accidents. Reception. My Father dislikes the proposal. I return to New York and Philadelphia. Governor Burnet. J. Collins. The Money for Vernon. The Governor's Deceit. Collins not finding employment goes to Barbados much in my Debt. Ralph and I go to England. Disappointment of Governor's Letters. Colonel French his Friend. Cornwallis's Letters. Cabbin. Denham. Hamilton. Arrival in England. Get employment. Ralph not. He is an expense to me. Adventures in England. Write a Pamphlet and print 100. Schemes. Lyons. Dr. Pemberton. My diligence, and

6

yet poor through Ralph. My Landlady. Her character. Wygate. Wilkes. Cibber. Plays. Books I borrowed. Preachers I heard. Redmayne. At Watts's. Temperance. Ghost. Conduct and Influence among the Men. Persuaded by Mr. Denham to return with him to Philadelphia and be his clerk. Our voyage and arrival. My resolutions in Writing. My Sickness. His Death. Found D. R. married. Go to work again with Keimer. Terms. His ill-usage of me. My Resentment. Saying of Decow. My Friends at Burlington. Agreement with H. Meredith to set up in Partnership. Do so. Success with the Assembly. Hamilton's Friendship. Sewell's History. Gazette. Paper money. Webb. Writing Busy Body. Breintnal. Godfrey. His character. Suit against us. Offer of my Friends, Coleman and Grace. Continue the Business, and M. goes to Carolina. Pamphlet on Paper Money. Gazette from Keimer. Junto credit; its plan. Marry. Library erected. Manner of conducting the project. Its plan and utility. Children. Almanac. The use I made of it. Great industry. Constant study. Father's Remark and Advice upon Diligence. Carolina Partnership. Learn French and German. Journey to Boston after ten years. Affection of my Brother. His Death, and leaving me his Son. Art of Virtue. Occasion. City Watch amended. Post-office. Spotswood. Bradford's Behaviour. Clerk of Assembly. Lose one of my Sons. Project of subordinate Juntos. Write occasionally in the papers. Success in Business. Fire companies. Engines. Go again to Boston in 1743. See Dr. Spence[r]. Whitefield. My connection with him. His generosity to me. My returns. Church Differences. My part in them. Propose a College. Not then prosecuted. Propose and establish a Philosophical Society. War. Electricity. My first knowledge of it. Partnership with D. Hall, etc. Dispute in Assembly upon Defence. Project for it. Plain Truth. Its success. Ten thousand Men raised and disciplined. Lotteries. Battery built. New Castle. My influence in the Council. Colors, Devices, and Mottos. Ladies' Military Watch. Quakers chosen of the Common Council. Put in the commission of the peace. Logan fond of me. His Library. Appointed Postmaster-General. Chosen Assemblyman. Commissioner to treat with Indians at Carlisle

and at Easton. Project and establish Academy. Pamphlet on it.
Journey to Boston. At Albany. Plan of union of the colonies.
Copy of it. Remarks upon it. It fails, and how. Journey to Boston in 1754. Disputes about it in our Assembly. My part in
them. New Governor. Disputes with him. His character and
sayings to me. Chosen Alderman. Project of Hospital. My share
in it. Its success. Boxes. Made a Commissioner of the Treasury.
My commission to defend the frontier counties. Raise Men and
build Forts. Militia Law of my drawing. Made Colonel. Parade
of my Officers. Offence to Proprietor. Assistance to Boston Ambassadors. Journey with Shirley, etc. Meet with Braddock. Assistance to him. To the Officers of his Army. Furnish him with
Forage. His concessions to me and character of me. Success of
my Electrical Experiments. Medal sent me. Present Royal Society, and Speech of President. Denny's Arrival and Courtship
to me. His character. My service to the Army in the affair of
Quarters. Disputes about the Proprietor's Taxes continued.
Project for paving the City. I am sent to England. Negotiation
there. *Canada delenda est.* My Pamphlet. Its reception and effect. Projects drawn from me concerning the Conquest. Acquaintance made and their services to me—Mrs. S. M. Small,
Sir John P., Mr. Wood, Sargent Strahan, and others. Their characters. Doctorate from Edinburgh, St. Andrew's. Doctorate from
Oxford. Journey to Scotland. Lord Leicester. Mr. Prat. De Grey.
Jackson. State of Affairs in England. Delays. Eventful Journey
into Holland and Flanders. Agency from Maryland. Son's appointment. My Return. Allowance and thanks. Journey to Boston. John Penn, Governor. My conduct toward him. The Paxton
Murders. My Pamphlet. Rioters march to Philadelphia. Governor retires to my House. My conduct. Sent out to the In-
surgents. Turn them back. Little thanks. Disputes revived.
Resolutions against continuing under Proprietary Government.
Another Pamphlet. Cool thoughts. Sent again to England with
Petition. Negotiation there. Lord H. His character. Agencies
from New Jersey, Georgia, Massachusetts. Journey into Germany, 1766. Civilities received there. Göttingen Observations.

Ditto into France in 1767. Ditto in 1769. Entertainment there at the Academy. Introduced to the King and the Mesdames, Mad. Victoria and Mrs. Lamagnon. Duc de Chaulnes, M. Beaumont, Le Roy, D'Alibard, Nollet. See Journals. Holland. Reprint my papers and add many. Books presented to me from many authors. My Book translated into French. Lightning Kite. Various Discoveries. My manner of prosecuting that Study. King of Denmark invites me to dinner. Recollect my Father's Proverb. Stamp Act. My opposition to it. Recommendation of J. Hughes. Amendment of it. Examination in Parliament. Reputation it gave me. Caressed by Ministry. Charles Townsend's Act. Opposition to it. Stoves and chimney-plates. Armonica. Acquaintance with Ambassadors. Russian Intimation. Writing in newspapers. Glasses from Germany. Grant of Land in Nova Scotia. Sicknesses. Letters to America returned hither. The consequences. Insurance Office. My character. Costs me nothing to be civil to inferiors; a good deal to be submissive to superiors, etc., etc. Farce of Perpetual Motion. Writing for Jersey Assembly. Hutchinson's Letters. Temple. Suit in Chancery. Abuse before the Privy Council. Lord Hillsborough's character and conduct. Lord Dartmouth. Negotiation to prevent the War. Return to America. Bishop of St. Asaph. Congress. Assembly. Committee of Safety. Chevaux-de-frise. Sent to Boston, to the Camp. To Canada, to Lord Howe. To France. Treaty, etc.

Autobiography

Twyford, at the Bishop of St. Asaph's, 1771.

DEAR SON: I have ever had pleasure in obtaining any little anecdotes of my ancestors. You may remember the inquiries I made
among the remains of my relations when you were with me in
England, and the journey I undertook for that purpose. Imagining it may be equally agreeable to you to know the circumstances
of my life, many of which you are yet unacquainted with, and
expecting the enjoyment of a week's uninterrupted leisure in
my present country retirement, I sit down to write them for
you. To which I have besides some other inducements. Having
emerged from the poverty and obscurity in which I was born
and bred, to a state of affluence and some degree of reputation
in the world, and having gone so far through life with a considerable share of felicity, the conducing means I made use of,
which with the blessing of God so well succeeded, my posterity
may like to know, as they may find some of them suitable to
their own situations, and therefore fit to be imitated.

That felicity, when I reflected on it, has induced me sometimes to say, that were it offered to my choice, I should have no
objection to a repetition of the same life from its beginning,
only asking the advantages authors have in a second edition to
correct some faults of the first. So I might, besides correcting
the faults, change some sinister accidents and events of it for
others more favourable. But though this were denied, I should
still accept the offer. Since such a repetition is not to be expected, the next thing most like living one's life over again
seems to be a recollection of that life, and to make that recol-

lection as durable as possible by putting it down in writing. Hereby, too, I shall indulge the inclination so natural in old men, to be talking of themselves and their own past actions; and I shall indulge it without being tiresome to others, who, through respect to age, might conceive themselves obliged to give me a hearing, since this may be read or not as any one pleases. And, lastly (I may as well confess it, since my denial of it will be believed by nobody), perhaps I shall a good deal gratify my own *vanity*. Indeed, I scarce ever heard or saw the introductory words, *"Without vanity I may say,"* etc., but some vain thing immediately followed. Most people dislike vanity in others, whatever share they have of it themselves; but I give it fair quarter wherever I meet with it, being persuaded that it is often productive of good to the possessor, and to others that are within his sphere of action; and therefore, in many cases, it would not be altogether absurd if a man were to thank God for his vanity among the other comforts of life.

And now I speak of thanking God, I desire with all humility to acknowledge that I owe the mentioned happiness of my past life to His kind providence, which led me to the means I used and gave them success. My belief of this induces me to *hope*, though I must not *presume*, that the same goodness will still be exercised toward me, in continuing that happiness, or enabling me to bear a fatal reverse, which I may experience as others have done; the complexion of my future fortune being known to Him only in whose power it is to bless to us even our afflictions.

The notes one of my uncles (who had the same kind of curiosity in collecting family anecdotes) once put into my hands, furnished me with several particulars relating to our ancestors. From these notes I learned that the family had lived in the same village, Ecton, in Northamptonshire, for three hundred years, and how much longer he knew not (perhaps from the time when the name of Franklin, that before was the name of an order of people, was assumed by them as a surname when others took surnames all over the kingdom), on a freehold of about

thirty acres, aided by the smith's business, which had continued
in the family till his time, the eldest son being always bred to
that business; a custom which he and my father followed as to
their eldest sons. When I searched the registers at Ecton, I
found an account of their births, marriages and burials from
the year 1555 only, there being no registers kept in that parish
at any time preceding. By that register I perceived that I was the
youngest son of the youngest son for five generations back.
My grandfather Thomas, who was born in 1598, lived at Ecton
till he grew too old to follow business longer, when he went to
live with his son John, a dyer at Banbury, in Oxfordshire, with
whom my father served an apprenticeship. There my grandfather died and lies buried. We saw his gravestone in 1758. His
eldest son Thomas lived in the house at Ecton, and left it with
the land to his only child, a daughter, who, with her husband,
one Fisher, of Wellingborough, sold it to Mr. Isted, now lord
of the manor there. My grandfather had four sons that grew up,
viz.: Thomas, John, Benjamin and Josiah. I will give you what
account I can of them, at this distance from my papers, and if
these are not lost in my absence, you will among them find
many more particulars.

Thomas was bred a smith under his father; but, being ingenious, and encouraged in learning (as all my brothers were)
by an Esquire Palmer, then the principal gentleman in that
parish, he qualified himself for the business of scrivener; became a considerable man in the county; was a chief mover of all
public-spirited undertakings for the county or town of North-
ampton, and his own village, of which many instances were
related of him; and much taken notice of and patronized by the
then Lord Halifax. He died in 1702, January 6, old style, just
four years to a day before I was born [January 17, 1706, New
Style]. The account we received of his life and character from
some old people at Ecton, I remember, struck you as something
extraordinary, from its similarity to what you knew of mine.
"Had he died on the same day," you said, "one might have supposed a transmigration."

John was bred a dyer, I believe of woolens. Benjamin was bred a silk dyer, serving an apprenticeship at London. He was an ingenious man. I remember him well, for when I was a boy he came over to my father in Boston, and lived in the house with us some years. He lived to a great age. His grandson, Samuel Franklin, now lives in Boston. He left behind him two quarto volumes, MS., of his own poetry, consisting of little occasional pieces addressed to his friends and relations, of which the following, sent to me, is a specimen. He had formed a short-hand of his own, which he taught me, but, never practising it, I have now forgot it. I was named after this uncle, there being a particular affection between him and my father. He was very pious, a great attender of sermons of the best preachers, which he took down in his short-hand, and had with him many volumes of them. He was also much of a politician; too much, perhaps, for his station. There fell lately into my hands, in London, a collection he had made of all the principal pamphlets relating to public affairs, from 1641 to 1717; many of the volumes are wanting as appears by the numbering, but there still remain eight volumes in folio, and twenty-four in quarto and in octavo. A dealer in old books met with them, and knowing me by my sometimes buying of him, he brought them to me. It seems my uncle must have left them here when he went to America, which was above fifty years since. There are many of his notes in the margins.

This obscure family of ours was early in the Reformation, and continued Protestants through the reign of Queen Mary, when they were sometimes in danger of trouble on account of their zeal against popery. They had got an English Bible, and to conceal and secure it, it was fastened open with tapes under and within the cover of a joint-stool. When my great-great-grandfather read it to his family, he turned up the joint-stool upon his knees, turning over the leaves then under the tapes. One of the children stood at the door to give notice if he saw the apparitor coming, who was an officer of the spiritual court. In that case the stool was turned down again upon its feet, when the Bible remained concealed under it as before. This ancedote I had from my uncle Benjamin. The family continued all of the Church of England till about the end of Charles the Second's reign, when some of the ministers that had been outed for non-conformity holding conventicles in Northamptonshire, Benjamin and Josiah adhered to them, and so continued all their lives: the rest of the family remained with the Episcopal Church.

Josiah, my father, married young, and carried his wife with three children into New England, about 1682. The conventicles having been forbidden by law, and frequently disturbed, induced some considerable men of his acquaintance to remove to that country, and he was prevailed with to accompany them thither, where they expected to enjoy their mode of religion with freedom. By the same wife he had four children more born there, and by a second wife ten more, in all seventeen; of which I remember thirteen sitting at one time at his table, who all grew up to be men and women, and married; I was the youngest son, and the youngest child but two, and was born in Boston, New England. My mother, the second wife, was Abiah Folger, daughter of Peter Folger, one of the first settlers of New England, of whom honorable mention is made by Cotton Mather, in his church history of that country, entitled Magnalia Christi Americana, as "a godly, learned Englishman," if I remember the words rightly. I have heard that he wrote sundry small occasional pieces, but only one of them was printed, which I saw now many years since. It was written in 1675, in the home-spun verse of that time and people, and addressed to those then concerned in the government there. It was in favor of liberty of conscience, and in behalf of the Baptists, Quakers, and other sectaries that had been under persecution, ascribing the Indian wars, and other distresses that had befallen the country, to that persecution, as so many judgments of God to punish so heinous an offense, and exhorting a repeal of those uncharitable laws. The whole appeared to me as written with a good deal of decent plainness and manly freedom. The six concluding lines I remember, though I have forgotten the two first of the stanza;

The birthplace of Franklin in Boston on Milk Street, between Marlborough and Hawley Streets. The house burned down in 1810.

but the purport of them was, that his censures proceeded from good-will, and, therefore, he would be known to be the author.

> Because to be a libeller (says he)
> I hate it with my heart;
> From Sherburne town, where now I dwell
> My name I do put here;
> Without offense your real friend,
> It is Peter Folgier.

My elder brothers were all put apprentices to different trades. I was put to the grammar-school at eight years of age, my father intending to devote me, as the tithe of his sons, to the service of the Church. My early readiness in learning to read (which must have been very early, as I do not remember when I could not read), and the opinion of all his friends, that I should certainly make a good scholar, encouraged him in this purpose of his. My uncle Benjamin, too, approved of it, and proposed to give me all his shorthand volumes of sermons, I suppose as a stock to set up with, if I would learn his [shorthand] character. I continued, however, at the grammar-school not quite one year, though in that time I had risen gradually from the middle of the class of that year to be the head of it, and farther was removed into the next class above it, in order to go with that into the third at the end of the year. But my father, in the meantime, from a view of the expense of a college education, which having so large a family he could not well afford, and the mean living many so educated were afterwards able to obtain—reasons that he gave his friends in my hearing—altered his first intention, took me from the grammar-school, and sent me to a school for writing and arithmetic, kept by a then famous man, Mr. George Brownell, very successful in his profession generally, and that by mild, encouraging methods. Under him I acquired fair writing pretty soon, but I failed in the arithmetic, and made no progress in it. At ten years old I was taken home to assist my father in his business, which was that of a tallow-chandler and sope-boiler; a business he was not bred to, but had assumed on his arrival in New England, and on finding his dying trade would not maintain his family, being in little request. Accordingly, I was employed in cutting wick for the candles, filling the dipping mold and the molds for cast candles, attending the shop, going of errands, etc.

I disliked the trade, and had a strong inclination for the sea, but my father declared against it; however, living near the water, I was much in and about it, learnt early to swim well, and to manage boats; and when in a boat or canoe with other boys, I was commonly allowed to govern, especially in any case of difficulty; and upon other occasions I was generally a leader among the boys, and sometimes led them into scrapes, of which I will mention one instance, as it shows an early projecting public spirit, tho' not then justly conducted.

There was a salt-marsh that bounded part of the mill-pond, on the edge of which, at high water, we used to stand to fish for minnows. By much tramping, we had made it a mere quagmire. My proposal was to build a wharff there fit for us to stand upon, and I showed my comrades a large heap of stones, which were intended for a new house near the marsh, and which would very well suit our purpose. Accordingly, in the evening, when the workmen were gone, I assembled a number of my play-fellows, and working with them diligently like so many emmets, sometimes two or three to a stone, we brought them all away and built our little wharff. The next morning the workmen were surprised at missing the stones, which were found in our wharff. Inquiry was made after the removers; we were discovered and complained of; several of us were corrected by our fathers; and, though I pleaded the usefulness of the work, mine convinced me that nothing was useful which was not honest.

I think you may like to know something of his person and character. He had an excellent constitution of body, was of middle stature, but well set, and very strong; he was ingenious, could draw prettily, was skilled a little in music, and had a clear pleasing voice, so that when he played psalm tunes on his violin and sung withal, as he sometimes did in an evening after the business of the day was over, it was extremely agreeable to hear. He had a mechanical genius too, and, on occasion, was very handy in the use of other tradesmen's tools; but his great excellence lay in a sound understanding and solid judgment in prudential matters, both in private and publick affairs. In the latter, indeed, he was never employed, the numerous family he had to educate and the straitness of his circumstances keeping him close to his trade; but I remember well his being frequently visited by leading people, who consulted him for his opinion in affairs of the town or of the church he belonged to, and showed a good deal of respect for his judgment and advice: he was also much consulted by private persons about their affairs when any difficulty occurred, and frequently chosen an arbitrator between contending parties. At his table he liked to have, as often as he could, some sensible friend or neighbor to converse with, and always took care to start some ingenious or useful topic for discourse, which might tend to improve the minds of his children. By this means he turned our attention to what was good, just, and prudent in the conduct of life; and little or no notice was ever taken of what related to the victuals on the table, whether it was well or ill dressed, in or out of season, of good or bad flavor, preferable or inferior to this or that other thing of the kind, so that I was bro't up in such a perfect inattention to those matters as to be quite indifferent what kind of food was set before me, and so unobservant of it, that to this day if I am asked I can scarce tell a few hours after dinner what I dined upon. This has been a convenience to me in travelling, where my companions have been sometimes very unhappy for want of a suitable gratification of their more delicate, because better instructed, tastes and appetites.

My mother had likewise an excellent constitution: she suckled all her ten children. I never knew either my father or mother to have any sickness but that of which they dy'd, he at 89, and she at 85 years of age. They lie buried together at Boston, where I some years since placed a marble over their grave, with this inscription:

JOSIAH FRANKLIN,
and
ABIAH his wife,
lie here interred.
They lived lovingly together in wedlock
fifty-five years.
Without an estate, or any gainful employment,
By constant labor and industry,
with God's blessing,
They maintained a large family
comfortably,
and brought up thirteen children
and seven grandchildren
reputably.
From this instance, reader,
Be encouraged to diligence in thy calling,
And distrust not Providence.
He was a pious and prudent man;
She, a discreet and virtuous woman.
Their youngest son,
In filial regard to their memory,
Places this stone.
J. F. born 1655, died 1744, Ætat 89.
A. F. born 1667, died 1752, — 85.

By my rambling digressions I perceive myself to be grown old. I us'd to write more methodically. But one does not dress for private company as for a publick ball. 'Tis perhaps only negligence.

To return: I continued thus employed in my father's business for two years, that is, till I was twelve years old; and my brother John, who was bred to that business, having left my father, married, and set up for himself at Rhode Island, there was all appearance that I was destined to supply his place, and become a tallow-chandler. But my dislike to the trade continuing, my father was under apprehensions that if he did not find one for me more agreeable, I should break away and get to sea, as his son Josiah had done, to his great vexation. He therefore sometimes took me to walk with him, and see joiners, bricklayers, turners, braziers, etc., at their work, that he might observe my inclination, and endeavor to fix it on some trade or other on land. It has ever since been a pleasure to me to see good workmen handle their tools; and it has been useful to me, having learnt so much by it as to be able to do little jobs myself in my house when a workman could not readily be got, and to construct little machines for my experiments, while the intention of making the experiment was fresh and warm in my mind. My father at last fixed upon the cutler's trade, and my uncle Benjamin's son Samuel, who was bred to that business in London, being about that time established in Boston, I was sent to be with him some time on liking. But his expectations of a fee with me displeasing my father, I was taken home again.

From a child I was fond of reading, and all the little money that came into my hands was ever laid out in books. Pleased with the Pilgrim's Progress, my first collection was of John Bunyan's works in separate little volumes. I afterward sold them to enable me to buy R. Burton's Historical Collections; they were small chapmen's books, and cheap, 40 or 50 in all. My father's little library consisted chiefly of books in polemic divinity, most of which I read, and have since often regretted that, at a time when I had such a thirst for knowledge, more proper books had not fallen in my way, since it was now resolved I should not be a clergyman. Plutarch's Lives there was in which I read abundantly, and I still think that time spent to great advantage. There was also a book of De Foe's, called an Essay on Projects, and another of Dr. Mather's, called Essays to do Good, which perhaps gave me a turn of thinking that had an influence on some of the principal future events of my life.

This bookish inclination at length determined my father to make me a printer, though he had already one son (James) of that profession. In 1717 my brother James returned from England with a press and letters to set up his business in Boston. I liked it much better than that of my father, but still had a hankering for the sea. To prevent the apprehended effect of such an inclination, my father was impatient to have me bound to my brother. I stood out some time, but at last was persuaded, and signed the indentures when I was yet but twelve years old. I was to serve as an apprentice till I was twenty-one years of age, only I was to be allowed a journeyman's wages during the last year. In a little time I made great proficiency in the business, and became a useful hand to my brother. I now had access to better books. An acquaintance with the apprentices of booksellers enabled me sometimes to borrow a small one, which I was careful to return soon and clean. Often I sat up in my room reading the greatest part of the night, when the book was borrowed in the evening and to be returned early in the morning, lest it should be missed or wanted.

And after some time an ingenious tradesman, Mr. Matthew Adams, who had a pretty collection of books, and who frequented our printing-house, took notice of me, invited me to his library, and very kindly lent me such books as I chose to read. I now took a fancy to poetry, and made some little pieces; my brother, thinking it might turn to account, encouraged me, and put me on composing occasional ballads. One was called *The Lighthouse Tragedy*, and contained an account of the drowning of Captain Worthilake, with his two daughters: the other was a sailor's song, on the taking of *Teach* (or Blackbeard) the pirate. They were wretched stuff, in the Grub-street-ballad style; and when they were printed he sent me about the town to sell them. The first sold wonderfully, the event being recent, having made a great noise. This flattered my vanity; but my father discouraged me by ridiculing my performances, and telling me verse-makers were generally beggars. So I escaped being a poet, most probably a very bad one; but as prose writing has been of great use to me in the course of my life, and was a principal means of my advancement, I shall tell you how, in such a situation, I acquired what little ability I have in that way.

There was another bookish lad in the town, John Collins by name, with whom I was intimately acquainted. We sometimes disputed, and very fond we were of argument, and very desirous of confuting one another, which disputatious turn, by the way, is apt to become a very bad habit, making people often extremely disagreeable in company by the contradiction that is necessary to bring it into practice; and thence, besides souring and spoiling the conversation, is productive of disgusts and, perhaps enmities where you may have occasion for friendship. I had caught it by reading my father's books of disputes about religion. Persons of good sense, I have since observed, seldom fall into it, except lawyers, university men, and men of all sorts that have been bred at Edinborough.

A question was once, somehow or other, started between Collins and me, of the propriety of educating the female sex in learning, and their abilities for study. He was of opinion that it was improper, and that they were naturally unequal to it. I took the contrary side, perhaps a little for dispute's sake. He was naturally more eloquent, had a ready plenty of words; and sometimes, as I thought, bore me down more by his fluency than by the strength of his reasons. As we parted without settling the point, and were not to see one another again for some time, I sat down to put my arguments in writing, which I copied fair and sent to him. He answered, and I replied. Three or four letters of a side had passed, when my father happened to find my papers and read them. Without entering into the discussion, he took occasion to talk to me about the manner of my writing; observed that, though I had the advantage of my antagonist in correct spelling and pointing (which I ow'd to the printing-house), I fell far short in elegance of expression, in method and in perspicuity, of which he convinced me by several instances. I saw the justice of his remarks, and thence grew more attentive to the manner in writing, and determined to endeavor at improvement.

About this time I met with an odd volume of the *Spectator*. It was the third. I had never before seen any of them. I bought it, read it over and over, and was much delighted with it. I thought the writing excellent, and wished, if possible, to imitate it. With this view I took some of the papers, and, making short hints of the sentiment in each sentence, laid them by a few days, and then, without looking at the book, try'd to compleat the papers again, by expressing each hinted sentiment at length, and as fully as it had been expressed before, in any suitable words that should come to hand. Then I compared my *Spectator* with the original, discovered some of my faults, and corrected them. But I found I wanted a stock of words, or a readiness in recollecting and using them, which I thought I should have acquired before that time if I had gone on making verses; since the continual occasion for words of the same import, but of different length, to suit the measure, or of different sound for the rhyme, would have laid me under a constant necessity of searching for variety, and also have tended to fix that variety in my mind, and make me master of it. Therefore I took some of the tales and turned them into verse; and, after a time, when I had pretty well forgotten the prose, turned them back again. I also sometimes jumbled my collections of hints into confusion, and after some weeks endeavored to reduce them into the best order, before I began to form the full sentences and compleat the paper. This was to teach me method in the arrangement of thoughts. By comparing my work afterwards with the original, I discovered many faults and amended them; but I sometimes had the pleasure of fancying that, in certain particulars of small import, I had been lucky enough to improve the method or the language, and this encouraged me to think I might possibly in time come to be a tolerable English writer, of which I was extreamly ambitious. My time for these exercises and for reading was at night, after work or before it began in the morning, or on Sundays, when I contrived to be in the printing-house alone, evading as much as I could the common attendance on public worship which my father used to exact on me when I was under his care, and which indeed I still thought a duty, though I could not, as it seemed to me, afford time to practise it.

When about 16 years of age I happened to meet with a book, written by one Tryon, recommending a vegetable diet. I determined to go into it. My brother, being yet unmarried, did not keep house, but boarded himself and his apprentices in another family. My refusing to eat flesh occasioned an inconveniency, and I was frequently chid for my singularity. I made myself acquainted with Tryon's manner of preparing some of his dishes, such as boiling potatoes or rice, making hasty pudding, and a few others, and then proposed to my brother, that if he would give me, weekly, half the money he paid for my board, I would board myself. He instantly agreed to it, and I presently found that I could save half what he paid me. This was an additional fund for buying books. But I had another advantage in it. My brother and the rest going from the printing-house to their meals, I remained there alone, and, despatching presently my light repast, which often was no more than a bisket or a slice of bread, a handful of raisins or a tart from the pastry-cook's, and a glass of water, had the rest of the time till their return for study, in which I made the greater progress, from that greater clearness of head and quicker apprehension which usually attend temperance in eating and drinking.

And now it was that, being on some occasion made asham'd of my ignorance in figures, which I had twiced failed in learning when at school, I took Cocker's book of Arithmetick, and went through the whole by myself with great ease. I also read Seller's and Shermy's books of Navigation, and became acquainted with the little geometry they contain; but never proceeded far in that science. And I read about this time Locke *on Human Understanding,* and the *Art of Thinking,* by Messrs. du Port Royal.

While I was intent on improving my language, I met with an English grammar (I think it was Greenwood's), at the end of which there were two little sketches of the arts of rhetoric and logic, the latter finishing with a specimen of a dispute in the Socratic method; and soon after I procur'd Xenophon's Memorable Things of Socrates, wherein there are many instances of the same method. I was charm'd with it, adopted it, dropt my abrupt contradiction and positive argumentation, and put on the humble inquirer and doubter. And being then, from reading Shaftesbury and Collins, become a real doubter in many points of our religious doctrine, I found this method safest for myself and very embarrassing to those against whom I used it; therefore I took a delight in it, practis'd it continually, and grew very artful and expert in drawing people, even of superior knowledge, into concessions, the consequences of which they did not foresee, entangling them in difficulties out of which they could not extricate themselves, and so obtaining victories that neither myself nor my cause always deserved. I continu'd this method some few years, but gradually left it, retaining only the habit of expressing myself in terms of modest diffidence; never using, when I advanced anything that may possibly be disputed, the words *certainly, undoubtedly,* or any others that give the air of positiveness to an opinion; but rather say, I conceive or apprehend a thing to be so and so; it appears to me, or *I should think it so or so,* for such and such reasons; or *I imagine it to be so;* or *it is so, if I am not mistaken.* This habit, I believe, has been of great advantage to me when I have had occasion to inculcate my opinions, and persuade me into measures that I have been from time to time engag'd in promoting; and, as the chief ends of conversation are to *inform* or to be *informed,* to *please* or to *persuade,* I wish well-meaning, sensible men would not lessen their power of doing good by a positive, assuming manner, that seldom fails to disgust, tends to create opposition, and to defeat every one of those purposes for which speech was given to us, to wit, giving or receiving information or pleasure. For, if you would inform, a positive and dogmatical manner in advancing your sentiments may provoke contradiction and prevent a candid attention. If you wish information and improvement from the knowledge of others, and yet at the same time express yourself as firmly fix'd in your present opinions, modest, sensible men, who do not love disputation, will probably leave you undisturbed in the possession of your error. And by such a manner, you can seldom hope to recommend yourself in *pleasing* your hearers, or to persuade those whose concurrence you desire. Pope says, judiciously:

Men should be taught as if you taught them not,
And things unknown propos'd as things forgot;

farther recommending to us

To speak, tho' sure, with seeming diffidence.

And he might have coupled with this line that which he has coupled with another, I think, less properly,

For want of modesty is want of sense.

If you ask, Why less properly? I must repeat the lines,

Immodest words admit of no defense.
For want of modesty is want of sense.

Now, is not *want of sense* (where a man is so unfortunate as to want it) some apology for his *want of modesty?* and would not the lines stand more justly thus?

Immodest words admit *but* this defense,
That want of modesty is want of sense.

This, however, I should submit to better judgments.

My brother had, in 1720 or 1721, begun to print a newspaper. It was the second that appeared in America, and was called the New England Courant. The only one before it was the Boston News-Letter. I remember his being dissuaded by some of his friends from the undertaking, as not likely to succeed, one newspaper being, in their judgment, enough for America. At this time (1771) there are not less than five-and-twenty. He went on, however, with the undertaking, and after having worked in composing the types and printing off the sheets, I was employed to carry the papers thro' the streets to the customers.

He had some ingenious men among his friends, who amus'd themselves by writing little pieces for this paper, which gain'd it credit and made it more in demand, and these gentlemen often visited us. Hearing their conversations, and their accounts of the approbation their papers were received with, I was excited to try my hand among them; but, being still a boy, and suspecting that my brother would object to printing anything of mine in his paper if he knew it to be mine, I contrived to disguise my hand, and, writing an anonymous paper, I put it in at night under the door of the printing-house. It was found in the morning, and communicated to his writing friends when they call'd in as usual. They read it, commented on it in my hearing, and I had the exquisite pleasure of finding it met with their approbation, and that, in their different guesses at the author, none were named but men of some character among us for learning and ingenuity. I suppose now that I was rather lucky in my judges, and that perhaps they were not really so very good ones as I then esteem'd them.

Encourag'd, however, by this, I wrote and convey'd in the same way to the press several more papers which were equally approv'd; and I kept my secret till my small fund of sense for such performances was pretty well exhausted, and then I discovered it, when I began to be considered, a little more by my brother's acquaintance, and in a manner that did not quite please him, as he thought, probably with reason, that it tended to make me too vain. And, perhaps, this might be one occasion of the differences that we began to have about this time. Though a brother, he considered himself as my master, and me as his apprentice, and, accordingly, expected the same services from me as he would from another, while I thought he demean'd me too much in some he requir'd of me, who from a brother expected more indulgence. Our disputes were often brought before our father, and I fancy I was either generally in the right, or else a better pleader, because the judgment was generally in my favor. But my brother was passionate, and had often beaten me, which I took extreamly amiss; and, thinking my apprenticeship very tedious, I was continually wishing for some opportunity of shortening it, which at length offered in a manner unexpected. [I fancy his harsh and tyrannical treatment of me might be a means of impressing me with that aversion to arbitrary power that has stuck to me through my whole life.]

One of the pieces in our newspaper on some political point, which I have now forgotten, gave offense to the Assembly. He was taken up, censur'd, and imprison'd for a month, by the speaker's warrant, I suppose, because he would not discover his author. I too was taken up and examin'd before the council; but, tho' I did not give them any satisfaction, they content'd themselves with admonishing me, and dismissed me, considering me, perhaps, as an apprentice, who was bound to keep his master's secrets.

During my brother's confinement, which I resented a good deal, notwithstanding our private differences, I had the management of the paper; and I made bold to give our rulers some rubs in it, which my brother took very kindly, while others began to consider me in an unfavorable light, as a young genius that had a turn for libelling and satyr. My brother's discharge was accompany'd with an order of the House (a very odd one), that *"James Franklin should no longer print the paper called the New England Courant."*

There was a consultation held in our printing-house among his friends, what he should do in this case. Some proposed to evade the order by changing the name of the paper; but my brother, seeing inconveniences in that, it was finally concluded on as a better way, to let it be printed for the future under the name of BENJAMIN FRANKLIN; and to avoid the censure of the Assembly, that might fall on him as still printing it by his apprentice, the contrivance was that my old indenture should be return'd to me, with a full discharge on the back of it, to be shown on occasion, but to secure to him the benefit of my service, I was to sign new indentures for the remainder of the term, which were to be kept private. A very flimsy scheme it was; however, it was immediately executed, and the paper went on accordingly, under my name for several months.

At length, a fresh difference arising between my brother and me, I took upon me to assert my freedom, presuming that he would not venture to produce the new indentures. It was not fair in me to take this advantage, and this I therefore reckon one of the first errata of my life; but the unfairness of it weighed little with me, when under the impressions of resent-

ment for the blows his passion too often urged him to bestow
upon me, though he was otherwise not an ill-natur'd man: perhaps I was too saucy and provoking.

When he found I would leave him, he took care to prevent
my getting employment in any other printing-house of the
town, by going round and speaking to every master, who accordingly refus'd to give me work. I then thought of going to New
York, as the nearest place where there was a printer; and I was
rather inclin'd to leave Boston when I reflected that I had already made myself a little obnoxious to the governing party,
and, from the arbitrary proceedings of the Assembly in my
brother's case, it was likely I might, if I stay'd, soon bring myself into scrapes; and farther, that my indiscrete disputations
about religion began to make me pointed at with horror by
good people as an infidel or atheist. I determin'd on the point,
but my father now siding with my brother, I was sensible that,
if I attempted to go openly, means would be used to prevent
me. My friend Collins, therefore, undertook to manage a little
for me. He agreed with the captain of a New York sloop for my
passage, under the notion of my being a young acquaintance of
his, that had got a naughty girl with child, whose friends would
compel me to marry her, and therefore I could not appear or
come away publicly. So I sold some of my books to raise a little
money, was taken on board privately, and as we had a fair wind,
in three days I found myself in New York, near 300 miles from
home, a boy of but 17, without the least recommendation to, or
knowledge of any person in the place, and with very little
money in my pocket.

My inclinations for the sea were by this time worne out, or I
might now have gratify'd them. But, having a trade, and supposing myself a pretty good workman, I offer'd my service to
the printer in the place, old Mr. William Bradford, who had
been the first printer in Pennsylvania, but removed from thence
upon the quarrel of George Keith. He could give me no employment, having little to do, and help enough already; but
says he, "My son at Philadelphia has lately lost his principal

hand, Aquila Rose, by death; if you go thither, I believe he may employ you." Philadelphia was a hundred miles further; I set out, however, in a boat for Amboy, leaving my chest and things to follow me round by sea.

In crossing the bay, we met with a squall that tore our rotten sails to pieces, prevented our getting into the Kill [VanKull], and drove us upon Long Island. In our way, a drunken Dutchman, who was a passenger too, fell overboard; when he was sinking, I reached through the water to his shock pate, and drew him up, so that we got him in again. His ducking sobered him a little, and he went to sleep, taking first out of his pocket a book, which he desir'd I would dry for him. It proved to be my old favorite author, Bunyan's Pilgrim's Progress, in Dutch, finely printed on good paper, with copper cuts, a dress better than I had ever seen it wear in its own language. I have since found that it has been translated into most of the languages of Europe, and suppose it has been more generally read than any other book, except perhaps the Bible. Honest John was the first that I know of who mix'd narration and dialogue; a method of writing very engaging to the reader, who in the most interesting parts finds himself, as it were, brought into the company and present at the discourse. De Foe in his Cruso, his Moll Flanders, Religious Courtship, Family Instructor, and other pieces, has imitated it with success; and Richardson has done the same in his Pamela, etc.

When we drew near the island, we found it was at a place where there could be no landing, there being a great surff on the stony beach. So we dropt anchor, and swung round towards the shore. Some people came down to the water edge and hallow'd to us, as we did to them; but the wind was so high, and the surff so loud, that we could not hear so as to understand each other. There were canoes on the shore, and we made signs, and hallow'd that they should fetch us; but they either did not understand us, or thought it impracticable, so they went away, and night coming on, we had no remedy but to wait till the wind should abate; and, in the mean time, the boatman and I concluded to sleep, if we could; and so crowded into the scuttle, with the Dutchman, who was still wet, and the spray beating over the head of our boat, leak'd thro' to us, so that we were soon almost as wet as he. In this manner we lay all night, with very little rest; but, the wind abating the next day, we made a shift to reach Amboy before night, having been thirty hours on the water, without victuals, or any drink but a bottle of filthy rum, and the water we sail'd on being salt.

In the evening I found myself very feverish, and went into bed; but, having read somewhere that cold water drank plentifully was good for a fever, I follow'd the prescription, sweat plentiful most of the night, my fever left me, and in the morning, crossing the ferry, I proceeded on my journey on foot, having fifty miles to Burlington, where I was told I should find boats that would carry me the rest of the way to Philadelphia.

It rained very hard all the day; I was thoroughly soak'd, and by noon a good deal tired; so I stopt at a poor inn, where I staid all night, beginning now to wish that I had never left home. I cut so miserable a figure, too, that I found, by the questions ask'd me, I was suspected to be some run-away servant, and in danger of being taken up on that suspicion. However, I proceeded the next day, and got in the evening to an inn, within eight or ten miles of Burlington, kept by one Dr. Brown. He entered into conversation with me while I took some refreshment, and, finding I had read a little, became very sociable and friendly. Our acquaintance continu'd as long as he liv'd. He had been, I imagine, an itinerant doctor, for there was no town in England, or country in Europe, of which he could not give a very particular account. He had some letters, and was ingenious, but much of an unbeliever, and wickedly undertook, some years after, to travestie the Bible in doggrel verse, as [Charles] Cotton had done Virgil. By this means he set many of the facts in a very ridiculous light, and might have hurt weak minds if his work had been published; but it never was.

At his house I lay that night, and the next morning reach'd Burlington, but had the mortification to find that the regular

boats were gone a little before my coming, and no other expected to go before Tuesday, this being Saturday; wherefore I
returned to an old woman in the town, of whom I had bought
gingerbread to eat on the water, and ask'd her advice. She invited me to lodge at her house till a passage by water should
offer; and being tired with my foot travelling, I accepted the
invitation. She understanding I was a printer, would have had
me stay at that town and follow my business, being ignorant of
the stock necessary to begin with. She was very hospitable, gave
me a dinner of ox-cheek with great good will, accepting only of
a pot of ale in return; and I thought myself fixed till Tuesday
should come. However, walking in the evening by the side of
the river, a boat came by, which I found was going towards
Philadelphia, with several people in her. They took me in, and,
as there was no wind, we row'd all the way; and about midnight, not having yet seen the city, some of the company were
confident we must have passed it, and would row no farther; the
others knew not where we were; so we put toward the shore, got
into a creek, landed near an old fence, with the rails of which
we made a fire, the night being cold, in October, and there we
remained till daylight. Then one of the company knew the
place to be Cooper's Creek, a little above Philadelphia, which
we saw as soon as we got out of the creek, and arriv'd there
about eight or nine o'clock on the Sunday morning, and landed
at the Market-street wharf.

I have been the more particular in this description of my
journey, and shall be so of my first entry into that city, that you
may in your mind compare such unlikely beginnings with the
figure I have since made there. I was in my working dress, my
best clothes being to come round by sea. I was dirty from my
journey; my pockets were stuff'd out with shirts and stockings,
and I knew no soul nor where to look for lodging. I was fa-
tigued with travelling, rowing, and want of rest, I was very
hungry; and my whole stock of cash consisted of a Dutch dollar,
and about a shilling in copper. The latter I gave the people of
the boat for my passage, who at first refus'd it, on account of my

rowing; but I insisted on their taking it. A man being some-times more generous when he has but a little money than when he has plenty, perhaps thro' fear of being thought to have but little.

Then I walked up the street, gazing about till near the market-house I met a boy with bread. I had made many a meal on bread, and, inquiring where he got it, I went immediately to the baker's he directed me to, in Second-street, and ask'd for bisket, intending such as we had in Boston; but they, it seems, were not made in Philadelphia. Then I asked for a three-penny loaf, and was told they had none such. So not considering or knowing the difference of money, and the greater cheapness nor the names of his bread, I bad him give me three-penny worth of any sort. He gave me, accordingly, three great puffy rolls. I was surpriz'd at the quantity, but took it, and, having no room in my pockets, walk'd off with a roll under each arm, and eating the other. Thus I went up Market-street as far as Fourth-street, passing by the door of Mr. Read, my future wife's father; when she, standing at the door, saw me, and thought I made, as I certainly did, a most awkward, ridiculous appearance. Then I turned and went down Chestnut-street and part of Walnut-street, eating my roll all the way, and, coming round, found myself again at Market-street wharf, near the boat I came in, to which I went for a draught of the river water; and, being filled with one of my rolls, gave the other two to a woman and her child that came down the river in the boat with us, and were waiting to go farther.

Thus refreshed, I walked again up the street, which by this time had many clean-dressed people in it, who were all walking the same way. I joined them, and thereby was led into the great meeting-house of the Quakers near the market. I sat down among them, and, after looking round awhile and hearing noth-ing said, being very drowsy thro' labor and want of rest the preceding night, I fell fast asleep, and continued so till the meeting broke up, when one was kind enough to rouse me. This was, therefore, the first house I was in or slept in, in Philadelphia.

Walking down again toward the river, and, looking in the faces of people, I met a young Quaker man, whose countenance I lik'd, and, accosting him, requested he would tell me where a stranger could get lodging. We were then near the sign of the Three Mariners. "Here," says he, "is one place that entertains strangers, but it is not a reputable house; if thee wilt walk with me, I'll show thee a better." He brought me to the Crooked Billet in Water-street. Here I got a dinner; and, while I was eating it, several sly questions were asked me, as it seemed to be suspected from my youth and appearance, that I might be some runaway.

After dinner, my sleepiness return'd, and being shown to a bed, I lay down without undressing, and slept till six in the evening, was call'd to supper, went to bed again very early, and slept soundly till next morning. Then I made myself as tidy as I could, and went to Andrew Bradford the printer's. I found in the shop the old man his father, whom I had seen at New York, and who, travelling on horseback, had got to Philadelphia before me. He introduc'd me to his son, who receiv'd me civilly, gave me a breakfast, but told me he did not at present want a hand, being lately suppli'd with one; but there was another printer in town, lately set up, one [Samuel] Keimer, who, perhaps, might employ me; if not, I should be welcome to lodge at his house, and he would give me a little work to do now and then till fuller business should offer.

The old gentleman said he would go with me to the new printer; and when we found him, "Neighbor," says Bradford, "I have brought to see you a young man of your business; perhaps you may want such a one." He ask'd me a few questions, put a composing stick in my hand to see how I work'd, and then said he would employ me soon, though he had just then nothing for me to do; and, taking old Bradford, whom he had never seen before, to be one of the town's people that had a good will for him, enter'd into a conversation on his present undertaking and prospects; while Bradford, not discovering that he was the other printer's father, on Keimer's saying he expected soon to get the greatest part of the business into his own hands, drew him on by artful questions, and starting little doubts, to explain all his views, what interest he reli'd on, and in what manner he intended to proceed. I, who stood by and heard all, saw immediately that one of them was a crafty old sophister, and the other a mere novice. Bradford left me with Keimer, who was greatly surprised when I told him who the old man was.

Keimer's printing-house, I found, consisted of an old shatter'd press, and one small, worn-out font of English, which he was then using himself, composing an Elegy on Aquila Rose, before mentioned, an ingenious young man, of excellent character, much respected in the town, clerk of the Assembly, and a pretty poet. Keimer made verses too, but very indifferently. He could not be said to write them, for his manner was to compose them in the types directly out of his head. So there being no copy, but one pair of cases, and the Elegy likely to require all the letter, no one could help him. I endeavor'd to put his press (which he had not yet us'd, and of which he understood nothing) into order fit to be work'd with; and, promising to come and print off his Elegy as soon as he should have got it ready, I return'd to Bradford's, who gave me a little job to do for the present, and there I lodged and dieted. A few days after, Keimer sent for me to print off the Elegy. And now he had got another pair of cases, and a pamphlet to reprint, on which he set me to work.

These two printers I found poorly qualified for their business. Bradford had not been bred to it, and was very illiterate; and Keimer, tho' something of a scholar, was a mere compositor, knowing nothing of presswork. He had been one of the French prophets, and could act their enthusiastic agitations. At this time he did not profess any particular religion, but something of all on occasion; was very ignorant of the world, and had, as I afterward found, a good deal of the knave in his composition. He did not like my lodging at Bradford's while I work'd with him. He had a house, indeed, but without furniture, so he could not lodge me; but he got me a lodging at Mr. Read's, before mentioned, who was the owner of his house; and, my chest and clothes being come by this time, I made rather a more respectable appearance in the eyes of Miss Read than I had done when she first happen'd to see me eating my roll in the street.

I began now to have some acquaintance among the young people of the town, that were lovers of reading, with whom I spent my evenings very pleasantly; and gaining money by my industry and frugality, I lived very agreeably, forgetting Boston as much as I could, and not desiring that any there should know where I resided, except my friend Collins, who was in my secret, and kept it when I wrote to him. At length, an incident happened that sent me back again much sooner than I had intended. I had a brother-in-law, Robert Holmes, master of a sloop that traded between Boston and Delaware. He being at Newcastle, forty miles below Philadelphia, heard there of me, and wrote me a letter mentioning the concern of my friends in Boston at my abrupt departure, assuring me of their good will to me, and that every thing would be accommodated to my mind if I would return, to which he exhorted me very earnestly. I wrote an answer to his letter, thank'd him for his advice, but stated my reasons for quitting Boston fully and in such a light as to convince him I was not so wrong as he had apprehended.

Sir William Keith, governor of the province, was then at Newcastle, and Captain Holmes, happening to be in company with him when my letter came to hand, spoke to him of me, and show'd him the letter. The governor read it, and seem'd surpris'd when he was told of my age. He said I appear'd a young man of promising parts, and therefore should be encouraged; the printers at Philadelphia were wretched ones; and, if I would set up there, he made no doubt that I should succeed; for his part, he would procure me the public business, and do me every other service in his power. This my brother-in-law afterwards told me in Boston, but I knew as yet nothing of it; when, one day, Keimer and I being at work together near the window, we saw the governor and another gentleman (which proved to be Colonel French of Newcastle), finely dress'd, come directly across the street to our house, and heard them at the door.

Keimer ran down immediately, thinking it a visit to him; but the governor inquir'd for me, came up, and with a condescension and politeness I had been quite unus'd to, made me many compliments, desired to be acquainted with me, blam'd me kindly for not having made myself known to him when I first came to the place, and would have me away with him to the tavern, where he was going with Colonel French to taste, as he said, some excellent Madeira. I was not a little surprised, and Keimer star'd like a pig poison'd. I went, however, with the governor and Colonel French to a tavern, at the corner of Third-street, and over the Madeira he propos'd my setting up my business, laid before me the probabilities of success, and both he and Colonel French assur'd me I should have their interest and influence in procuring the public business of both governments [Pennsylvania and Delaware]. On my doubting whether my father would assist me in it, Sir William said he would give me a letter to him, in which he would state the advantages, and he did not doubt of prevailing with him. So it was concluded I should return to Boston in the first vessel, with the governor's letter recommending me to my father. In the mean time the intention was to be kept a secret, and I went on working with Keimer as usual, the governor sending for me now and then to dine with him, a very great honor I thought it, and conversing with me in the most affable, familiar, and friendly manner imaginable.

About the end of April, 1724, a little vessel offer'd for Boston. I took leave of Keimer as going to see my friends. The governor gave me an ample letter, saying many flattering things of me to my father, and strongly recommending the project of my setting up at Philadelphia as a thing that must make my fortune.

We struck on a shoal in going down the bay, and sprung a leak; we had a blustering time at sea, and were oblig'd to pump almost continually, at which I took my turn. We arriv'd safe, however, at Boston in about a fortnight. I had been absent seven months, and my friends had heard nothing of me; for my br. Holmes was not yet return'd, and had not written about me. My unexpected appearance surpriz'd the family; all were, however, very glad to see me, and made me welcome, except my brother. I went to see him at his printing-house. I was better dress'd than ever while in his service, having a genteel new suit from head to foot, a watch, and my pockets lin'd with near five pounds sterling in silver. He receiv'd me not very frankly, look'd me all over, and turn'd to his work again.

The journeymen were inquisitive where I had been, what sort of a country it was, and how I lik'd it. I prais'd it much, and the happy life I led in it, expressing strongly my intention of returning to it; and, one of them asking what kind of money we had there, I produc'd a handful of silver, and spread it before them, which was a kind of raree-show they had not been us'd to, paper being the money of Boston. Then I took an opportunity of letting them see my watch; and lastly (my brother still grum and sullen), I gave them a piece of eight to drink, and took my leave. This visit of mine offended him extreamly; for, when my mother some time after spoke to him of a reconciliation, and of her wishes to see us on good terms together, and that we might live for the future as brothers, he said I had insulted him in such a manner before his people that he could never forget or forgive it. In this, however, he was mistaken.

My father received the governor's letter with some apparent surprise; but said little of it to me for some days, when Capt. Holmes returning he showed it to him, ask'd him if he knew Keith, and what kind of man he was; adding his opinion that he must be of small discretion to think of setting a boy up in business who wanted yet three years of being at man's estate. Holmes said what he could in favor of the project, but my father was clear in the impropriety of it, and at last gave a flat denial to it. Then he wrote a civil letter to Sir William, thanking him for the patronage he had so kindly offered me, but declining to assist me as yet in setting up, I being, in his opinion, too young to be trusted with the management of a business so important, and for which the preparation must be so expensive.

My friend and companion Collins, who was a clerk in the post-office, pleas'd with the account I gave him of my new country, determined to go thither also; and, while I waited for my father's determination, he set out before me by land to Rhode Island, leaving his books, which were a pretty collection of mathematicks and natural philosophy, to come with mine and me to New York, where he propos'd to wait for me.

My father, tho' he did not approve Sir William's proposition, was yet pleas'd that I had been able to obtain so advantageous a character from a person of such note where I had resided, and that I had been so industrious and careful as to equip myself so handsomely in so short a time; therefore, seeing no prospect of an accommodation between my brother and me, he gave his consent to my returning again to Philadelphia, advis'd me to behave respectfully to the people there, endeavor to obtain the general esteem, and avoid lampooning and libeling, to which he thought I had too much inclination; telling me, that by steady industry and a prudent parsimony I might save enough by the time I was one-and-twenty to set me up; and that, if I came near the matter, he would help me out with the rest. This was all I could obtain, except some small gifts as tokens of his and my mother's love, when I embark'd again for New York, now with their approbation and their blessing.

The sloop putting in at Newport, Rhode Island, I visited my brother John, who had been married and settled there some years. He received me very affectionately, for he always lov'd me. A friend of his, one Vernon, having some money due to him in Pennsylvania, about thirty-five pounds currency, desired I would receive it for him, and keep it till I had his directions what to remit it in. Accordingly, he gave me an order. This afterwards occasion'd me a good deal of uneasiness.

At Newport we took in a number of passengers for New York, among which were two young women, companions, and a grave, sensible, matron-like Quaker woman, with her attendants. I had shown an obliging readiness to do her some little services, which impress'd her I suppose with a degree of good will toward me; therefore, when she saw a daily growing familiarity between me and the two young women, which they appear'd to encourage, she took me aside, and said, "Young man, I am concern'd for thee, as thou has no friend with thee, and seems not to know much of the world, or of the snares youth is expos'd to; depend upon it, those are very bad women; I can see it in all their actions; and if thee art not upon thy guard, they will draw thee into some danger; they are strangers to thee, and I advise thee, in a friendly concern for thy welfare, to have no acquaintance with them." As I seem'd at first not to think so ill of them as she did, she mentioned some thing she had observ'd and heard that had escap'd my notice, but now convinc'd me she was right. I thank'd her for her kind advice, and promis'd to follow it. When we arriv'd at New York, they told me where they liv'd, and invited me to come and see them; but I avoided it, and it was well I did; for the next day the captain miss'd a silver spoon and some other things, that had been taken out of his cabbin, and, knowing that these were a couple of strumpets, he got a warrant to search their lodgings, found the stolen goods, and had the thieves punish'd. So, tho' we had escap'd a sunken rock, which we scrap'd upon in the passage, I thought this escape of rather more importance to me.

At New York I found my friend Collins, who had arriv'd there some time before me. We had been intimate from children, and had read the same books together; but he had the advantage of more time for reading and studying, and a wonderful genius for mathematical learning, in which he far outstript me. While I liv'd in Boston, most of my hours of leisure for conversation were spent with him, and he continu'd a sober

as well as an industrious lad; was much respected for his learning by several of the clergy and other gentlemen, and seemed
to promise making a good figure in life. But, during my absence,
he had acquir'd a habit of sotting with brandy; and I found by
his own account, and what I heard from others, that he had been
drunk every day since his arrival at New York, and behav'd very
oddly. He had gam'd, too, and lost his money, so that I was
oblig'd to discharge his lodgings, and defray his expenses to
and at Philadelphia, which prov'd extremely inconvenient to
me.

The then governor of New York, [William] Burnet (son of
Bishop Burnet), hearing from the captain that a young man,
one of his passengers, had a great many books, desir'd he would
bring me to see him. I waited upon him accordingly, and
should have taken Collins with me but that he was not sober.
The gov'r treated me with great civility, show'd me his library,
which was a very large one, and we had a good deal of conversation about books and authors. This was the second governor
who had done me the honor to take notice of me; which, to a
poor boy like me, was very pleasing.

We proceeded to Philadelphia. I received on the way Vernon's money, without which we could hardly have finish'd our
journey. Collins wished to be employ'd in some counting-house;
but, whether they discover'd his dramming by his breath, or by
his behaviour, tho' he had some recommendations, he met with
no success in any application, and continu'd lodging and boarding at the same house with me, and at my expense. Knowing I
had that money of Vernon's, he was continually borrowing of
me, still promising repayment as soon as he should be in business. At length he had got so much of it that I was distress'd to
think what I should do in case of being call'd on to remit it.

His drinking continu'd, about which we sometimes quar-
rell'd; for, when a little intoxicated, he was very fractious.
Once, in a boat on the Delaware with some other young men,
he refused to row in his turn. "I will be row'd home," says he.
"We will not row you," says I. "You must, or stay all night on

the water," says he, "just as you please." The others said, "Let
us row; what signifies it?" But, my mind being soured with his
other conduct, I continu'd to refuse. So he swore he would
make me row, or throw me overboard; and coming along, step-
ping on the thwarts, toward me, when he came up and struck at
me, I clapped my hand under his crutch, and, rising, pitched
him head-foremost into the river. I knew he was a good swim-
mer, and so was under little concern about him; but before he
could get round to lay hold of the boat, we had with a few
strokes pull'd her out of his reach; and ever when he drew near
the boat, we ask'd if he would row, striking a few strokes to
slide her away from him. He was ready to die with vexation,
and obstinately would not promise to row. However, seeing
him at last beginning to tire, we lifted him in and brought him
home dripping wet in the evening. We hardly exchang'd a civil
word afterwards, and a West India captain, who had a commission to procure a tutor for the sons of a gentleman at Barbadoes,
happening to meet with him, agreed to carry him thither. He
left me then, promising to remit me the first money he should
receive in order to discharge the debt; but I never heard of him
after.

The breaking into this money of Vernon's was one of the
first great errata of my life; and this affair show'd that my father
was not much out in his judgment when he suppos'd me too
young to manage business of importance. But Sir William, on
reading his letter, said he was too prudent. There was great
difference in persons; and discretion did not always accompany
years, nor was youth always without it. "And since he will not
set you up," says he, "I will do it myself. Give me an inventory
of the things necessary to be had from England, and I will send
for them. You shall repay me when you are able; I am resolv'd
to have a good printer here, and I am sure you must succeed."
This was spoken with such an appearance of cordiality, that I
had not the least doubt of his meaning what he said. I had
hitherto kept the proposition of my setting up, a secret in Philadelphia, and I still kept it. Had it been known that I depended

on the governor, probably some friend, that knew him better, would have advis'd me not to rely on him, as I afterwards heard it as his known character to be liberal of promises which he never meant to keep. Yet, unsolicited as he was by me, how could I think his generous offer insincere? I believ'd him one of the best men in the world.

I presented him an inventory of a little print'g-house, amounting by my computation to about one hundred pounds sterling. He lik'd it, but ask'd me if my being on the spot in England to chuse the types, and see that every thing was good of the kind, might not be of some advantage. "Then," says he, "when there, you may make acquaintances, and establish correspondences in the bookselling and stationery way." I agreed that this might be advantageous. "Then," says he, "get yourself ready to go with Annis"; which was the annual ship, and the only one at that time usually passing between London and Philadelphia. But it would be some months before Annis sail'd, so I continu'd working with Keimer, fretting about the money Collins had got from me, and in daily apprehensions of being call'd upon by Vernon, which, however, did not happen for some years after.

I believe I have omitted mentioning that, in my first voyage from Boston, being becalm'd off Block Island, our people set about catching cod, and hauled up a great many. Hitherto I had stuck to my resolution of not eating animal food, and on this occasion I consider'd, with my master Tryon, the taking every fish as a kind of unprovoked murder, since none of them had, or ever could do us any injury that might justify the slaughter. All this seemed very reasonable. But I had formerly been a great lover of fish, and, when this came hot out of the frying-pan, it smelt admirably well. I balanc'd some time between principle and inclination, till I recollected that, when the fish were opened, I saw smaller fish taken out of their stomachs; then thought I, "If you eat one another, I don't see why we mayn't eat you." So I din'd upon cod very heartily, and continued to eat with other people, returning only now and then occasionally to a vegetable diet. So convenient a thing is it to be a *reasonable creature,* since it enables one to find or make a reason for every thing one has a mind to do.

Keimer and I liv'd on a pretty good familiar footing, and agreed tolerably well, for he suspected nothing of my setting up. He retained a great deal of his old enthusiasms and lov'd argumentation. We therefore had many disputations. I used to work him so with my Socratic method, and had trepann'd him so often by questions apparently so distant from any point we had in hand, and yet by degrees led to the point, and brought him into difficulties and contradictions, that at last he grew ridiculously cautious, and would hardly answer me the most common question, without asking first, *"What do you intend to infer from that?"* However, it gave him so high an opinion of my abilities in the confuting way, that he seriously proposed my being his colleague in a project he had of setting up a new sect. He was to preach the doctrines, and I was to confound all opponents. When he came to explain with me upon the doctrines, I found several conundrums which I objected to, unless I might have my way a little to, and introduce some of mine.

Keimer wore his beard at full length, because somewhere in the Mosaic law it is said, *"Thou shalt not mar the corners of thy beard."* He likewise kept the Seventh day, Sabbath; and these two points were essentials with him. I dislik'd both; but agreed to admit them upon condition of his adopting the doctrine of using no animal food. "I doubt," said he, "my constitution will not bear that." I assur'd him it would, and that he would be the better for it. He was usually a great glutton, and I promised myself some diversion in half starving him. He agreed to try the practice, if I would keep him company. I did so, and we held it for three months. We had our victuals dress'd, and brought to us regularly by a woman in the neighborhood, who had from me a list of forty dishes, to be prepar'd for us at different times, in all which there was neither fish, flesh, nor fowl, and the whim suited me the better at this time from the cheapness of it, not costing us above eighteenpence sterling each per week. I have since kept several Lents most strictly, leaving the common diet for that, and that for the common, abruptly, without the least inconvenience, so that I think there is little in the advice of making those changes by easy gradations. I went on pleasantly, but poor Keimer suffered grievously, tired of the project, long'd for the flesh-pots of Egypt, and order'd a roast pig. He invited me and two women friends to dine with him; but, it being brought too soon upon table, he could not resist the temptation, and ate the whole before we came.

I had made some courtship during this time to Miss [Deborah] Read. I had a great respect and affection for her, and had some reason to believe she had the same for me; but, as I was about to take a long voyage, and we were both very young, only a little above eighteen, it was thought most prudent by her mother to prevent our going too far at present, as a marriage, if it was to take place, would be more convenient after my return, when I should be, as I expected, set up in my business. Perhaps, too, she thought my expectations not so well founded as I imagined them to be.

My chief acquaintances at this time were Charles Osborne, Joseph Watson, and James Ralph, all lovers of reading. The two first were clerks to an eminent scrivener or conveyancer in the town, Charles Brogden; the other was clerk to a merchant. Watson was a pious, sensible young man, of great integrity; the others rather more lax in their principles of religion, particularly Ralph, who, as well as Collins, had been unsettled by me, for which they both made me suffer. Osborne was sensible, candid, frank; sincere and affectionate to his friends; but, in literary matters, too fond of criticising. Ralph was ingenious, genteel in his manners, and extremely eloquent; I think I never knew a prettier talker. Both of them great admirers of poetry, and began to try their hands in little pieces. Many pleasant walks we four had together on Sundays into the woods, near Schuylkill, where we read to one another, and conferr'd on what we read.

Ralph was inclin'd to pursue the study of poetry, not doubting but he might become eminent in it, and make his fortune by it, alleging that the best poets must, when they first began to write, make as many faults as he did. Osborne dissuaded him, assur'd him he had no genius for poetry, and advis'd him to think of nothing beyond the business he was bred to; that, in the mercantile way, tho' he had no stock, he might, by his diligence and punctuality, recommend himself to employment as a factor, and in time acquire wherewith to trade on his own account. I approv'd the amusing one's self with poetry now and then, so far as to improve one's language, but no farther.

On this it was propos'd that we should each of us, at our next meeting, produce a piece of our own composing, in order to improve by our mutual observations, criticisms, and corrections. As language and expression were what we had in view, we excluded all considerations of invention by agreeing that the task should be a version of the eighteenth Psalm, which describes the descent of a Deity. When the time of our meeting drew nigh, Ralph called on me first, and let me know his piece was ready. I told him I had been busy, and, having little inclination, had done nothing. He then show'd me his piece for my opinion, and I much approv'd it, as it appear'd to me to have great merit. "Now," says he, "Osborne never will allow the least merit in any thing of mine, but makes 1000 criticisms out of mere envy. He is not so jealous of you; I wish, therefore, you would take this piece, and produce it as yours; I will pretend not to have had time, and so produce nothing. We shall then see what he will say to it." It was agreed, and I immediately transcrib'd it, that it might appear in my own hand.

We met; Watson's performance was read; there were some beauties in it, but many defects. Osborne's was read; it was much better; Ralph did it justice; remarked some faults, but applauded the beauties. He himself had nothing to produce. I was backward; seemed desirous of being excused; had not had sufficient time to correct, etc.; but no excuse could be admitted; produce I must. It was read and repeated; Watson and Osborne gave up the contest, and join'd in applauding it. Ralph only made some criticisms, and propos'd some amendments; but I defended my text. Osborne was against Ralph, and told him he was no better a critic than poet, so he dropt the argument. As they two went home together, Osborne expressed himself still more strongly in favor of what he thought my production; having restrain'd himself before, as he said, lest I should think it flattery. "But who would have imagin'd," said he, "that Franklin had been capable of such a performance; such painting, such force, such fire! He has even improv'd the original. In his common conversation he seems to have no choice of words; he hesitates and blunders; and yet, good God! how he writes!" When we next met, Ralph discovered the trick we had plaid him, and Osborne was a little laught at.

This transaction fixed Ralph in his resolution of becoming a poet. I did all I could to dissuade him from it, but he continued scribbling verses till *Pope* cured him. He became, however, a pretty good prose writer. More of him hereafter. But, as I may not have occasion again to mention the other two, I shall just remark here, that Watson died in my arms a few years after, much lamented, being the best of our set. Osborne went to the West Indies, where he became an eminent lawyer and made money, but died young. He and I had made a serious agreement, that the one who happen'd first to die should, if possible, make a friendly visit to the other, and acquaint him how he found things in that separate state. But he never fulfill'd his promise.

The governor, seeming to like my company, had me frequently to his house, and his setting me up was always mention'd as a fixed thing. I was to take with me letters recommendatory to a number of his friends, besides the letter of credit to furnish me with the necessary money for purchasing the press and types, paper, etc. For these letters I was appointed to call at different times, when they were to be ready; but a future time was still named. Thus he went on till the ship, whose departure too had been several times postponed, was on the point of sailing. Then, when I call'd to take my leave and receive the letters, his secretary, Dr. Bard, came out to me and said the governor was extremely busy in writing, but would be down at Newcastle before the ship, and there the letters would be delivered to me.

Ralph, though married, and having one child, had determined to accompany me in this voyage. It was thought he intended to establish a correspondence, and obtain goods to sell on commission; but I found afterwards, that, thro' some discontent with his wife's relations, he purposed to leave her on their hands, and never return again. Having taken leave of my friends, and interchang'd some promises with Miss Read, I left Philadelphia in the ship, which anchor'd at Newcastle. The governor was there; but when I went to his lodging, the secretary came to me from him with the civillest message in the world, that he could not then see me, being engaged in business of the utmost importance, but should send the letters to me on board, wished me heartily a good voyage and a speedy return, etc. I returned on board a little puzzled, but still not doubting.

Mr. Andrew Hamilton, a famous lawyer of Philadelphia, had taken passage in the same ship for himself and son, and with Mr. Denham, a Quaker merchant, and Messrs. Onion and Russel, masters of an iron work in Maryland; had engag'd the great cabin; so that Ralph and I were forced to take up with a berth in the steerage, and none on board knowing us, were considered as ordinary persons. But Mr. Hamilton and his son (it was James, since Governor) return'd from Newcastle to Philadelphia, the father being recall'd by a great fee to plead for a seized ship; and, just before we sail'd, Colonel French coming on board, and showing me great respect, I was more taken notice of, and, with my friend Ralph, invited by the other gentlemen to come into the cabin, there being now room. Accordingly, we remov'd thither.

Understanding that Colonel French had brought on board the governor's despatches, I ask'd the captain for those letters

that were to be under my care. He said all were put into the
bag together and he could not then come at them; but, before
we landed in England, I should have an opportunity of picking
them out; so I was satisfied for the present, and we proceeded
on our voyage. We had a sociable company in the cabin, and
lived uncommonly well, having the addition of all Mr. Hamilton's stores, who had laid in plentifully. In this passage Mr.
Denham contracted a friendship for me that continued during
his life. The voyage was otherwise not a pleasant one, as we
had a great deal of bad weather.

When we came into the Channel, the captain kept his word
with me, and gave me an opportunity of examining the bag
for the governor's letters. I found none upon which my name
was put as under my care. I picked out six or seven, that, by the
handwriting, I thought might be the promised letters, especially as one of them was directed to Basket, the king's printer,
and another to some stationer. We arriv'd in London the 24th
of December, 1724. I waited upon the stationer, who came first
in my way, delivering the letter as from Governor Keith. "I
don't know such a person," says he; but, opening the letter, "O!
this is from Riddlesden. I have lately found him to be a compleat rascal, and I will have nothing to do with him, nor receive
any letters from him." So, putting the letter into my hand, he
turn'd on his heel and left me to serve some customer. I was
surprised to find these were not the governor's letters; and, after
recollecting and comparing circumstances, I began to doubt his
sincerity. I found my friend Denham, and opened the whole
affair to him. He let me into Keith's character; told me there
was not the least probability that he had written any letters for
me; that no one, who knew him, had the smallest dependence
on him; and he laught at the notion of the governor's giving
me a letter of credit, having, as he said, no credit to give. On
my expressing some concern about what I should do, he advised
me to endeavor getting some employment in the way of my
business. "Among the printers here," he said, "you will improve

Franklin the printer's apprentice. Reproduced from a painting by Charles B. Mills in the Franklin Union, Boston.

yourself, and when you return to America, you will set up to greater advantage."

We both of us happen'd to know, as well as the stationer, that Riddlesden, the attorney, was a very knave. He had half ruin'd Miss Read's father by persuading him to be bound for him. By this letter it appear'd there was a secret scheme on foot to the prejudice of Hamilton (suppos'd to be then coming over with us); and that Keith was concerned in it with Riddlesden. Denham, who was a friend of Hamilton's, thought he ought to be acquainted with it; so, when he arriv'd in England, which was soon after, partly from resentment and ill-will to Keith and Riddlesden, and partly from good-will to him, I waited on him, and gave him the letter. He thank'd me cordially, the information being of importance to him; and from that time he became my friend, greatly to my advantage afterwards on many occasions.

But what shall we think of a governor's playing such pitiful tricks, and imposing so grossly on a poor ignorant boy! It was a habit he had acquired. He wish'd to please everybody; and, having little to give, he gave expectations. He was otherwise an ingenious, sensible man, a pretty good writer, and a good governor for the people, tho' not for his constituents, the proprietaries, whose instructions he sometimes disregarded. Several of our best laws were of his planning and passed during his administration.

Ralph and I were inseparable companions. We took lodgings together in Little Britain at three shillings and six-pence a week —as much as we could then afford. He found some relations, but they were poor, and unable to assist him. He now let me know his intentions of remaining in London, and that he never meant to return to Philadelphia. He had brought no money with him, the whole he could muster having been expended in paying his passage. I had fifteen pistoles; so he borrowed occasionally of me to subsist, while he was looking out for business. He first endeavored to get into the playhouse, believing himself qualify'd for an actor; but [Robert] Wilkes, to whom he apply'd, advis'd him candidly not to think of that employment, as it was impossible he should succeed in it. Then he propos'd to Roberts, a publisher in Paternoster Row, to write for him a weekly paper like the Spectator, on certain conditions, which Roberts did not approve. Then he endeavored to get employment as a hackney writer, to copy for the stationers and lawyers about the Temple, but could find no vacancy.

I immediately got into work at Palmer's, then a famous printing-house in Bartholomew Close, and here I continu'd near a year. I was pretty diligent, but spent with Ralph a good deal of my earnings in going to plays and other places of amusement. We had together consumed all my pistoles, and now just rubbed on from hand to mouth. He seem'd quite to forget his wife and child, and I, by degrees, my engagements with Miss Read, to whom I never wrote more than one letter, and that was to let her know I was not likely soon to return. This was another of the great errata of my life, which I should wish to correct if I were to live it over again. In fact, by our expenses, I was constantly kept unable to pay my passage.

At Palmer's I was employed in composing for the second edition of [William] Wollaston's "Religion of Nature." Some of his reasonings not appearing to me well founded, I wrote a little metaphysical piece in which I made remarks on them. It was entitled "A Dissertation on Liberty and Necessity, Pleasure and Pain." I inscribed it to my friend Ralph; I printed a small number. It occasion'd my being more consider'd by Mr. Palmer as a young man of some ingenuity, tho' he seriously expostulated with me upon the principles of my pamphlet, which to him appear'd abominable. My printing this pamphlet was another erratum. While I lodg'd in Little Britain, I made an acquaintance with one Wilcox, a bookseller, whose shop was at the next door. He had an immense collection of second-hand books. Circulating libraries were not then in use; but we agreed that, on certain reasonable terms, which I have now forgotten, I might take, read, and return any of his books. This I esteem'd a great advantage, and I made as much use of it as I could.

My pamphlet by some means falling into the hands of one Lyons, a surgeon, author of a book entitled "The Infallibility of Human Judgment," it occasioned an acquaintance between us. He took great notice of me, called on me often to converse on those subjects, carried me to the Horns, a pale alehouse in —— Lane, Cheapside, and introduced me to Dr. [Bernard] Mandeville, author of the "Fable of the Bees," who had a club there, of which he was the soul, being a most facetious, entertaining companion. Lyons, too, introduced me to Dr. [Henry] Pemberton, at Batson's Coffee-house, who promis'd to give me an opportunity, some time or other, of seeing Sir Isaac Newton, of which I was extremely desirous; but this never happened.

I had brought over a few curiosities, among which the principal was a purse made of the asbestos, which purifies by fire. Sir Hans Sloane heard of it, came to see me, and invited me to his house in Bloomsbury Square, where he show'd me all his curiosities, and persuaded me to let him add that to the number, for which he paid me handsomely.

In our house there lodg'd a young woman, a milliner, who, I think, had a shop in the Cloisters. She had been genteelly bred, was sensible and lively, and of most pleasing conversation. Ralph read plays to her in the evenings, they grew intimate, she took another lodging, and he followed her. They liv'd together some time; but, he being still out of business, and her income not sufficient to maintain them with her child, he took a resolution of going from London, to try for a country school, which he thought himself well qualified to undertake, as he wrote an excellent hand, and was a master of arithmetic and accounts. This, however, he deemed a business below him, and confident of future better fortune, when he should be unwilling to have it known that he once was so meanly employed, he changed his name, and did me the honor to assume mine; for I soon after had a letter from him, acquainting me that he was settled in a small village (in Berkshire, I think it was, where he taught reading and writing to ten or a dozen boys, at sixpence each per week), recommending Mrs. T—— to my care, and desiring me to write to him, directing for Mr. Franklin, schoolmaster, at such a place.

He continued to write frequently, sending me large specimens of an epic poem which he was then composing, and desiring my remarks and corrections. These I gave him from time to time, but endeavor'd rather to discourage his proceeding. One of [Edward] Young's Satires was then just published. I copy'd and sent him a great part of it, which set in a strong light the folly of pursuing the Muses with any hope of advancement by them. All was in vain; sheets of the poem continued to come by every post. In the mean time, Mrs. T——, having on his account lost her friend and business, was often in distresses, and us'd to send for me, and borrow what I could spare to help her out of them. I grew fond of her company, and, being at that time under no religious restraint, and presuming upon my importance to her, I attempted familiarities (another erratum) which she repuls'd with a proper resentment, and acquainted him with my behaviour. This made a breach between us; and, when he returned again to London, he let me know he thought I had cancell'd all the obligations he had been under to me. So I found I was never to expect his repaying me what I lent to him, or advanc'd for him. This, however, was not then of much consequence, as he was totally unable; and in the loss of his friendship I found myself relieved from a burthen. I now began to think of getting a little money beforehand, and, expecting better work, I left Palmer's to work at Watts's, near Lincoln's Inn Fields, a still greater printing-house. Here I continued all the rest of my stay in London.

At my first admission into this printing-house I took to working at press, imagining I felt a want of the bodily exercise I had been us'd to in America, where presswork is mix'd with composing. I drank only water; the other workmen, nearly fifty in number, were great guzzlers of beer. On occasion, I carried up and down stairs a large form of types in each hand, when others carried but one in both hands. They wondered to see, from this and several instances, that the *Water-American,* as they called me, was *stronger* than themselves, who drank *strong* beer! We had an alehouse boy who attended always in the house to supply the workmen. My companion at the press drank every day a pint before breakfast, a pint at breakfast with his bread and cheese, a pint between breakfast and dinner, a pint at dinner, a pint in the afternoon about six o'clock, and another when he had done his day's work. I thought it a detestable custom; but it was necessary, he suppos'd, to drink *strong* beer, that he might be *strong* to labor. I endeavored to convince him that the bodily strength afforded by beer could only be in proportion to the grain or flour of the barley dissolved in the water of which it was made; that there was more flour in a penny-worth of bread; and therefore, if he would eat that with a pint of water, it would give him more strength than a quart of beer. He drank on, however, and had four or five shillings to pay out of his wages every Saturday night for that muddling liquor; an expense I was free from. And thus these poor devils keep themselves always under.

Watts, after some weeks, desiring to have me in the composing-room, I left the pressmen; a new bien venu or sum for drink, being five shillings, was demanded of me by the compositors. I thought it an imposition, as I had paid below; the master thought so too, and forbad my paying it. I stood out two or three weeks, was accordingly considered as an excommunicate, and had so many little pieces of private mischief done me, by mixing my sorts, transposing my pages, breaking my matter, etc., etc., if I were ever so little out of the room, and all ascribed to the chappel ghost, which they said ever haunted those not regularly admitted, that, notwithstanding the master's protection, I found myself oblig'd to comply and pay the money, convinc'd of the folly of being on ill terms with those one is to live with continually.

I was now on a fair footing with them, and soon acquir'd considerable influence. I propos'd some reasonable alterations in their chappel [1] laws, and carried them against all opposition. From my example, a great part of them left their muddling breakfast of beer, and bread, and cheese, finding they could with me be suppl'd from a neighboring house with a large porringer of hot water-gruel, sprinkled with pepper, crumb'd with bread, and a bit of butter in it, for the price of a pint of beer, viz., three half-pence. This was a more comfortable as well as cheaper breakfast, and kept their heads clearer. Those who continued sotting with beer all day, were often, by not paying, out of credit at the alehouse, and us'd to make interest with me to get beer; their *light,* as they phrased it, *being out.* I watch'd the pay-table on Saturday night, and collected what I stood engag'd for them, having to pay sometimes near thirty shillings a week on their accounts. This, and my being esteem'd a pretty good *riggite,* that is, a jocular verbal satirist, supported my consequence in the society. My constant attendance (I never making a St. Monday) recommended me to the master; and my uncommon quickness at composing occasioned my being put upon all work of dispatch, which was generally better paid. So I went on now very agreeably.

My lodging in Little Britain being too remote, I found another in Duke-street, opposite to the Romish Chapel. It was two pair of stairs backwards, at an Italian warehouse. A widow lady kept the house; she had a daughter, and a maid servant, and a journeyman who attended the warehouse, but lodg'd abroad. After sending to inquire my character at the house where I last lodg'd she agreed to take me in at the same rate, 3s. 6d. per week; cheaper, as she said, from the protection she expected in having a man lodge in the house. She was a widow, an elderly woman; had been bred a Protestant, being a clergy-

---

[1] "A printing-house is always called a chapel by the workmen, the origin of which appears to have been, that printing was first carried on in England in an ancient chapel converted into a printing-house, and the title has been preserved by tradition. The bien venu among the printers answers to the terms entrance and footing among mechanics; thus a journeyman, on entering a printing-house, was accustomed to pay one or more gallons of beer for the good of the chapel: this custom was falling into disuse thirty years ago; it is very properly rejected entirely in the United States."—W. T. F.

man's daughter, but was converted to the Catholic religion by her husband, whose memory she much revered; had lived much among people of distinction, and knew a thousand anecdotes of them as far back as the times of Charles the Second. She was lame in her knees with the gout, and, therefore, seldom stirred out of her room, so sometimes wanted company; and hers was so highly amusing to me, that I was sure to spend an evening with her whenever she desired it. Our supper was only half an anchovy each, on a very little strip of bread and butter, and half a pint of ale between us; but the entertainment was in her conversation. My always keeping good hours, and giving little trouble in the family, made her unwilling to part with me; so that, when I talk'd of a lodging I had heard of, nearer my business, for two shillings a week, which, intent as I now was on saving money, made some difference, she bid me not think of it, for she would abate me two shillings a week for the future; so I remained with her at one shilling and sixpence as long as I staid in London.

In a garret of her house there lived a maiden lady of seventy, in the most retired manner, of whom my landlady gave me this account: that she was a Roman Catholic, had been sent abroad when young, and lodg'd in a nunnery with an intent of becoming a nun; but, the country not agreeing with her, she returned to England, where, there being no nunnery, she had vow'd to lead the life of a nun, as near as might be done in those circumstances. Accordingly, she had given all her estate to charitable uses, reserving only twelve pounds a year to live on, and out of this sum she still gave a great deal in charity, living herself on water-gruel only, and using no fire but to boil it. She had lived many years in that garret, being permitted to remain there gratis by successive Catholic tenants of the house below, as they deemed it a blessing to have her there. A priest visited her to confess her every day. "I have ask'd her," says my landlady, "how she, as she liv'd, could possibly find so much employment for a confessor?" "Oh," said she, "it is impossible to avoid *vain thoughts.*" I was permitted once to visit her. She was chearful and polite, and convers'd pleasantly. The room was clean, but had no other furniture than a matras, a table with a crucifix and book, a stool which she gave me to sit on, and a picture over the chimney of Saint Veronica displaying her handkerchief, with the miraculous figure of Christ's bleeding face on it, which she explained to me with great seriousness. She look'd pale, but was never sick; and I give it as another instance on how small an income, life and health may be supported.

At Watts's printing-house I contracted an acquaintance with an ingenious young man, one Wygate, who, having wealthy relations, had been better educated than most printers; was a tolerable Latinist, spoke French, and lov'd reading. I taught him and a friend of his to swim at twice going into the river, and they soon became good swimmers. They introduc'd me to some gentlemen from the country, who went to Chelsea by water to see the College and Don Saltero's curiosities. In our return, at the request of the company, whose curiosity Wygate had excited, I stripped and leaped into the river, and swam from near Chelsea to Blackfriar's, performing on the way many feats of activity, both upon and under water, that surpris'd and pleas'd those to whom they were novelties.

I had from a child been ever delighted with this exercise, had studied and practis'd all Thevenot's motions and positions, added some of my own, aiming at the graceful and easy as well as the useful. All these I took this occasion of exhibiting to the company, and was much flatter'd by their admiration; and Wygate, who was desirous of becoming a master, grew more and more attach'd to me on that account, as well as from the similarity of our studies. He at length proposed to me travelling all over Europe together, supporting ourselves everywhere by working at our business. I was once inclined to it; but, mentioning it to my good friend Mr. Denham, with whom I often spent an hour when I had leisure, he dissuaded me from it, advising me to think only of returning to Pennsylvania, which he was now about to do.

I must record one trait of this good man's character. He had

formerly been in business at Bristol, but failed in debt to a
number of people, compounded and went to America. There,
by a close application to business as a merchant, he acquir'd
a plentiful fortune in a few years. Returning to England in the
ship with me, he invited his old creditors to an entertainment,
at which he thank'd them for the easy composition they had
favored him with, and, when they expected nothing but the
treat, every man at the first remove found under his plate an
order on a banker for the full amount of the unpaid remainder
with interest.

He now told me he was about to return to Philadelphia, and
should carry over a great quantity of goods in order to open a
store there. He propos'd to take me over as his clerk, to keep
his books, in which he would instruct me, copy his letters, and
attend the store. He added, that, as soon as I should be acquainted with mercantile business, he would promote me by
sending me with a cargo of flour and bread, etc., to the West
Indies, and procure me commissions from others which would
be profitable; and, if I manag'd well, would establish me hand-
somely. The thing pleas'd me; for I was grown tired of London, remembered with pleasure the happy months I had spent
in Pennsylvania, and wish'd again to see it; therefore I immediately agreed on the terms of fifty pounds a year, Pennsylvania
money; less, indeed, than my present gettings as a compositor,
but affording a better prospect.

I now took leave of printing, as I thought, for ever, and was
daily employed in my new business, going about with Mr. Denham among the tradesmen to purchase various articles, and
seeing them pack'd up, doing errands, calling upon workmen
to dispatch, etc.; and, when all was on board, I had a few days'
leisure. On one of these days, I was, to my surprise, sent for by
a great man I knew only by name, a Sir William Wyndham, and
I waited upon him. He had heard by some means or other of
my swimming from Chelsea to Blackfriar's, and of my teaching
Wygate and another young man to swim in a few hours. He had
two sons, about to set out on their travels; he wished to have

them first taught swimming, and proposed to gratify me hand-somely if I would teach them. They were not yet come to town, and my stay was uncertain, so I could not undertake it; but, from this incident, I thought it likely that, if I were to remain in England and open a swimming-school, I might get a good deal of money; and it struck me so strongly, that, had the over-ture been sooner made me, probably I should not so soon have returned to America. After many years, you and I had some-thing of more importance to do with one of these sons of Sir William Wyndham, become Earl of Egremont, which I shall mention in its place.

Thus I spent about eighteen months in London; most part of the time I work'd hard at my business, and spent but little upon myself except in seeing plays and in books. My friend Ralph had kept me poor; he owed me about twenty-seven pounds, which I was now never likely to receive; a great sum out of my small earnings! I lov'd him, notwithstanding, for he had many amiable qualities. I had by no means improv'd my fortune; but I had picked up some very ingenious acquaintance, whose conversation was of great advantage to me; and I had read considerably.

We sail'd from Gravesend on the 23rd of July, 1726. For the incidents of the voyage, I refer you to my Journal, where you will find them all minutely related. Perhaps the most important part of that journal is the *plan* to be found in it, which I formed at sea, for regulating my future conduct in life. It is the more remarkable, as being formed when I was so young, and yet being pretty faithfully adhered to quite thro' to old age.

We landed in Philadelphia on the 11th of October, where I found sundry alterations. Keith was no longer governor, being superseded by Major Gordon. I met him walking the streets as a common citizen. He seem'd a little asham'd at seeing me, but pass'd without saying any thing. I should have been as much asham'd at seeing Miss Read, had not her friends, despairing with reason of my return after the receipt of my letter, per-suaded her to marry another, one Rogers, a potter, which was done in my absence. With him, however, she was never happy, and soon parted from him, refusing to cohabit with him or bear his name, it being now said that he had another wife. He was a worthless fellow, tho' an excellent workman, which was the temptation to her friends. He got into debt, ran away in 1727 or 1728, went to the West Indies, and died there. Keimer had got a better house, a shop well supply'd with stationery, plenty of new types, a number of hands, tho' none good, and seem'd to have a great deal of businesss.

Mr. Denham took a store in Water-street, where we open'd our goods; I attended the business diligently, studied accounts, and grew, in a little time, expert at selling. We lodg'd and boarded together; he counsell'd me as a father, having a sincere regard for me. I respected and loved him, and we might have gone on together very happy; but, in the beginning of February, 172$\frac{6}{7}$, when I had just pass'd my twenty-first year, we both were taken ill. My distemper was pleurisy, which very nearly carried me off. I suffered a good deal, gave up the point in my mind, and was rather disappointed when I found myself recovering, regretting, in some degree, that I must now, some time or other, have all that disagreeable work to do over again. I forget what his distemper was; it held him a long time, and at length carried him off. He left me a small legacy in a nuncupative will, as a token of his kindness for me, and he left me once more to the wide world; for the store was taken into the care of his executors, and my employment under him ended.

My brother-in-law, Holmes, being now at Philadelphia, advised my return to my business; and Keimer tempted me, with an offer of large wages by the year, to come and take the management of his printing-house, that he might better attend his stationer's shop. I had heard a bad character of him in London from his wife and her friends, and was not fond of having any more to do with him. I tri'd for farther employment as a merchant's clerk; but, not readily meeting with any, I clos'd again with Keimer. I found in his house these hands: Hugh Meredith, a Welsh Pensilvanian, thirty years of age, bred to country work;

honest, sensible, had a great deal of solid observation, was something of a reader, but given to drink. Stephen Potts, a young countryman of full age, bred to the same, of uncommon natural parts, and great wit and humour, but a little idle. These he had agreed with at extream low wages per week, to be rais'd a shilling every three months, as they would deserve by improving in their business; and the expectation of these high wages, to come on hereafter, was what he had drawn them in with. Meredith was to work at press, Potts at book-binding, which he, by agreement, was to teach them, though he knew neither one nor t'other. John ——, a wild Irishman, brought up to no business, whose service, for four years, Keimer had purchased from the captain of a ship; he, too, was to be made a pressman. George Webb, an Oxford scholar, whose time for four years he had likewise bought, intending him for a compositor, of whom more presently; and David Harry, a country boy, whom he had taken apprentice.

I soon perceiv'd that the intention of engaging me at wages so much higher than he had been us'd to give, was, to have these raw, cheap hands form'd thro' me; and, as soon as I had instructed them, then they being all articled to him, he should be able to do without me. I went on, however, very cheerfully, put his printing-house in order, which had been in great confussion, and brought his hands by degrees to mind their business and to do it better.

It was an odd thing to find an Oxford scholar in the situation of a bought servant. He was not more than eighteen years of age, and gave me this account of himself; that he was born in Gloucester, educated at a grammar-school there, had been distinguish'd among the scholars for some apparent superiority in performing his part, when they exhibited plays; belong'd to the Witty Club there, and had written some pieces in prose and verse, which were printed in the Gloucester newspapers; thence he was sent to Oxford; where he continued about a year, but not well satisfi'd, wishing of all things to see London, and become a player. At length, receiving his quarterly allowance of fifteen guineas, instead of discharging his debts he walk'd out of town, hid his gown in a furze bush, and footed it to London, where, having no friends to advise him, he fell into bad company, soon spent his guineas, found no means of being introduc'd among the players, grew necessitous, pawn'd his cloaths, and wanted bread. Walking the street very hungry, and not knowing what to do with himself, a crimp's bill was put into his hand, offering immediate entertainment and encouragement to such as would bind themselves to serve in America. He went directly, sign'd the indentures, was put into the ship, and came over, never writing a line to acquaint his friends what was become of him. He was lively, witty, good-natur'd, and a pleasant companion, but idle, thoughtless, and imprudent to the last degree.

John, the Irishman, soon ran away; with the rest I began to live very agreeably, for they all respected me the more, as they found Keimer incapable of instructing them, and that from me they learned something daily. We never worked on Saturday, that being Keimer's Sabbath, so I had two days for reading. My acquaintance with ingenious people in the town increased. Keimer himself treated me with great civility and apparent regard, and nothing now made me uneasy but my debt to Vernon, which I was yet unable to pay, being hitherto but a poor œconomist. He, however, kindly made no demand of it.

Our printing-house often wanted sorts, and there was no letter-founder in America; I had seen types cast at James's in London, but without much attention to the manner; however, I now contrived a mould, made use of the letters we had as puncheons, struck the matrices in lead, and thus supply'd in a pretty tolerable way all deficiencies. I also engrav'd several things on occasion; I made the ink; I was warehouseman, and everything, and, in short, quite a fac-totum.

But, however serviceable I might be, I found that my services became every day of less importance, as the other hands improv'd in the business; and, when Keimer paid my second quarter's wages, he let me know that he felt them too heavy, and thought I should make an abatement. He grew by degrees less civil, put on more of the master, frequently found fault, was captious, and seem'd ready for an outbreaking. I went on, nevertheless, with a good deal of patience, thinking that his encumber'd circumstances were partly the cause. At length a trifle snapt our connections; for, a great noise happening near the court-house, I put my head out of the window to see what was the matter. Keimer, being in the street, look'd up and saw me, call'd out to me in a loud voice and angry tone to mind my business, adding some reproachful words, that nettled me the more for their publicity, all the neighbors who were looking out on the same occasion being witnesses how I was treated. He came up immediately into the printing-house, continu'd the quarrel, high words pass'd on both sides, he gave me the quarter's warning we had stipulated, expressing a wish that he had not been oblig'd to so long a warning. I told him his wish was unnecessary, for I would leave him that instant; and so, taking my hat, walk'd out of doors, desiring Meredith, whom I saw below, to take care of some things I left, and bring them to my lodgings.

Meredith came accordingly in the evening, when we talked my affair over. He had conceiv'd a great regard for me, and was very unwilling that I should leave the house while he remain'd in it. He dissuaded me from returning to my native country, which I began to think of; he reminded me that Keimer was in debt for all he possess'd; that his creditors began to be uneasy; that he kept his shop miserably, sold often without profit for ready money, and often trusted without keeping accounts; that he must therefore fail, which would make a vacancy I might profit of. I objected my want of money. He then let me know that his father had a high opinion of me, and, from some discourse that had pass'd between them, he was sure would advance money to set us up, if I would enter into partnership with him. "My time," says he, "will be out with Keimer in the spring; by that time we may have our press and types in from London. I am sensible I am no workman; if you like it, your skill in the business shall be set against the stock I furnish, and we will share the profits equally."

The proposal was agreeable, and I consented; his father was in town and approv'd of it; the more as he saw I had great influence with his son, had prevail'd on him to abstain long from dram-drinking, and he hop'd might break him off that wretched habit entirely, when we came to be so closely connected. I gave an inventory to the father, who carry'd it to a merchant; the things were sent for, the secret was to be kept till they should arrive, and in the mean time I was to get work, if I could, at the other printing-house. But I found no vacancy there, and so remain'd idle a few days, when Keimer, on a prospect of being employ'd to print some paper money in New Jersey, which would require cuts and various types that I only could supply, and apprehending Bradford might engage me and get the job from him, sent me a very civil message, that old friends should not part for a few words, the effect of sudden passion, and wishing me to return. Meredith persuaded me to comply, as it would give more opportunity for his improvement under my daily instructions; so I return'd, and we went on more smoothly than for some time before. The New Jersey jobb was obtain'd, I contriv'd a copperplate press for it, the first that had been seen in the country; I cut several ornaments and checks for the bills. We went together to Burlington, where I executed the whole to satisfaction; and he received so large a sum for the work as to be enabled thereby to keep his head much longer above water.

At Burlington I made an acquaintance with many principal people of the province. Several of them had been appointed by the Assembly a committee to attend the press, and take care that no more bills were printed than the law directed. They were therefore, by turns, constantly with us, and generally he who attended, brought with him a friend or two for company. My mind having been much more improv'd by reading than Keimer's, I suppose it was for that reason my conversation seem'd to be more valu'd. They had me to their houses, introduced me to their friends, and show'd me much civility; while he, tho' the master, was a little neglected. In truth, he was an odd fish; ignorant of common life, fond of rudely opposing receiv'd opinions, slovenly to extream dirtiness, enthusiastic in some points of religion, and a little knavish withal.

We continu'd there near three months; and by that time I could reckon among my acquired friends, Judge Allen, Samuel Bustill, the secretary of the Province, Isaac Pearson, Joseph Cooper, and several of the Smiths, members of Assembly, and Isaac Decow, the surveyor-general. The latter was a shrewd, sagacious old man, who told me that he began for himself, when young, by wheeling clay for the brickmakers, learned to write after he was of age, carri'd the chain for surveyors, who taught him surveying, and he had now by his industry, acquir'd a good estate; and says he, "I foresee that you will soon work this man out of his business, and make a fortune in it at Philadelphia." He had not then the least intimation of my intention to set up there or anywhere. These friends were afterwards of great use to me, as I occasionally was to some of them. They all continued their regard for me as long as they lived.

Before I enter upon my public appearance in business, it may be well to let you know the then state of my mind with regard to my principles and morals, that you may see how far those influenc'd the future events of my life. My parents had early given me religious impressions, and brought me through my childhood piously in the Dissenting way. But I was scarce fifteen, when, after doubting by turns of several points, as I found them disputed in the different books I read, I began to doubt of Revelation itself. Some books against Deism fell into my hands; they were said to be the substance of sermons preached at Boyle's Lectures. It happened that they wrought an effect on me quite contrary to what was intended by them; for the arguments of the Deists, which were quoted to be refuted, appeared to me much stronger than the refutations; in short, I soon became a thorough Deist. My arguments perverted some others, particularly Collins and Ralph; but, each of them having afterwards wrong'd me greatly without the least compunction, and recollecting Keith's conduct toward me (who was another free-thinker), and my own towards Vernon and Miss Read, which at times gave me great trouble, I began to suspect that this doc-trine, tho' it might be true, was not very useful. My London pamphlet, which had for its motto these lines of Dryden:

> "Whatever is is right. Though purblind man
> Sees but a part o' the chain, the nearest link:
> His eyes not carrying to the equal beam,
> That poises all above;"

and from the attributes of God, his infinite wisdom, goodness and power, concluded that nothing could possibly be wrong in the world, and that vice and virtue were empty distinctions, no such things existing, appear'd now not so clever a perform-ance as I once thought it; and I doubted whether some error had not insinuated itself unperceiv'd into my argument, so as to infect all that follow'd, as is common in metaphysical rea-sonings.

I grew convinc'd that *truth, sincerity* and *integrity* in deal-ings between man and man were of the utmost importance to the felicity of life; and I form'd written resolutions, which still remain in my journal book, to practice them ever while I lived. Revelation had indeed no weight with me, as such; but I en-tertain'd an opinion that, though certain actions might not be bad *because* they were forbidden by it, or good *because* it com-manded them, yet probably these actions might be forbidden *because* they were bad for us, or commanded *because* they were beneficial to us, in their own natures, all the circumstances of things considered. And this persuasion, with the kind hand of Providence, or some guardian angel, or accidental favorable circumstances and situations, or all together, preserved me, thro' this dangerous time of youth, and the hazardous situations I was sometimes in among strangers, remote from the eye and advice of my father, without any willful gross immorality or injustice, that might have been expected from my want of religion. I say willful, because the instances I have mentioned had something of *necessity* in them, from my youth, inexperience, and the knavery of others. I had therefore a tolerable character to begin the world with; I valued it properly, and determin'd to preserve it.

We had not been long return'd to Philadelphia before the new types arriv'd from London. We settled with Keimer, and left him by his consent before he heard of it. We found a house to hire near the market, and took it. To lessen the rent, which was then but twenty-four pounds a year, tho' I have since known it to let for seventy, we took in Thomas Godfrey, a glazier, and his family, who were to pay a considerable part of it to us, and we to board with them. We had scarce opened our letters and put our press in order, before George House, an acquaintance of mine, brought a countryman to us, whom he had met in the street inquiring for a printer. All our cash was now expended in the variety of particulars we had been obliged to procure, and this countryman's five shillings, being our first-fruits, and coming so seasonably, gave me more pleasure than any crown I have since earned; and the gratitude I felt toward House has made me often more ready than perhaps I should otherwise have been to assist young beginners.

There are croakers in every country, always boding its ruin. Such a one then lived in Philadelphia; a person of note, an elderly man, with a wise look and a very grave manner of speaking; his name was Samuel Mickle. This gentleman, a stranger to me, stopt one day at my door, and asked me if I was the young man who had lately opened a new printing-house. Being answered in the affirmative, he said he was sorry for me, because it was an expensive undertaking, and the expense would be lost; for Philadelphia was a sinking place, the people already half-bankrupts, or near being so; all appearances to the contrary, such as new buildings and the rise of rents, being to his certain knowledge fallacious; for they were, in fact, among the things that would soon ruin us. And he gave me such a detail of misfortunes now existing, or that were soon to exist, that he left me half melancholy. Had I known him before I engaged in this business, probably I never should have done it. This man continued to live in this decaying place, and to declaim in the same strain, refusing for many years to buy a house there, because all was going to destruction; and at last I had the pleasure of seeing him give five times as much for one as he might have bought it for when he first began his croaking.

I should have mentioned before, that, in the autumn of the preceding year, I had form'd most of my ingenious acquaintance into a club of mutual improvement, which we called the JUNTO; we met on Friday evenings. The rules that I drew up required that every member, in his turn, should produce one or more queries on any point of Morals, Politics, or Natural Philosophy, to be discuss'd by the company; and once in three months produce and read an essay of his own writing, on any subject he pleased. Our debates were to be under the direction of a president, and to be conducted in the sincere spirit of inquiry after truth, without fondness for dispute, or desire of victory; and, to prevent warmth, all expressions of positiveness in opinions, or direct contradiction, were after some time made contraband, and prohibited under small pecuniary penalties.

The first members were Joseph Breintnal, a copyer of deeds for the scriveners, a good-natur'd, friendly, middle-ag'd man, a great lover of poetry, reading all he could meet with, and writing some that was tolerable; very ingenious in many little Nicknackeries, and of sensible conversation.

Thomas Godfrey, a self-taught mathematician, great in his way, and afterwards inventor of what is now called Hadley's Quadrant. But he knew little out of his way, and was not a pleasing companion; as, like most great mathematicians I have met with, he expected universal precision in everything said, or was for ever denying or distinguishing upon trifles, to the disturbance of all conversation. He soon left us.

Nicholas Scull, a surveyor, afterwards surveyor-general, who lov'd books, and sometimes made a few verses.

William Parsons, bred a shoemaker, but, loving reading, had

acquir'd a considerable share of mathematics, which he first studied with a view to astrology, that he afterwards laught at it. He also became surveyor-general.

William Maugridge, a joiner, a most exquisite mechanic, and a solid, sensible man.

Hugh Meredith, Stephen Potts, and George Webb I have characteriz'd before.

Robert Grace, a young gentleman of some fortune, generous, lively, and witty; a lover of punning and of his friends.

And William Coleman, then a merchant's clerk, about my age, who had the coolest, clearest head, the best heart, and the exactest morals of almost any man I ever met with. He became afterwards a merchant of great note, and one of our provincial judges. Our friendship continued without interruption to his death, upwards of forty years; and the club continued almost as long, and was the best school of philosophy, morality, and politics that then existed in the province; for our queries, which were read the week preceding their discussion, put us upon reading with attention upon the several subjects, that we might speak more to the purpose; and here, too, we acquired better habits of conversation, every thing being studied in our rules which might prevent our disgusting each other. From thence the long continuance of the club, which I shall have frequent occasion to speak further of hereafter.

But my giving this account of it here to show something of the interest I had, every one of these exerting themselves in recommending business to us. Breintnal particularly procur'd us from the Quakers the printing forty sheets of their history, the rest being to be done by Keimer; and upon this we work'd exceedingly hard, for the price was low. It was a folio, pro patria size, in pica, with long primer notes. I compos'd of it a sheet a day, and Meredith worked it off at press; it was often eleven at night, and sometimes later, before I had finished my distribution for the next day's work, for the little jobbs sent in by our other friends now and then put us back. But so determin'd I was to continue doing a sheet a day of the folio, that one night, when, having impos'd my forms, I thought my day's work over, one of them by accident was broken, and two pages reduced to pi, I immediately distributed and compos'd it over again before I went to bed; and this industry, visible to our neighbors, began to give us character and credit; particularly, I was told, that mention being made of the new printing-office at the merchants' Every-night club, the general opinion was that it must fail, there being already two printers in the place, Keimer and Bradford; but Dr. Baird (whom you and I saw many years after at his native place, St. Andrew's in Scotland) gave a contrary opinion: "For the industry of that Franklin," says he, "is superior to any thing I ever saw of the kind; I see him still at work when I go home from club, and he is at work again before his neighbors are out of bed." This struck the rest, and we soon after had offers from one of them to supply us with stationery; but as yet we did not chuse to engage in shop business.

I mention this industry the more particularly and the more freely, tho' it seems to be talking in my own praise, that those of my posterity, who shall read it, may know the use of that virtue, when they see its effects in my favour throughout this relation.

George Webb, who had found a female friend that lent him wherewith to purchase his time of Keimer, now came to offer himself as a journeyman to us. We could not then employ him; but I foolishly let him know as a secret that I soon intended to begin a newspaper, and might then have work for him. My hopes of success, as I told him, were founded on this, that the then only newspaper, printed by Bradford, was a paltry thing, wretchedly manag'd, no way entertaining, and yet was profitable to him; I therefore thought a good paper would scarcely fail of good encouragement. I requested Webb not to mention it; but he told it to Keimer, who immediately, to be beforehand with me, published proposals for printing one himself, on which Webb was to be employed. I resented this; and, to counteract them, as I could not yet begin our paper, I wrote several pieces of entertainment for Bradford's paper, under the title of the BUSY BODY, which Breintnal continu'd some months. By this means the attention of the publick was fixed on that paper, and Keimer's proposals, which we burlesqu'd and ridicul'd, were disregarded. He began his paper, however, and, after carrying it on three quarters of a year, with at most only ninety subscribers, he offered it me for a trifle; and I, having been ready some time to go on with it, took it in hand directly; and it prov'd in a few years extremely profitable to me.

I perceive that I am apt to speak in the singular number, though our partnership still continu'd; the reason may be that, in fact, the whole management of the business lay upon me Meredith was no compositor, a poor pressman, and seldom sober. My friends lamented my connection with him, but I was to make the best of it.

Our first papers made a quite different appearance from any before in the province; a better type, and better printed; but some spirited remarks of my writing, on the dispute then going on between Governor Burnet and the Massachusetts Assembly, struck the principal people, occasioned the paper and the manager of it to be much talk'd of, and in a few weeks brought them all to be our subscribers.

Their example was follow'd by many, and our number went on growing continually. This was one of the first good effects of my having learnt a little to scribble; another was, that the leading men, seeing a newspaper now in the hands of one who could also handle a pen, thought it convenient to oblige and encourage me. Bradford still printed the votes, and laws, and other publick business. He had printed an address of the House to the governor, in a coarse, blundering manner, we reprinted it elegantly and correctly, and sent one to every member. They were sensible of the difference: it strengthened the hands of our friends in the House, and they voted us their printers for the year ensuing.

Among my friends in the House I must not forget Mr. Hamilton, before mentioned, who was then returned from England, and had a seat in it. He interested himself for me strongly in that instance, as he did in many others afterward, continuing his patronage till his death. [I got his son once £500.]

Mr. Vernon, about this time, put me in mind of the debt I ow'd him, but did not press me. I wrote him an ingenuous letter of acknowledgment, crav'd his forbearance a little longer, which he allow'd me, and as soon as I was able, I paid the principal with interest, and many thanks; so that erratum was in some degree corrected.

But now another difficulty came upon me which I had never the least reason to expect. Mr. Meredith's father, who was to have paid for our printing-house, according to the expectations given me, was able to advance only one hundred pounds currency, which had been paid; and a hundred more was due to the merchant, who grew impatient, and su'd us all. We gave bail, but saw that, if the money could not be rais'd in time, the suit must soon come to a judgment and execution, and our hopeful prospects must, with us, be ruined, as the press and letters must be sold for payment, perhaps at half price.

In this distress two true friends, whose kindness I have never forgotten, nor ever shall forget while I can remember any thing, came to me separately, unknown to each other, and, without any application from me, offering each of them to advance me all the money that should be necessary to enable me to take the whole business upon myself, if that should be practicable; but they did not like my continuing the partnership with Meredith, who, as they said, was often seen drunk in the streets, and playing at low games in alehouses, much to our discredit. These two friends were William Coleman and Robert Grace. I told them I could not propose a separation while any prospect remain'd of the Meredith's fulfilling their part of our agreement, because I thought myself under great obligations to them for what they had done, and would do if they could; but, if they fail'd in their performance, and our partnership must be dissolv'd, I should then think myself at liberty to accept the assistance of my friends.

Thus the matter rested for some time, when I said to my

partner, "Perhaps your father is dissatisfied at the part you have undertaken in this affair of ours, and is unwilling to advance for you and me what he would for you alone. If that is the case, tell me, and I will resign the whole to you, and go about my business." "No," said he, "my father has really been disappointed, and is really unable; and I am unwilling to distress him farther. I see this is a business I am not fit for. I was bred a farmer, and it was a folly in me to come to town, and put myself, at thirty years of age, an apprentice to learn a new trade. Many of our Welsh people are going to settle in North Carolina, where land is cheap. I am inclin'd to go with them, and follow my old employment. You may find friends to assist you. If you will take the debts of the company upon you; return to my father the hundred pound he has advanced; pay my little personal debts, and give me thirty pounds and a new saddle, I will relinquish the partnership, and leave the whole in your hands." I agreed to this proposal: it was drawn up in writing, sign'd, and seal'd immediately. I gave him what he demanded, and he went soon after to Carolina, from whence he sent me next year two long letters, containing the best account that had been given of that country, the climate, the soil, husbandry, etc., for in those matters he was very judicious. I printed them in the papers, and they gave great satisfaction to the publick.

As soon as he was gone, I recurr'd to my two friends; and because I would not give an unkind preference to either, I took half of what each had offered and I wanted of one, and half of the other; paid off the company's debts, and went on with the business in my own name, advertising that the partnership was dissolved. I think this was in or about the year 1729. [July 14, 1730.]

About this time there was a cry among the people for more paper money, only fifteen thousand pounds being extant in the province, and that soon to be sunk. The wealthy inhabitants oppos'd any addition, being against all paper currency, from an apprehension that it would depreciate, as it had done in New England, to the prejudice of all creditors. We had discuss'd this point in our Junto, where I was on the side of an addition, being persuaded that the first small sum struck in 1723 had done much good by increasing the trade, employment, and number of inhabitants in the province, since I now saw all the old houses inhabited, and many new ones building: whereas I remembered well, that when I first walk'd about the streets of Philadelphia, eating my roll, I saw most of the houses in Walnut Street, between Second and Front streets, with bills on their doors, "To be let"; and many likewise in Chestnut-street and other streets, which made me then think the inhabitants of the city were deserting it one after another.

Our debates possess'd me so fully of the subject, that I wrote and printed an anonymous pamphlet on it, entitled *"The Nature and Necessity of a Paper Currency."* It was well receiv'd by the common people in general; but the rich men dislik'd it, for it increas'd and strengthen'd the clamor for more money, and they happening to have no writers among them that were able to answer it, their opposition slacken'd, and the point was carried by a majority in the House. My friends there, who conceiv'd I had been of some service, thought fit to reward me by employing me in printing the money; a very profitable jobb and a great help to me. This was another advantage gain'd by my being able to write.

The utility of this currency became by time and experience so evident as never afterwards to be much disputed; so that it grew soon to fifty-five thousand pounds, and in 1739 to eighty thousand pounds, since which it arose during war to upwards of three hundred and fifty thousand pounds, trade, building, and inhabitants all the while increasing, tho' I now think there are limits beyond which the quantity may be hurtful.

I soon after obtain'd, thro' my friend Hamilton, the printing of the Newcastle paper money, another profitable jobb as I then thought it; small things appearing great to those in small circumstances; and these, to me, were really great advantages, as they were great encouragements. He procured for me, also, the printing of the laws and votes of that government, which continu'd in my hands as long as I follow'd the business.

I now open'd a little stationer's shop. I had in it blanks of all sorts, the correctest that ever appear'd among us, being assisted in that by my friend Breintnal. I had also paper, parchment, chapmen's books, etc. One Whitemash, a compositor I had known in London, an excellent workman, now came to me, and work'd with me constantly and diligently; and I took an apprentice, the son of Aquila Rose.

I began now gradually to pay off the debt I was under for the printing-house. In order to secure my credit and character as a tradesman, I took care not only to be in *reality* industrious and frugal, but to avoid all appearances to the contrary. I drest plainly; I was seen at no places of idle diversion. I never went out a fishing or shooting; a book, indeed, sometimes debauch'd me from my work, but that was seldom, snug, and gave no scandal; and, to show that I was not above my business, I sometimes brought home the paper I purchas'd at the stores thro' the streets on a wheelbarrow. Thus being esteem'd an industrious, thriving young man, and paying duly for what I bought, the merchants who imported stationery solicited my custom; others proposed supplying me with books, and I went on swimmingly. In the mean time, Keimer's credit and business declining daily, he was at last forc'd to sell his printing-house to satisfy his creditors. He went to Barbadoes, and there lived some years in very poor circumstances.

His apprentice, David Harry, whom I had instructed while I work'd with him, set up in his place at Philadelphia, having bought his materials. I was at first apprehensive of a powerful rival in Harry, as his friends were very able, and had a good deal of interest. I therefore propos'd a partnership to him, which he, fortunately for me, rejected with scorn. He was very proud, dress'd like a gentleman, liv'd expensively, too much diversion and pleasure abroad, ran in debt, and neglected his business; upon which, all business left him; and, finding nothing to do, he followed Keimer to Barbadoes, taking the printing-house with him. There this apprentice employ'd his former master as a journeyman; they quarrel'd often; Harry went continually behindhand, and at length was forc'd to sell his types and return to his country work in Pensilvania. The person that bought them employ'd Keimer to use them, but in a few years he died.

There remained now no competitor with me in Philadelphia but the old one, Bradford; who was rich and easy, did a little printing now and then by straggling hands, but was not very anxious about the business. However, as he kept the post-office, it was imagined he had better opportunities of obtaining news; his paper was thought a better distributer of advertisements than mine, and therefore had many more, which was a profitable thing to him, and a disadvantage to me; for, tho' I did indeed receive and send papers by the post, yet the publick opinion was otherwise, for what I did send was by bribing the riders, who took them privately, Bradford being unkind enough to forbid it, which occasion'd some resentment on my part; and I thought so meanly of him for it, that, when I afterward came into his situation, I took care never to imitate it.

I had hitherto continu'd to board with Godfrey, who lived in part of my house with his wife and children, and had one side of the shop for his glazier's business, tho' he worked little, being always absorbed in his mathematics. Mrs. Godfrey projected a match for me with a relation's daughter, took opportunities of bringing us often together, till a serious courtship on my part ensu'd, the girl being in herself very deserving. The old folks encourag'd me by continual invitations to supper, and by leaving us together, till at length it was time to explain. Mrs. Godfrey manag'd our little treaty. I let her know that I expected as much money with their daughter as would pay off my remaining debt for the printing-house, which I believe was not then above a hundred pounds. She brought me word they had no such sum to spare; I said they might mortgage their house in the loan-office. The answer to this, after some days, was, that they did not approve the match; that, on inquiry of Bradford, they had been informed the printing business was not a profit-able one; the types would soon be worn out, and more wanted; that S. Keimer and D. Harry had failed one after the other, and I should probably soon follow them; and, therefore, I was forbidden the house, and the daughter shut up.

Whether this was a real change of sentiment or only artifice, on a supposition of our being too far engaged in affection to retract, and therefore that we should steal a marriage, which would leave them at liberty to give or withhold what they pleas'd, I know not; but I suspected the latter, resented it, and went no more. Mrs. Godfrey brought me afterward some more favorable accounts of their disposition, and would have drawn me on again; but I declared absolutely my resolution to have nothing more to do with that family. This was resented by the Godfreys; we differ'd, and they removed, leaving me the whole house, and I resolved to take no more inmates.

But this affair having turned my thoughts to marriage, I look'd around me and made overtures of acquaintance in other places; but soon found that, the business of a printer being gen-erally thought a poor one, I was not to expect money with a wife, unless with such a one as I should not otherwise think agreeable. In the mean time, that hard-to-be-governed passion of youth hurried me frequently into intrigues with low women that fell in my way, which were attended with some expense and great inconvenience, besides a continual risque to my health by a distemper which of all things I dreaded, though by great good luck I escaped it. A friendly correspondence as neighbors and old acquaintances had continued between me and Mrs. Read's family, who all had a regard for me from the time of my first lodging in their house. I was often invited there and consulted in their affairs, wherein I sometimes was of service. I piti'd poor Miss Read's unfortunate situation, who was generally dejected, seldom cheerful, and avoided company. I considered my giddi-ness and inconstancy when in London as in a great degree the cause of her unhappiness, tho' the mother was good enough to think the fault more her own than mine, as she had prevented our marrying before I went thither, and persuaded the other match in my absence. Our mutual affection was revived, but there were now great objections to our union. The match was indeed looked upon as invalid, a preceding wife being said to be living in England; but this could not easily be prov'd, because of the distance; and, tho' there was a report of his death, it was not certain. Then, tho' it should be true, he had left many debts, which his successor might be call'd upon to pay. We ventured, however, over all these difficulties, and I took her to wife, September 1st, 1730. None of the inconveniences happened that we had apprehended; she proved a good and faithful helpmate, assisted me much by attending the shop; we throve together, and have ever mutually endeavor'd to make each other happy. Thus I corrected that great *erratum* as well as I could.

About this time, our club meeting, not at a tavern, but in a little room of Mr. Grace's, set apart for that purpose, a proposition was made by me, that, since our books were often referr'd to in our disquisitions upon the queries, it might be convenient to us to have them altogether where we met, that upon occasion they might be consulted; and by thus clubbing our books to a common library, we should, while we lik'd to keep them together, have each of us the advantage of using the books of all the other members, which would be nearly as beneficial as if each owned the whole. It was lik'd and agreed to, and we fill'd one end of the room with such books as we could best spare. The number was not so great as we expected; and tho' they had been of great use, yet some inconveniences occurring for want of due care of them, the collection, after about a year, was separated, and each took his books home again.

And now I set on foot my first project of a public nature, that for a subscription library. I drew up the proposals, got them put into form by our great scrivener, Brockden, and, by the help of my friends in the Junto, procured fifty subscribers of forty shillings each to begin with, and ten shillings a year for fifty years, the term our company was to continue. We afterwards obtain'd a charter, the company being increased to one

hundred: this was the mother of all the North American subscription libraries, now so numerous. It is become a great thing
itself, and continually increasing. These libraries have improved the general conversation of the Americans, made the
common tradesmen and farmers as intelligent as most gentlemen from other countries, and perhaps have contributed in
some degree to the stand so generally made throughout the colonies in defence of their privileges.

Mem°. Thus far was written with the intention express'd in
the beginning and therefore contains several little family anecdotes of no importance to others. What follows was written
many years after in compliance with the advice contain'd in
these letters, and accordingly intended for the public. The affairs of the Revolution occasion'd the interruption.

Letter from Mr. Abel James, with Notes of my Life (received in Paris)

"My Dear and Honored Friend: I have often been desirous
of writing to thee, but could not be reconciled to the thought,
that the letter might fall into the hands of the British, lest some
printer or busy-body should publish some part of the contents,
and give our friend pain, and myself censure.

"Some time since there fell into my hands, to my great joy,
about twenty-three sheets in thy own handwriting, containing
an account of the parentage and life of thyself, directed to thy
son, ending in the year 1730, with which there were notes, likewise in thy writing; a copy of which I inclose, in hopes it may
be a means, if thou continued it up to a later period, that the
first and latter part may be put together; and if it is not yet
continued, I hope thee will not delay it. Life is uncertain, as
the preacher tells us; and what will the world say if kind, hu-
mane, and benevolent Ben. Franklin should leave his friends
and the world deprived of so pleasing and profitable a work;
a work which would be useful and entertaining not only to a

few, but to millions? The influence writings under that classs have on the minds of youth is very great, and has nowhere appeared to me so plain, as in our public friend's journals. It almost insensibly leads the youth into the resolution of endeavoring to become as good and eminent as the journalist. Should thine, for instance, when published (and I think it could not fail of it), lead the youth to equal the industry and temperance of thy early youth, what a blessing with that class would such a work be! I know of no character living, nor many of them put together, who has so much in his power as thyself to promote a greater spirit of industry and early attention to business, frugality, and temperance with the American youth. Not that I think the work would have no other merit and use in the world, far from it; but the first is of such vast importance that I know nothing that can equal it."

The foregoing letter and the minutes accompanying it being shown to a friend, I received from him the following:

Letter from Mr. Benjamin Vaughn

"Paris, January 31, 1783.

"My Dearest Sir: When I had read over your sheets of minutes of the principal incidents of your life, recovered for you by your Quaker acquaintance, I told you I would send you a letter expressing my reasons why I thought it would be useful to complete and publish it as he desired. Various concerns have for some time past prevented this letter being written, and I do not know whether it was worth any expectation; happening to be at leisure, however, at present, I shall by writing, at least interest and instruct myself; but as the terms I am inclined to use may tend to offend a person of your manners, I shall only tell you how I would address any other person, who was as good and as great as yourself, but less diffident. I would say to him, Sir, I solicit the history of your life from the following motives: Your history is so remarkable, that if you do not give it, somebody else will certainly give it; and perhaps so as nearly to do as much harm, as your own management of the thing might do good. It will moreover present a table of the internal circumstances of your country, which will very much tend to invite to it settlers of virtuous and manly minds. And considering the eagerness with which such information is sought by them, and the extent of your reputation, I do not know of a more efficacious advertisement than your biography would give. All that has happened to you is also connected with the detail of the manners and situation of a rising people; and in this respect I do not think that the writings of Cæsar and Tacitus can be more interesting to a true judge of human nature and society. But these, sir, are small reasons, in my opinion, compared with the chance which your life will give for the forming of future great men; and in conjunction with your Art of Virtue (which you design to publish) of improving the features of private character, and consequently of aiding all happiness, both public and domestic. The two works I allude to, sir, will in particular give a noble rule and example of self-education. School and other education constantly proceed upon false principles, and show a clumsy apparatus pointed at a false mark; but your apparatus is simple, and the mark a true one; and while parents and young persons are left destitute of other just means of estimating and becoming prepared for a reasonable course in life, your discovery that the thing is in many a man's private power, will be invaluable! Influence upon the private character, late in life, is not only an influence late in life, but a weak influence. It is in youth that we plant our chief habits and prejudices; it is in youth that we take our party as to profession, pursuits and matrimony. In youth, therefore, the turn is given; in youth the education even of the next generation is given; in youth the private and public character is determined; and the term of life extending but from youth to age, life ought to begin well from youth, and more especially before we take our party as to our principal objects. But your biography will not merely teach self-education, but the education of a wise man; and the wisest

Franklin's printing press

man will receive lights and improve his progress, by seeing de-
tailed the conduct of another wise man. And why are weaker
men to be deprived of such helps, when we see our race has
been blundering on in the dark, almost without a guide in this
particular, from the farthest trace of time? Show then, sir, how
much is to be done, both to sons and fathers; and invite all wise
men to become like yourself, and other men to become wise.
When we see how cruel statesmen and warriors can be to the
human race, and how absurd distinguished men can be to their
acquaintance, it will be instructive to observe the instances
multiply of pacific, acquiescing manners; and to find how com-
patible it is to be great and domestic, enviable and yet good-
humored.

"The little private incidents which you will also have to
relate, will have considerable use, as we want, above all things,
rules of prudence in ordinary affairs; and it will be curious to
see how you have acted in these. It will be so far a sort of key
to life, and explain many things that all men ought to have
once explained to them, to give them a chance of becoming wise
by foresight. The nearest thing to having experience of one's
own, is to have other people's affairs brought before us in a
shape that is interesting; this is sure to happen from your pen;
our affairs and management will have an air of simplicity or
importance that will not fail to strike; and I am convinced you
have conducted them with as much originality as if you had
been conducting discussions in politics or philosophy; and what
more worthy of experiments and system (its importance and its
errors considered) than human life?

"Some men have been virtuous blindly, others have speculated fantastically, and others have been shrewd to bad purposes; but you, sir, I am sure, will give under your hand,
nothing but what is at the same moment, wise, practical and
good. Your account of yourself (for I suppose the parallel I am
drawing for Dr. Franklin, will hold not only in point of character, but of private history) will show that you are ashamed of
no origin; a thing the more important, as you prove how little

necessary all origin is to happiness, virtue, or greatness. As no end likewise happens without a means, so we shall find, sir, that even you yourself framed a plan by which you became considerable; but at the same time we may see that though the event is flattering, the means are as simple as wisdom could make them; that is, depending upon nature, virtue, thought and habit. Another thing demonstrated will be the propriety of every man's waiting for his time for appearing upon the stage of the world. Our sensations being very much fixed to the moment, we are apt to forget that more moments are to follow the first, and consequently that man should arrange his conduct so as to suit the whole of a life. Your attribution appears to have been applied to your life, and the passing moments of it have been enlivened with content and enjoyment, instead of being tormented with foolish impatience or regrets. Such a conduct is easy for those who make virtue and themselves in countenance by examples of other truly great men, of whom patience is so often the characteristic. Your Quaker correspondent, sir (for here again I will suppose the subject of my letter resembling Dr. Franklin), praised your frugality, diligence and temperance, which is considered as a pattern for all youth; but it is singular that he should have forgotten your modesty and your disinterestedness, without which you never could have waited for your advancement, or found your situation in the meantime comfortable; which is a strong lesson to show the poverty of glory and the importance of regulating our minds. If this correspondent had known the nature of your reputation as well as I do, he would have said, Your former writings and measures would secure attention to your Biography, and Art of Virtue; and your Biography and Art of Virtue, in return, would secure attention to them. This is an advantage attendant upon a various character, and which brings all that belongs to it into greater play; and it is the more useful, as perhaps more persons are at a loss for the means of improving their minds and characters, than they are for the time or the inclination to do it. But there is one concluding reflection, sir, that will shew the use of your life as a mere piece of biography. This style of writing seems a little gone out of vogue, and yet it is a very useful one; and your specimen of it may be particularly serviceable, as it will make a subject of comparison with the lives of various public cut-throats and intriguers, and with absurd monastic self-tormentors or vain literary triflers. If it encourages more writings of the same kind with your own, and induces more men to spend lives fit to be written, it will be worth all Plutarch's Lives put to-gether. But being tired of figuring to myself a character of which every feature suits only one man in the world, without giving him the praise of it, I shall end my letter, my dear Dr. Franklin, with a personal application to your proper self. I am earnestly desirous, then, my dear sir, that you should let the world into the traits of your genuine character, as civil broils may otherwise tend to disguise or traduce it. Considering your great age, the caution of your character, and your peculiar style of thinking, it is not likely that any one besides yourself can be sufficiently master of the facts of your life, or the intentions of your mind. Besides all this, the immense revolution of the pres-ent period, will necessarily turn our attention towards the au-thor of it, and when virtuous principles have been pretended in it, it will be highly important to shew that such have really in-fluenced; and, as your own character will be the principal one to receive a scrutiny, it is proper (even for its effects upon your vast and rising country, as well as upon England and upon Europe) that it should stand respectable and eternal. For the furtherance of human happiness, I have always maintained that it is necessary to prove that man is not even at present a vicious and detestable animal; and still more to prove that good man-agement may greatly amend him; and it is for much the same reason, that I am anxious to see the opinion established, that there are fair characters existing among the individuals of the race; for the moment that all men, without exception, shall be conceived abandoned, good people will cease efforts deemed to be hopeless, and perhaps think of taking their share in the scramble of life, or at least of making it comfortable principally for themselves. Take then, my dear sir, this work most speedily into hand: shew yourself good as you are good; temperate as you are temperate; and above all things, prove yourself as one, who from your infancy have loved justice, liberty and concord, in a way that has made it natural and consistent for you to have acted, as we have seen you act in the last seventeen years of your life. Let Englishmen be made not only to respect, but even to love you. When they think well of individuals in your native country, they will go nearer to thinking well of your country; and when your countrymen see themselves well thought of by Englishmen, they will go nearer to thinking well of England. Extend your views even further; do not stop at those who speak the English tongue, but after having settled so many points in nature and politics, think of bettering the whole race of men. As I have not read any part of the life in question, but know only the character that lived it, I write somewhat at hazard. I am sure, however, that the life and the treatise I allude to (on the Art of Virtue) will necessarily fulfil the chief of my expectations; and still more so if you take up the measure of suiting these performances to the several views above stated. Should they even prove unsuccessful in all that a sanguine admirer of yours hopes from them, you will at least have framed pieces to interest the human mind; and whoever gives a feeling of pleasure that is innocent to man, has added so much to the fair side of a life otherwise too much darkened by anxiety and too much injured by pain. In the hope, therefore, that you will listen to the prayer addressed to you in this letter, I beg to subscribe myself, my dearest sir, etc., etc.,

"Signed,   Benj. Vaughan."

Continuation of the Account of my Life, begun at Passy, near Paris, 1784

It is some time since I receiv'd the above letters, but I have been too busy till now to think of complying with the request they contain. It might, too, be much better done if I were at home among my papers, which would aid my memory, and help to ascertain dates; but my return being uncertain, and having just now a little leisure, I will endeavor to recollect and write what I can; if I live to get home, it may there be corrected and improv'd.

Not having any copy here of what is already written, I know not whether an account is given of the means I used to establish the Philadelphia public library, which, from a small beginning, is now become so considerable, though I remember to have come down to near the time of that transaction (1730). I will therefore begin here with an account of it, which may be struck out if found to have been already given.

At the time I establish'd myself in Pennsylvania, there was not a good bookseller's shop in any of the colonies to the southward of Boston. In New York and Philad'a the printers were indeed stationers; they sold only paper, etc., almanacs, ballads, and a few common school-books. Those who lov'd reading were oblig'd to send for their books from England; the members of the Junto had each a few. We had left the alehouse, where we first met, and hired a room to hold our club in. I propos'd that we should all of us bring our books to that room, where they would not only be ready to consult in our conferences, but become a common benefit, each of us being at liberty to borrow such as he wish'd to read at home. This was accordingly done, and for some time contented us.

Finding the advantage of this little collection, I propos'd to render the benefit from books more common, by commencing a public subscription library. I drew a sketch of the plan and rules that would be necessary, and got a skilful conveyancer, Mr. Charles Brockden, to put the whole in form of articles of agreement to be subscribed, by which each subscriber engag'd to pay a certain sum down for the first purchase of books, and an annual contribution for increasing them. So few were the readers at that time in Philadelphia, and the majority of us so poor, that I was not able, with great industry, to find more than fifty persons, mostly young tradesmen, willing to pay down for this purpose forty shillings each, and ten shillings per annum. On this little fund we began. The books were imported; the library was opened one day in the week for lending to the subscribers, on their promissory notes to pay double the value if not duly returned. The institution soon manifested its utility, was imitated by other towns, and in other provinces. The libraries were augmented by donations; reading became fashionable; and our people, having no publick amusements to divert their attention from study, became better acquainted with books, and in a few years were observ'd by strangers to be better instructed and more intelligent than people of the same rank generally are in other countries.

When we were about to sign the above-mentioned articles, which were to be binding on us, our heirs, etc., for fifty years, Mr. Brockden, the scrivener, said to us, "You are young men, but it is scarcely probable that any of you will live to see the expiration of the term fix'd in the instrument." A number of us, however, are yet living; but the instrument was after a few years rendered null by a charter that incorporated and gave perpetuity to the company.

The objections and reluctances I met with in soliciting the subscriptions, made me soon feel the impropriety of presenting one's self as the proposer of any useful project, that might be suppos'd to raise one's reputation in the smallest degree above that of one's neighbors, when one has need of their assistance to accomplish that project. I therefore put myself as much as I could out of sight, and stated it as a scheme of a *number of friends,* who had requested me to go about and propose it to such as they thought lovers of reading. In this way my affair went on more smoothly, and I ever after practis'd it on such occasions; and, from my frequent successes, can heartily recommend it. The present little sacrifice of your vanity will afterwards be amply repaid. If it remains a while uncertain to whom the merit belongs, some one more vain than yourself will be encouraged to claim it, and then even envy will be disposed to do you justice by plucking those assumed feathers, and restoring them to their right owner.

This library afforded me the means of improvement by constant study, for which I set apart an hour or two each day, and thus repair'd in some degree the loss of the learned education my father once intended for me. Reading was the only amusement I allow'd myself. I spent no time in taverns, games, or frolicks of any kind; and my industry in my business continu'd as indefatigable as it was necessary. I was indebted for my printing-house; I had a young family coming on to be educated, and I had to contend with for business two printers, who were established in the place before me. My circumstances, however, grew daily easier. My original habits of frugality continuing, and my father having, among his instructions to me when a boy, frequently repeated a proverb of Solomon, "Seest thou a man diligent in his calling, he shall stand before kings, he shall not stand before mean men," I from thence considered industry as a means of obtaining wealth and distinction, which encourag'd me, tho' I did not think that I should ever literally *stand before kings,* which, however, has since happened; for I have stood before *five,* and even had the honour of sitting down with one, the King of Denmark, to dinner.

We have an English proverb that says, *"He that would thrive, must ask his wife."* It was lucky for me that I had one as much dispos'd to industry and frugality as myself. She assisted me cheerfully in my business, folding and stitching pamphlets, tending shop, purchasing old linen rags for the paper-makers, etc., etc. We kept no idle servants, our table was plain and simple, our furniture of the cheapest. For instance, my breakfast was a long time bread and milk (no tea), and I ate it out of a twopenny earthen porringer, with a pewter spoon. But mark how luxury will enter families, and make a progress, in spite of principle: being call'd one morning to breakfast, I found it in a China bowl, with a spoon of silver! They had been bought for me without my knowledge by my wife, and had cost her the enormous sum of three-and-twenty shillings, for which she had no other excuse or apology to make, but that she thought *her* husband deserv'd a silver spoon and China bowl as well as any of his neighbors. This was the first appearance of plate and China in our house, which afterward, in a course of years, as our wealth increas'd, augmented gradually to several hundred pounds in value.

I had been religiously educated as a Presbyterian; and tho' some of the dogmas of that persuasion, such as *the eternal decrees of God, election, reprobation, etc.,* appeared to me unintelligible, others doubtful, and I early absented myself from the public assemblies of the sect, Sunday being my studying day, I never was without some religious principles. I never doubted, for instance, the existence of the Deity; that he made the world, and govern'd it by his Providence; that the most acceptable service of God was the doing good to man; that our souls are immortal; and that all crime will be punished, and virtue rewarded, either here or hereafter. These I esteem'd the essentials of every religion; and, being to be found in all the religions we had in our country, I respected them all, tho' with different degrees of respect, as I found them more or less mix'd with other articles, which, without any tendency to inspire, promote, or confirm morality, serv'd principally to divide us, and make us unfriendly to one another. This respect to all, with an opinion that the worst had some good effects, induc'd me to avoid all discourse that might tend to lessen the good opinion another might have of his own religion; and as our province increas'd in people, and new places of worship were continually wanted, and generally erected by voluntary contribution, my mite for such purpose, whatever might be the sect, was never refused.

Tho' I seldom attended any public worship, I had still an opinion of its propriety, and of its utility when rightly conducted, and I regularly paid my annual subscription for the support of the only Presbyterian minister or meeting we had in Philadelphia. He us'd to visit me sometimes as a friend, and admonish me to attend his administrations, and I was now and then prevail'd on to do so, once for five Sundays successively.

Franklin's old bookshop, near Christ Church, Philadelphia

Had he been in my opinion a good preacher, perhaps I might have continued, notwithstanding the occasion I had for the Sunday's leisure in my course of study; but his discourses were chiefly either polemic arguments, or explications of the peculiar doctrines of our sect, and were all to me very dry, uninteresting, and unedifying, since not a single moral principle was inculcated or enforc'd, their aim seeming to be rather to make us Presbyterians than good citizens.

At length he took for his text that verse of the fourth chapter of Philippians, *"Finally, brethren, whatsoever things are true, honest, just, pure, lovely, or of good report, if there be any virtue, or any praise, think on these things."* And I imagin'd, in a sermon on such a text, we could not miss of having some morality. But he confin'd himself to five points only, as meant by the apostle, viz.: 1. Keeping holy the Sabbath day. 2. Being diligent in reading the holy Scriptures. 3. Attending duly the publick worship. 4. Partaking of the Sacrament. 5. Paying a due respect to God's ministers. These might be all good things; but, as they were not the kind of good things that I expected from that text, I despaired of ever meeting with them from any other, was disgusted, and attended his preaching no more. I had some years before compos'd a little Liturgy, or form of prayer, for my own private use (viz., in 1728), entitled, *Articles of Belief and Acts of Religion.* I return'd to the use of this, and went no more to the public assemblies. My conduct might be blameable, but I leave it, without attempting further to excuse it; my present purpose being to relate facts, and not to make apologies for them.

It was about this time I conceiv'd the bold and arduous project of arriving at moral perfection. I wish'd to live without committing any fault at any time; I would conquer all that either natural inclination, custom, or company might lead me into. As I knew, or thought I knew, what was right and wrong, I did not see why I might not always do the one and avoid the other. But I soon found I had undertaken a task of more difficulty than I had imagined. While my care was employ'd in guarding against one fault, I was often surprised by another;

habit took the advantage of inattention; inclination was sometimes too strong for reason. I concluded, at length, that the
mere speculative conviction that it was our interest to be completely virtuous, was not sufficient to prevent our slipping; and
that the contrary habits must be broken, and good ones acquired and established, before we can have any dependence on
a steady, uniform rectitude of conduct. For this purpose I therefore contrived the following method.

In the various enumerations of the moral virtues I had met
with in my reading, I found the catalogue more or less numerous, as different writers included more or fewer ideas under the
same name. Temperance, for example, was by some confined to
eating and drinking, while by others it was extended to mean
the moderating every other pleasure, appetite, inclination, or
passion, bodily or mental, even to our avarice and ambition. I
propos'd to myself, for the sake of clearness, to use rather more
names, with fewer ideas annex'd to each, than a few names with
more ideas; and I included under thirteen names of virtues all
that at that time occurr'd to me as necessary or desirable, and
annexed to each a short precept, which fully express'd the
extent I gave to its meaning.

These names of virtues, with their precepts, were:

1. TEMPERANCE

Eat not to dullness; drink not to elevation.

2. SILENCE

Speak not but what may benefit others or yourself; avoid
trifling conversation.

3. ORDER

Let all your things have their places; let each part of your
business have its time.

4. RESOLUTION

Resolve to perform what you ought; perform without fail
what you resolve.

5. FRUGALITY

Make no expense but to do good to others or yourself; *i.e.,* waste nothing.

6. INDUSTRY

Lose no time; be always employ'd in something useful; cut off all unnecessary actions.

7. SINCERITY

Use no hurtful deceit; think innocently and justly, and, if you speak, speak accordingly.

8. JUSTICE

Wrong none by doing injuries, or omitting the benefits that are your duty.

9. MODERATION

Avoid extreams; forbear resenting injuries so much as you think they deserve.

10. CLEANLINESS

Tolerate no uncleanliness in body, cloaths, or habitation.

11. TRANQUILLITY

Be not disturbed at trifles, or at accidents common or unavoidable.

12. CHASTITY

Rarely use venery but for health or offspring, never to dulness, weakness, or the injury of your own or another's peace or reputation.

13. HUMILITY

Imitate Jesus and Socrates.

My intention being to acquire the *habitude* of all these virtues, I judg'd it would be well not to distract my attention by attempting the whole at once, but to fix it on one of them at a time; and, when I should be master of that, then to proceed to another, and so on, till I should have gone thro' the thirteen; and, as the previous acquisition of some might facilitate the acquisition of certain others, I arrang'd them with that view, as they stand above. Temperance first, as it tends to procure that coolness and clearness of head, which is so necessary where constant vigilance was to be kept up, and guard maintained against the unremitting attraction of ancient habits, and the force of perpetual temptations. This being acquir'd and establish'd, Silence would be more easy; and my desire being to gain knowledge at the same time that I improv'd in virtue, and considering that in conversation it was obtain'd rather by the use of the ears than of the tongue, and therefore wishing to break a habit I was getting into of prattling, punning, and joking, which only made me acceptable to trifling company, I gave *Silence* the second place. This and the next, *Order,* I expected would allow me more time for attending to my project and my studies. *Resolution,* once become habitual, would keep me firm in my endeavors to obtain all the subsequent virtues; *Frugality* and Industry freeing me from my remaining debt, and producing affluence and independence, would make more easy the practice of Sincerity and Justice, etc., etc. Conceiving then, that, agreeably to the advice of Pythagoras in his Golden Verses, daily examination would be necessary, I contrived the following method for conducting that examination [on next page].

I made a little book, in which I allotted a page for each of the virtues. I rul'd each page with red ink, so as to have seven columns, one for each day of the week, marking each column with a letter for the day. I cross'd these columns with thirteen red lines, marking the beginning of each line with the first letter of one of the virtues, on which line, and in its proper column, I might mark, by a little black spot, every fault I found upon examination to have been committed respecting that virtue upon that day.

I determined to give a week's strict attention to each of the virtues successively. Thus, in the first week, my great guard was to avoid every the least offence against *Temperance,* leav-

FORM OF THE PAGES

TEMPERANCE							
Eat not to Dulness. *Drink not to Elevation.*							
	SUN.	MON.	TUES.	WED.	THURS.	FRI.	SAT.
T [Temperance]							
S [Silence]	● ●	●		●		●	
O [Order]	●	●	●		●	●	●
R [Resolution]			●			●	
F [Frugality]		●			●		
I [Industry]			●				
S [Sincerity]							
J [Justice]							
M [Moderation]							
Cl. [Cleanliness]							
T [Tranquility]							
Ch. [Chastity]							
H [Humility]							

ing the other virtues to their ordinary chance, only marking every evening the faults of the day. Thus, if in the first week I could keep my first line, marked T, clear of spots, I suppos'd the habit of that virtue so much strengthen'd, and its opposite weaken'd, that I might venture extending my attention to include the next, and for the following week keep both lines clear of spots. Proceeding thus to the last, I could go thro' a course compleat in thirteen weeks, and four courses in a year. And like him who, having a garden to weed, does not attempt to eradicate all the bad herbs at once, which would exceed his reach and his strength, but works on one of the beds at a time, and, having accomplish'd the first, proceeds to a second, so I should have, I hoped, the encouraging pleasure of seeing on my pages the progress I made in virtue, by clearing successively my lines of their spots, till in the end, by a number of courses, I should be happy in viewing a clean book, after a thirteen weeks' daily examination.

This my little book had for its motto these lines from Addison's *Cato*:

> "Here will I hold. If there's a power above us
> (And that there is, all nature cries aloud
> Thro' all her works), He must delight in virtue;
> And that which he delights in must be happy."

Another from Cicero,

"O vitæ Philosophia dux! O virtutum indagatrix expultrixque vitiorum! Unus dies, bene et ex præceptis tuis actus, peccanti immortalitati est anteponendus."

Another from the Proverbs of Solomon, speaking of wisdom or virtue:

"Length of days is in her right hand, and in her left hand riches and honour. Her ways are ways of pleasantness, and all her paths are peace." iii. 16, 17.

And conceiving God to be the fountain of wisdom, I thought it right and necessary to solicit his assistance for obtaining it;

to this end I formed the following little prayer, which was pre-fix'd to my tables of examination, for daily use.

"O powerful Goodness! bountiful Father! merciful Guide! Increase in me that wisdom which discovers my truest interest. Strengthen my resolutions to perform what that wisdom dictates. Accept my kind offices to thy other children as the only return in my power for thy continual favours to me."

I used also sometimes a little prayer which I took from Thomson's Poems, viz.:

> "Father of light and life, thou Good Supreme!
> O teach me what is good; teach me Thyself!
> Save me from folly, vanity, and vice,
> From every low pursuit; and fill my soul
> With knowledge, conscious peace, and virtue pure;
> Sacred, substantial, never-fading bliss!"

The precept of *Order* requiring that *every part of my business should have its allotted time,* one page in my little book contain'd the following scheme of employment for the twenty-four hours of a natural day.

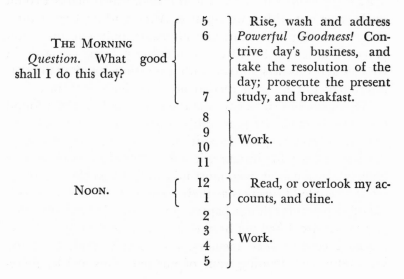

THE MORNING Question. What good shall I do this day?	5	Rise, wash and address *Powerful Goodness!* Contrive day's business, and take the resolution of the day; prosecute the present study, and breakfast.
	6	
	7	
	8	Work.
	9	
	10	
	11	
NOON.	12	Read, or overlook my accounts, and dine.
	1	
	2	Work.
	3	
	4	
	5	

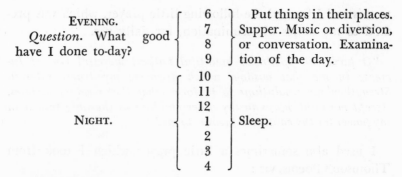

I enter'd upon the execution of this plan for self-examination, and continu'd it with occasional intermissions for some time. I was surpris'd to find myself so much fuller of faults than I had imagined; but I had the satisfaction of seeing them diminish. To avoid the trouble of renewing now and then my little book, which, by scraping out the marks on the paper of old faults to make room for new ones in a new course, became full of holes, I transferr'd my tables and precepts to the ivory leaves of a memorandum book, on which the lines were drawn with red ink, that made a durable stain, and on those lines I mark'd my faults with a black-lead pencil, which marks I could easily wipe out with a wet sponge. After a while I went thro' one course only in a year, and afterward only one in several years, till at length I omitted them entirely, being employ'd in voyages and business abroad, with a multiplicity of affairs that interfered; but I always carried my little book with me.

My scheme of ORDER gave me the most trouble; and I found that, tho' it might be practicable where a man's business was such as to leave him the disposition of his time, that of a journeyman printer, for instance, it was not possible to be exactly observed by a master, who must mix with the world, and often receive people of business at their own hours. Order, too, with regard to places for things, papers, etc., I found it extreamly difficult to acquire. I had not been early accustomed to it, and, having an exceeding good memory, I was not so sensible of the inconvenience attending want of method. This article, therefore, cost me so much painful attention, and my faults in it vexed me so much, and I made so little progress in amendment, and had such frequent relapses, that I was almost ready to give up the attempt, and content myself with a faulty character in that respect, like the man who, in buying an ax of a smith, my neighbour, desired to have the whole of its surface as bright as the edge. The smith consented to grind it bright for him if he would turn the wheel; he turn'd, while the smith press'd the broad face of the ax hard and heavily on the stone, which made the turning of it very fatiguing. The man came every now and then from the wheel to see how the work went on, and at length would take his ax as it was, without farther grinding. "No," said the smith, "turn on, turn on; we shall have it bright by-and-by; as yet, it is only speckled." "Yes," says the man, *"but I think I like a speckled ax best."* And I believe this may have been the case with many, who, having, for want of some such means as I employ'd, found the difficulty of obtaining good and breaking bad habits in other points of vice and virtue, have given up the struggle, and concluded that *"a speckled ax was best";* for something, that pretended to be reason, was every now and then suggesting to me that such extream nicety as I exacted of myself might be a kind of foppery in morals, which, if it were known, would make me ridiculous; that a perfect character might be attended with the inconvenience of being envied and hated; and that a benevolent man should allow a few faults in himself, to keep his friends in countenance.

In truth, I found myself incorrigible with respect to Order; and now I am grown old, and my memory bad, I feel very sensibly the want of it. But, on the whole, tho' I never arrived at the perfection I had been so ambitious of obtaining, but fell far short of it, yet I was, by the endeavor, a better and a happier man than I otherwise should have been if I had not attempted it; as those who aim at perfect writing by imitating the engraved copies, tho' they never reach the wish'd-for excellence of those copies, their hand is mended by the endeavor, and is tolerable while it continues fair and legible.

It may be well my posterity should be informed that to this little artifice, with the blessing of God, their ancestor ow'd the constant felicity of his life, down to his 79th year, in which this is written. What reverses may attend the remainder is in the hand of Providence; but, if they arrive, the reflection on past happiness enjoy'd ought to help his bearing them with more resignation. To Temperance he ascribes his long-continued health, and what is still left to him of a good constitution; to Industry and Frugality, the early easiness of his circumstances and acquisition of his fortune, with all that knowledge that enabled him to be a useful citizen, and obtained for him some degree of reputation among the learned; to Sincerity and Justice, the confidence of his country, and the honorable employs it conferred upon him; and to the joint influence of the whole mass of the virtues, even in the imperfect state he was able to acquire them, all that evenness of temper, and that cheerfulness in conversation, which makes his company still sought for, and agreeable even to his younger acquaintance. I hope, therefore, that some of my descendants may follow the example and reap the benefit.

It will be remark'd that, tho' my scheme was not wholly without religion, there was in it no mark of any of the distinguishing tenets of any particular sect. I had purposely avoided them; for, being fully persuaded of the utility and excellency of my method, and that it might be serviceable to people in all religions, and intending some time or other to publish it, I would not have any thing in it that should prejudice any one, of any sect, against it. I purposed writing a little comment on each virtue, in which I would have shown the advantages of possessing it, and the mischiefs attending its opposite vice; and I should have called my book THE ART OF VIRTUE, [Nothing so likely to make a man's fortune as virtue.] because it would have shown the means and manner of obtaining virtue, which would have distinguished it from the mere exhortation to be good, that does not instruct and indicate the means, but is like the apostle's man of verbal charity, who only without showing to the naked and hungry how or where they might get clothes or victuals, exhorted them to be fed and clothed.—James ii. 15, 16.

But it so happened that my intention of writing and publishing this comment was never fulfilled. I did, indeed, from time to time, put down short hints of the sentiments, reasonings, etc., to be made use of in it, some of which I have still by me; but the necessary close attention to private business in the earlier part of my life, and public business since, have occasioned my postponing it; for, it being connected in my mind with *a great and extensive project,* that required the whole man to execute, and which an unforeseen succession of employs prevented my attending to, it has hitherto remain'd unfinish'd.

In this piece it was my design to explain and enforce this doctrine, that vicious actions are not hurtful because they are forbidden, but forbidden because they are hurtful, the nature of man alone considered; that it was, therefore, every one's interest to be virtuous who wish'd to be happy even in this world; and I should, from this circumstance (there being always in the world a number of rich merchants, nobility, states, and princes, who have need of honest instruments for the management of their affairs, and such being so rare), have endeavored to convince young persons that no qualities were so likely to make a poor man's fortune as those of probity and integrity.

My list of virtues contain'd at first but twelve; but a Quaker friend having kindly informed me that I was generally thought proud; that my pride show'd itself frequently in conversation; that I was not content with being in the right when discussing any point, but was overbearing, and rather insolent, of which he convinc'd me by mentioning several instances; I determined endeavoring to cure myself, if I could, of this vice or folly among the rest, and I added *Humility* to my list, giving an extensive meaning to the word.

I cannot boast of much success in acquiring the *reality* of this virtue, but I had a good deal with regard to the *appearance* of it. I made it a rule to forbear all direct contradiction to the sentiments of others, and all positive assertion of my own. I even forbid myself, agreeably to the old laws of our Junto, the use of every word or expression in the language that imported a fix'd opinion, such as *certainly, undoubtedly,* etc., and I adopted, instead of them, *I conceive, I apprehend,* or *I imagine* a thing to be so or so; or it *so appears to me at present.* When another asserted something that I thought an error, I deny'd myself the pleasure of contradicting him abruptly, and of showing immediately some absurdity in his proposition; and in answering I began by observing that in certain cases or circumstances his opinion would be right, but in the present case there *appear'd* or *seem'd* to me some difference, etc. I soon found the advantage of this change in my manner; the conversations I engag'd in went on more pleasantly. The modest way in which I propos'd my opinions procur'd them a readier reception and less contradiction; I had less mortification when I was found to be in the wrong, and I more easily prevail'd with others to give up their mistakes and join with me when I happened to be in the right.

And this mode, which I at first put on with some violence to natural inclination, became at length so easy, and so habitual to me, that perhaps for these fifty years past no one has ever heard a dogmatical expression escape me. And to this habit (after my character of integrity) I think it principally owing that I had early so much weight with my fellow-citizens when I proposed new institutions, or alterations in the old, and so much influence in public councils when I became a member; for I was but a bad speaker, never eloquent, subject to much hesitation in my choice of words, hardly correct in language, and yet I generally carried my points.

In reality, there is, perhaps, no one of our national passions so hard to subdue as *pride.* Disguise it, struggle with it, beat it down, stifle it, mortify it as much as one pleases, it is still alive, and will every now and then peep out and show itself; you will see it, perhaps, often in this history; for, even if I could conceive that I had compleatly overcome it, I should probably be proud of my humility.

[Here ends the section written at Passy, 1784.]

"I am now about to write at home, August, 1788, but can not have the help expected from my papers, many of them being lost in the war. I have, however, found the following."

Having mentioned *a great and extensive project* which I had conceiv'd, it seems proper that some account should be here given of that project and its object. Its first rise in my mind appears in the following paper, accidentally preserv'd, viz.: *Observations* on my reading history, in Library, May 19th, 1731.

"That the great affairs of the world, the wars, revolutions, etc., are carried on and affected by parties.

"That the view of these parties is their present general interest, or what they take to be such.

"That the different views of these different parties occasion all confusion.

"That while a party is carrying on a general design, each man has his particular private interest in view.

"That as soon as a party has gain'd its general point, each member becomes intent upon his particular interest; which, thwarting others, breaks that party into divisions, and occasions more confusion.

"That few in public affairs act from a meer view of the good of their country, whatever they may pretend; and, tho' their actings bring real good to their country, yet men primarily considered that their own and their country's interest was united, and did not act from a principle of benevolence.

"That fewer still, in public affairs, act with a view to the good of mankind.

"There seems to me at present to be great occasion for raising a United Party for Virtue, by forming the virtuous and good men of all nations into a regular body, to be govern'd by suitable good and wise rules, which good and wise men may probably be more unanimous in their obedience to, than common people are to common laws.

"I at present think that whoever attempts this aright, and is well qualified, can not fail of pleasing God, and of meeting with success.   B. F."

Revolving this project in my mind, as to be undertaken hereafter, when my circumstances should afford me the necessary leisure, I put down from time to time, on pieces of paper, such thoughts as occurr'd to me respecting it. Most of these are lost; but I find one purporting to be the substance of an intended creed, containing, as I thought, the essentials of every known religion, and being free of every thing that might shock the professors of any religion. It is express'd in these words, viz.:

"That there is one God, who made all things.

"That he governs the world by his providence.

"That he ought to be worshiped by adoration, prayer, and thanksgiving.

"But that the most acceptable service of God is doing good to man.

"That the soul is immortal.

"And that God will certainly reward virtue and punish vice, either here or hereafter."

My ideas at that time were, that the sect should be begun and spread at first among young and single men only; that each person to be initiated should not only declare his assent to such creed, but should have exercised himself with the thirteen weeks' examination and practice of the virtues, as in the before-mention'd model; that the existence of such a society should be kept a secret, till it was become considerable, to prevent solicitations for the admission of improper persons, but that the members should each of them search among his acquaintance for ingenuous, well-disposed youths, to whom, with prudent caution, the scheme should be gradually communicated; that the members should engage to afford their advice, assistance, and support to each other in promoting one another's interests, business, and advancement in life; that, for distinction, we should be call'd *The Society of the Free and Easy:* free, as being, by the general practice and habit of the virtues, free from the dominion of vice; and particularly by the practice of industry and frugality, free from debt, which exposes a man to confinement, and a species of slavery to his creditors.

This is as much as I can now recollect of the project, except that I communicated it in part to two young men, who adopted it with some enthusiasm; but my then narrow circumstances, and the necessity I was under of sticking close to my business, occasion'd my postponing the further prosecution of it at that time; and my multifarious occupations, public and private, induc'd me to continue postponing, so that it has been omitted till I have no longer strength or activity left sufficient for such an enterprise; tho' I am still of opinion that it was a practicable scheme, and might have been very useful, by forming a great number of good citizens; and I was not discourag'd by the seeming magnitude of the undertaking, as I have always thought that one man of tolerable abilities may work great changes, and accomplish great affairs among mankind, if he first forms a good plan, and, cutting off all amusements or other employments that would divert his attention, makes the execution of that same plan his sole study and business.

In 1732 I first publish'd my Almanack, under the name of *Richard Saunders;* it was continu'd by me about twenty-five years, commonly call'd *Poor Richard's Almanack.* I endeavor'd to make it both entertaining and useful, and it accordingly came to be in such demand, that I reap'd considerable profit from it, vending annually near ten thousand. And observing that it was generally read, scarce any neighborhood in the province being without it, I consider'd it as a proper vehicle for conveying instruction among the common people, who bought scarcely any other books; I therefore filled all the little spaces that occurr'd between the remarkable days in the calendar with proverbial sentences, chiefly such as inculcated industry and frugality, as the means of procuring wealth, and thereby securing virtue; it being more difficult for a man in want, to act always honestly, as, to use here one of those proverbs, *it is hard for an empty sack to stand upright.*

These proverbs, which contained the wisdom of many ages and nations, I assembled and form'd into a connected discourse prefix'd to the Almanack of 1757, as the harangue of a wise old man to the people attending an auction. The bringing all these scatter'd counsels thus into a focus enabled them to make greater impression. The piece, being universally approved, was copied in all the newspapers of the Continent; reprinted in Britain on a broad side, to be stuck up in houses; two translations were made of it in French, and great numbers bought by the clergy and gentry, to distribute gratis among their poor parishioners and tenants. In Pennsylvania, as it discouraged useless expense in foreign superfluities, some thought it had its share of influence in producing that growing plenty of money which was observable for several years after its publication.

I considered my newspaper, also, as another means of communicating instruction, and in that view frequently reprinted in it extracts from the Spectator, and other moral writers; and sometimes publish'd little pieces of my own, which had been first compos'd for reading in our Junto. Of these are a Socratic dialogue, tending to prove that, whatever might be his parts and abilities, a vicious man could not properly be called a man of sense; and a discourse on self-denial, showing that virtue was not secure till its practice became a habitude, and was free from the opposition of contrary inclinations. These may be found in the papers about the beginning of 1735. [June 23 and July 7, 1730.]

In the conduct of my newspaper, I carefully excluded all libelling and personal abuse, which is of late years become so disgraceful to our country. Whenever I was solicited to insert any thing of that kind, and the writers pleaded, as they generally did, the liberty of the press, and that a newspaper was

Franklin working on models of his famous stove

like a stage-coach, in which any one who would pay had a right to a place, my answer was, that I would print the piece separately if desired, and the author might have as many copies as he pleased to distribute himself, but that I would not take upon me to spread his detraction; and that, having contracted with my subscribers to furnish them with what might be either useful or entertaining, I could not fill their papers with private altercation, in which they had no concern, without doing them manifest injustice. Now, many of our printers make no scruple of gratifying the malice of individuals by false accusations of the fairest characters among ourselves, augmenting animosity even to the producing of duels; and are, moreover, so indiscreet as to print scurrilous reflections on the government of neighboring states, and even on the conduct of our best national allies, which may be attended with the most pernicious consequences. These things I mention as a caution to young printers, and that they may be encouraged not to pollute their presses and disgrace their profession by such infamous practices, but refuse steadily, as they may see by my example that such a course of conduct will not, on the whole, be injurious to their interests.

In 1733 I sent one of my journeymen to Charleston, South Carolina, where a printer was wanting. I furnish'd him with a press and letters, on an agreement of partnership, by which I was to receive one-third of the profits of the business, paying one-third of the expense. He was a man of learning, and honest but ignorant in matters of account; and, tho' he sometimes made me remittances, I could get no account from him, nor any satisfactory state of our partnership while he lived. On his decease, the business was continued by his widow, who, being born and bred in Holland, where, as I have been inform'd, the knowledge of accounts makes a part of female education, she not only sent me as clear a state as she could find of the transactions past, but continued to account with the greatest regularity and exactness every quarter afterwards, and managed the business with such success, that she not only brought up reputably a family of children, but, at the expiration of the term, was able to purchase of me the printing-house, and establish her son in it.

I mention this affair chiefly for the sake of recommending that branch of education for our young females, as likely to be of more use to them and their children, in case of widowhood, than either music or dancing, by preserving them from losses by imposition of crafty men, and enabling them to continue, perhaps, a profitable mercantile house, with establish'd correspondence, till a son is grown up fit to undertake and go on with it, to the lasting advantage and enriching of the family.

About the year 1734 there arrived among us from Ireland a young Presbyterian preacher, named Hemphill, who delivered with a good voice, and apparently extempore, most excellent discourses, which drew together considerable numbers of different persuasions, who join'd in admiring them. Among the rest, I became one of his constant hearers, his sermons pleasing me, as they had little of the dogmatical kind, but inculcated strongly the practice of virtue, or what in the religious stile are called good works. Those, however, of our congregation, who considered themselves as orthodox Presbyterians, disapprov'd his doctrine, and were join'd by most of the old clergy, who arraign'd him of heterodoxy before the synod, in order to have him silenc'd. I became his zealous partisan, and contributed all I could to raise a party in his favour, and we combated for him a while with some hopes of success. There was much scribbling pro and con upon the occasion; and finding that, tho' an elegant preacher, he was but a poor writer, I lent him my pen and wrote for him two or three pamphlets, and one piece in the Gazette of April, 1735. Those pamphlets, as is generally the case with controversial writings, tho' eagerly read at the time, were soon out of vogue, and I question whether a single copy of them now exists.

During the contest an unlucky occurrence hurt his cause exceedingly. One of our adversaries having heard him preach a sermon that was much admired, thought he had somewhere read the sermon before, or at least part of it. On search, he found that part quoted at length, in one of the British Reviews, from a discourse of Dr. Foster's. This detection gave many of our party disgust, who accordingly abandoned his cause, and occasion'd our more speedy discomfiture in the synod. I stuck by him, however, as I rather approv'd his giving us good sermons compos'd by others, than bad ones of his own manufacture, tho' the latter was the practice of our common teachers. He afterward acknowledg'd to me that none of those he preach'd were his own; adding, that his memory was such as enabled him to retain and repeat any sermon after one reading only. On our defeat, he left us in search elsewhere of better fortune, and I quitted the congregation, never joining it after, tho' I continu'd many years my subscription for the support of its ministers.

I had begun in 1733 to study languages; I soon made myself so much a master of the French as to be able to read the books with ease. I then undertook the Italian. An acquaintance, who was also learning it, us'd often to tempt me to play chess with him. Finding this took up too much of the time I had to spare for study, I at length refus'd to play any more, unless on this condition, that the victor in every game should have a right to impose a task, either in parts of the grammar to be got by heart, or in translations, etc., which tasks the vanquish'd was to perform upon honour, before our next meeting. As we play'd pretty equally, we thus beat one another into that language. I afterwards with a little painstaking, acquir'd as much of the Spanish as to read their books also.

I have already mention'd that I had only one year's instruction in a Latin school, and that when very young, after which I neglected that language entirely. But, when I had attained an acquaintance with the French, Italian, and Spanish, I was surpriz'd to find, on looking over a Latin Testament, that I understood so much more of that language than I had imagined, which encouraged me to apply myself again to the study of it, and I met with more success, as those preceding languages had greatly smooth'd my way.

From these circumstances, I have thought that there is some

inconsistency in our common mode of teaching languages. We are told that it is proper to begin first with the Latin, and, having acquir'd that, it will be more easy to attain those modern languages which are deriv'd from it; and yet we do not begin with the Greek, in order more easily to acquire the Latin. It is true that, if you can clamber and get to the top of a staircase without using the steps, you will more easily gain them in descending; but certainly, if you begin with the lowest you will with more ease ascend to the top; and I would therefore offer it to the consideration of those who superintend the education of our youth, whether, since many of those who begin with the Latin quit the same after spending some years without having made any great proficiency, and what they have learnt becomes almost useless, so that their time has been lost, it would not have been better to have begun with the French, proceeding to the Italian, etc.; for, tho', after spending the same time, they should quit the study of languages and never arrive at the Latin, they would, however, have acquired another tongue or two, that, being in modern use, might be serviceable to them in common life.

After ten years' absence from Boston, and having become easy in my circumstances, I made a journey thither to visit my relations, which I could not sooner well afford. In returning, I call'd at Newport to see my brother, then settled there with his printing-house. Our former differences were forgotten, and our meeting was very cordial and affectionate. He was fast declining in his health, and requested of me that, in case of his death, which he apprehended not far distant, I would take home his son, then but ten years of age, and bring him up to the printing business. This I accordingly perform'd, sending him a few years to school before I took him into the office. His mother carried on the business till he was grown up, when I assisted him with an assortment of new types, those of his father being in a manner worn out. Thus it was that I made my brother ample amends for the service I had depriv'd him of by leaving him so early.

In 1736 I lost one of my sons, a fine boy of four years old, by the small-pox, taken in the common way. I long regretted bitterly, and still regret that I had not given it to him by inoculation. This I mention for the sake of parents who omit that operation, on the supposition that they should never forgive themselves if a child died under it; my example showing that the regret may be the same either way, and that, therefore, the safer should be chosen.

Our club, the Junto, was found so useful, and afforded such satisfaction to the members, that several were desirous of introducing their friends, which could not well be done without exceeding what we had settled as a convenient number, viz., twelve. We had from the beginning made it a rule to keep our institution a secret, which was pretty well observ'd; the intention was to avoid applications of improper persons for admittance, some of whom, perhaps, we might find it difficult to refuse. I was one of those who were against any addition to our number, but, instead of it, made in writing a proposal, that every member separately should endeavor to form a subordinate club, with the same rules respecting queries, etc., and without informing them of the connection with the Junto. The advantages proposed were, the improvement of so many more young citizens by the use of our institutions; our better acquaintance with the general sentiments of the inhabitants on any occasion, as the Junto member might propose what queries we should desire, and was to report to the Junto what pass'd in his separate club; the promotion of our particular interests in business by more extensive recommendation, and the increase of our influence in public affairs, and our power of doing good by spreading thro' the several clubs the sentiments of the Junto.

The project was approv'd, and every member undertook to form his club, but they did not all succeed. Five or six only were compleated, which were called by different names, as the Vine, the Union, the Band, etc. They were useful to themselves, and afforded us a good deal of amusement, information, and instruction, besides answering, in some considerable degree, our views of influencing the public opinion on particular occasions,

200	217	232	249	8	25	40	57	72	89	104	121	136	153	168	181
58	39	26	7	250	231	218	199	186	167	154	135	122	103	90	71
198	219	230	251	6	27	38	59	70	91	102	123	134	155	166	187
60	37	28	5	252	229	220	197	188	165	156	133	124	101	92	69
201	216	233	248	9	24	41	56	73	88	105	120	137	152	169	184
55	42	23	10	247	234	215	202	183	170	151	138	119	106	87	74
203	214	235	246	11	22	43	54	75	86	107	118	139	150	171	182
53	44	21	12	245	236	213	204	181	172	149	140	117	108	85	76
205	212	237	244	13	20	45	52	77	84	109	116	141	148	173	180
51	46	19	14	243	238	241	206	179	174	147	142	115	110	83	78
207	210	239	242	15	18	47	50	79	82	111	114	143	146	175	178
49	48	17	16	241	240	209	208	177	176	145	144	113	112	81	80
196	221	228	253	4	29	36	61	68	93	100	125	132	157	164	189
62	35	30	3	254	227	222	195	190	163	158	131	126	99	94	67
194	223	226	255	2	31	34	63	66	95	98	127	130	159	162	191
64	33	32	1	256	225	224	193	192	161	160	129	128	97	96	65

One of the "magic squares" made by Franklin to amuse himself during long sessions of the General Assembly while he was clerk. In a letter written many years later he described, and belittled, this mathematical exercise "... In my younger days, having once some leisure, (which I still think I might have employed more usefully) I had amused myself in making these kind of magic squares, and, at length, had acquired such a knack at it, that I could fill the cells of any magic square, of reasonable size, with a series of numbers as fast as I could write them, disposed in such a manner, as that the sums of every row, horizontal, perpendicular, or diagonal, should be equal. ..."

of which I shall give some instances in course of time as they happened.

My first promotion was my being chosen, in 1736, clerk of the General Assembly. The choice was made that year without opposition; but the year following, when I was again propos'd (the choice, like that of the members, being annual), a new member made a long speech against me, in order to favour some other candidate. I was, however, chosen, which was the more agreeable to me, as, besides the pay for the immediate service as clerk, the place gave me a better opportunity of keeping up an interest among the members, which secur'd to me the business of printing the votes, laws, paper money, and other occasional jobbs for the public, that, on the whole, were very profitable.

I therefore did not like the opposition of this new member, who was a gentleman of fortune and education, with talents that were likely to give him, in time, great influence in the House, which, indeed, afterwards happened. I did not, however, aim at gaining his favour by paying any servile respect to him, but, after some time, took this other method. Having heard that he had in his library a certain very scarce and curious book, I wrote a note to him, expressing my desire of perusing that book, and requesting he would do me the favour of lending it to me for a few days. He sent it immediately, and I return'd it in about a week with another note, expressing strongly my sense of the favour. When we next met in the House, he spoke to me (which he had never done before), and with great civility; and he ever after manifested a readiness to serve me on all occasions, so that we became great friends, and our friendship continued to his death. This is another instance of the truth of an old maxim I had learned, which says, *"He that has once done you a kindness will be more ready to do you another, than he whom you yourself have obliged."* And it shows how much more profitable it is prudently to remove, than to resent, return, and continue inimical proceedings.

In 1737, Colonel [Alexander] Spotswood, late governor of Virginia, and then postmaster-general, being dissatisfied with

the conduct of his deputy at Philadelphia, respecting some negligence in rendering, and inexactitude of his accounts, took
from him the commission and offered it to me. I accepted it
readily, and found it of great advantage; for, tho' the salary
was small, it facilitated the correspondence that improv'd my
newspaper, increas'd the number demanded, as well as the advertisements to be inserted, so that it came to afford me a
considerable income. My old competitor's newspaper declin'd
proportionably, and I was satisfy'd without retaliating his refusal, while postmaster, to permit my papers being carried by
the riders. Thus he suffer'd greatly from his neglect in due
accounting; and I mention it as a lesson to those young men
who may be employ'd in managing affairs for others, that they
should always render accounts, and make remittances, with
great clearness and punctuality. The character of observing such
a conduct is the most powerful of all recommendations to new
employments and increase of business.

I began now to turn my thoughts a little to public affairs,
beginning, however, with small matters. The city watch was one
of the first things that I conceiv'd to want regulation. It was
managed by the constables of the respective wards in turn; the
constable warned a number of housekeepers to attend him for
the night. Those who chose never to attend, paid him six shillings a year to be excus'd, which was suppos'd to be for hiring
substitutes, but was, in reality, much more than was necessary
for that purpose, and made the constableship a place of profit;
and the constable, for a little drink, often got such ragamuffins
about him as a watch, that respectable housekeepers did not
choose to mix with. Walking the rounds, too, was often neglected, and most of the nights spent in tippling. I thereupon
wrote a paper to be read in Junto, representing these irregu-
larities, but insisting more particularly on the inequality of this
six-shilling tax of the constables, respecting the circumstances of
those who paid it, since a poor widow housekeeper, all whose
property to be guarded by the watch did not perhaps exceed the
value of fifty pounds, paid as much as the wealthiest merchant,
who had thousands of pounds' worth of goods in his stores.

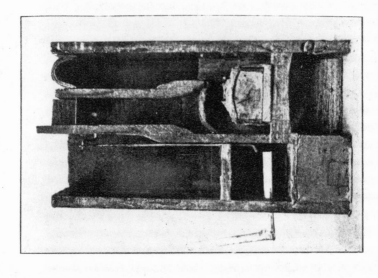

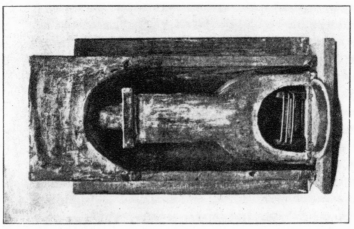

Franklin's model of "The Pennsylvania fire-place," in the American Philosophical Society, Philadelphia

On the whole, I proposed as a more effectual watch, the hiring of proper men to serve constantly in that business; and as a more equitable way of supporting the charge, the levying a tax that should be proportion'd to the property. This idea, being approv'd by the Junto, was communicated to the other clubs, but as arising in each of them; and though the plan was not immediately carried into execution, yet, by preparing the minds of people for the change, it paved the way for the law obtained a few years after, when the members of our clubs were grown into more influence.

About this time I wrote a paper (first to be read in Junto, but it was afterward publish'd) on the different accidents and carelessnesses by which houses were set on fire, with cautions against them, and means proposed of avoiding them. This was much spoken of as a useful piece, and gave rise to a project, which soon followed it, of forming a company for the more ready extinguishing of fires, and mutual assistance and removing and securing of goods when in danger. Associates in this scheme were presently found, amounting to thirty. Our articles of agreement oblig'd every member to keep always in good order, and fit for use, a certain number of leather buckets, with strong bags and baskets (for packing and transporting of goods), which were to be brought to every fire; and we agreed to meet once a month to spend a social evening together, in discoursing and communicating such ideas as occurred to us upon the subject of fires, as might be useful in our conduct on such occasions.

The utility of this institution soon appeared, and many more desiring to be admitted than we thought convenient for one company, they were advised to form another, which was accordingly done; and this went on, one new company being formed after another, till they became so numerous as to include most of the inhabitants who were men of property; and now, at the time of my writing this, tho' upward of fifty years since its establishment, that which I first formed, called the Union Fire Company, still subsists and flourishes, tho' the first members are all deceas'd but myself and one, who is older by a year than I am. The small fines that have been paid by members for absence at the monthly meetings have been apply'd to the purchase of fire-engines, ladders, fire-hooks, and other useful implements for each company, so that I question whether there is a city in the world better provided with the means of putting a stop to beginning conflagrations; and, in fact, since these institutions, the city has never lost by fire more than one or two houses at a time, and the flames have often been extinguished before the house in which they began has been half consumed.

In 1739 arrived among us from Ireland the Reverend Mr. [George] Whitefield, who had made himself remarkable there as an itinerant preacher. He was at first permitted to preach in some of our churches; but the clergy, taking a dislike to him, soon refus'd him their pulpits, and he was oblig'd to preach in the fields. The multitudes of all sects and denominations that attended his sermons were enormous, and it was a matter of speculation to me, who was one of the number, to observe the extraordinary influence of his oratory on his hearers, and how much they admir'd and respected him, notwithstanding his common abuse of them, by assuring them they were naturally *half beasts and half devils.* It was wonderful to see the change soon made in the manners of our inhabitants. From being thoughtless or indifferent about religion, it seem'd as if all the world were growing religious, so that one could not walk thro' the town in an evening without hearing psalms sung in different families of every street.

And it being found inconvenient to assemble in the open air, subject to its inclemencies, the building of a house to meet in was no sooner propos'd, and persons appointed to receive contributions, but sufficient sums were soon receiv'd to procure the ground and erect the building, which was one hundred feet long and seventy broad, about the size of Westminster Hall; and the work was carried on with such spirit as to be finished in a much shorter time than could have been expected. Both house and ground were vested in trustees, expressly for the use of any preacher of any religious persuasion who might desire to say something to the people at Philadelphia; the design in building not being to accommodate any particular sect, but the inhabitants in general; so that even if the Mufti of Constantinople were to send a missionary to preach Mohammedanism to us, he would find a pulpit at his service.

Mr. Whitefield, in leaving us, went preaching all the way thro' the colonies to Georgia. The settlement of that province had lately been begun, but, instead of being made with hardy, industrious husbandmen, accustomed to labor, the only people fit for such an enterprise, it was with families of broken shop-keepers and other insolvent debtors, many of indolent and idle habits, taken out of the jails, who, being set down in the woods, unqualified for clearing land, and unable to endure the hardships of a new settlement, perished in numbers, leaving many helpless children unprovided for. The sight of their miserable situation inspir'd the benevolent heart of Mr. Whitefield with the idea of building an Orphan House there, in which they might be supported and educated. Returning northward, he preach'd up this charity, and made large collections, for his eloquence had a wonderful power over the hearts and purses of his hearers, of which I myself was an instance.

I did not disapprove of the design, but, as Georgia was then destitute of materials and workmen, and it was proposed to send them from Philadelphia at a great expense, I thought it would have been better to have built the house there, and brought the children to it. This I advis'd; but he was resolute in his first project, rejected my counsel, and I therefor refus'd to contribute. I happened soon after to attend one of his sermons, in the course of which I perceived he intended to finish with a collection, and I silently resolved he should get nothing from me. I had in my pocket a handful of copper money, three or four silver dollars, and five pistoles in gold. As he proceeded I began to soften, and concluded to give the coppers. Another stroke of his oratory made me asham'd of that, and determin'd me to give the silver; and he finish'd so admirably, that I empty'd my pocket wholly into the collector's dish, gold and all. At this sermon there was also one of our club, who, being of my sentiments respecting the building in Georgia, and suspecting a collection might be intended, had, by precaution, emptied his pockets before he came from home. Towards the conclusion of the discourse, however, he felt a strong desire to give, and apply'd to a neighbour, who stood near him, to borrow some money for the purpose. The application was unfortunately [made] to perhaps the only man in the company who had the firmness not to be affected by the preacher. His answer was, *"At any other time, Friend Hopkinson, I would lend to thee freely; but not now, for thee seems to be out of thy right senses."*

Some of Mr. Whitefield's enemies affected to suppose that he would apply these collections to his own private emolument; but I, who was intimately acquainted with him (being employed in printing his Sermons and Journals, etc.), never had the least suspicion of his integrity, but am to this day decidedly of opinion that he was in all his conduct a perfectly *honest man;* and methinks my testimony in his favour ought to have the more weight, as we had no religious connection. He us'd, indeed, sometimes to pray for my conversion, but never had the satisfaction of believing that his prayers were heard. Ours was a mere civil friendship, sincere on both sides, and lasted to his death.

The following instance will show something of the terms on which we stood. Upon one of his arrivals from England at Boston, he wrote to me that he should come soon to Philadelphia, but knew not where he could lodge when there, as he understood his old friend and host, Mr. [Anthony] Benezet, was removed to Germantown. My answer was, "You know my house; if you can make shift with its scanty accommodations, you will be most heartily welcome." He reply'd, that if I made that kind offer for Christ's sake, I should not miss of a reward. And I returned, *"Don't let me be mistaken; it was not for Christ's sake, but for your sake."* One of our common acquaintance jocosely remark'd, that, knowing it to be the custom of the saints, when they received any favour, to shift the burden of the obligation from off their own shoulders, and place it in heaven, I had contriv'd to fix it on earth.

The last time I saw Mr. Whitefield was in London, when he consulted me about his Orphan House concern, and his purpose of appropriating it to the establishment of a college.

He had a loud and clear voice, and articulated his words and sentences so perfectly, that he might be heard and understood at a great distance, especially as his auditories, however numerous, observ'd the most exact silence. He preach'd one evening from the top of the Court-house steps, which are in the middle of Market-street, and on the west side of Second-street, which crosses it at right angles. Both streets were fill'd with his hearers to a considerable distance. Being among the hindmost in Market-street, I had the curiosity to learn how far he could be heard, by retiring backwards down the street towards the river; and I found his voice distinct till I came near Front-street, when some noise in that street obscur'd it. Imagining then a semicircle, of which my distance should be the radius, and that it were fill'd with auditors, to each of whom I allow'd two square feet, I computed that he might well be heard by more than thirty thousand. This reconcil'd me to the newspaper accounts of his having preach'd to twenty-five thousand people in the fields, and to the antient histories of generals haranguing whole armies, of which I had sometimes doubted.

By hearing him often, I came to distinguish easily between sermons newly compos'd, and those which he had often preach'd in the course of his travels. His delivery of the latter was so improv'd by frequent repetitions that every accent, every emphasis, every modulation of voice, was so perfectly well turn'd and well plac'd, that, without being interested in the subject, one could not help being pleas'd with the discourse; a pleasure of much the same kind with that receiv'd from an excellent piece of musick. This is an advantage itinerant preachers have over those who are stationary, as the latter can not well improve their delivery of a sermon by so many rehearsals.

His writing and printing from time to time gave great advantage to his enemies; unguarded expressions, and even erroneous opinions, delivered in preaching, might have been afterwards explain'd or qualifi'd by supposing others that might have accompani'd them, or they might have been deny'd; but *litera scripta manet*. Critics attack'd his writing violently, and with no such appearance of reason as to diminish the number of his votaries and prevent their encrease; so that I am of opinion if he had never written any thing, he would have left behind him a much more numerous and important sect, and his reputation might in that case have been still growing, even after his death, as there being nothing of his writing on which to found a censure and give him a lower character, his proselytes would be left at liberty to feign for him as great a variety of excellences as their enthusiastic admiration might wish him to have possessed.

My business was now continually augmenting and my circumstances growing daily easier, my newspaper having become very profitable, as being for a time almost the only one in this and the neighbouring provinces. I experienced, too, the truth of the observation, *"that after getting the first hundred pound, it is more easy to get the second,"* money itself being of a prolific nature.

The partnership at Carolina having succeeded, I was encourag'd to engage in others, and to promote several of my workmen, who had behaved well, by establishing them with printing-houses in different colonies, on the same terms with that in Carolina. Most of them did well, being enabled at the end of our term, six years, to purchase the types of me and go on working for themselves, by which means several families were raised. Partnerships often finish in quarrels; but I was happy in this, that mine were all carried on and ended amicably, owing, I think, a good deal to the precaution of having very explicitly settled, in our articles, every thing to be done by or expected from each partner, so that there was nothing to dispute, which precaution I would therefore recommend to all who enter into partnerships; for, whatever esteem partners may have for, and confidence in each other at the time of the contract, little jealousies and disgusts may arise, with ideas of inequality in the care and burden of the business, etc., which are attended often with breach of friendship and of the connection, perhaps with lawsuits and other disagreeable consequences.

I had, on the whole, abundant reason to be satisfied with my being established in Pennsylvania. There were, however, two things that I regretted, there being no provision for defense, nor for a compleat education of youth; no militia, nor any college. I therefore, in 1743, drew up a proposal for establishing an academy; and at that time, thinking the Reverend Mr. Peters, who was out of employ, a fit person to superintend such an institution, I communicated the project to him; but he, having more profitable views in the service of the proprietaries, which succeeded, declin'd the undertaking; and, not knowing another at that time suitable for such a trust, I let the scheme lie a while dormant. I succeeded better the next year, 1744, in proposing and establishing a Philosophical Society. The paper I wrote for that purpose will be found among my writings, when collected.

With respect to defense, Spain having been several years at war against Great Britain, and being at length join'd by France, which brought us into great danger; and the laboured and long-continued endeavour of our governor, Thomas, to prevail with our Quaker Assembly to pass a militia law, and make other provisions for the security of the province, having proved abortive, I determined to try what might be done by a voluntary association of the people. To promote this, I first wrote and published a pamphlet, entitled PLAIN TRUTH, in which I stated our defenceless situation in strong lights, with the necessity of union and discipline for our defense, and promis'd to propose in a few days an association, to be generally signed for that purpose. The pamphlet had a sudden and surprising effect. I was call'd upon for the instrument of association, and having settled the draft of it with a few friends, I appointed a meeting of the citizens in the large building before mentioned. The house was pretty full; I had prepared a number of printed copies, and provided pens and ink dispers'd all over the room. I harangued them a little on the subject, read the paper, and explained it, and then distributed the copies, which were eagerly signed, not the least objection being made.

When the company separated, and the papers were collected, we found above twelve thousand hands; and, other copies being dispersed in the country, the subscribers amounted at length to upward of ten thousand. These all furnished themselves as soon as they could with arms, formed themselves into companies and regiments, chose their own officers, and met every week to be instructed in the manual exercise, and other parts of military discipline. The women, by subscriptions among themselves, provided silk colors, which they presented to the companies, painted with different devices and mottos, which I supplied.

The officers of the companies composing the Philadelphia regiment, being met, chose me for their colonel; but, conceiving myself unfit, I declin'd that station, and recommended Mr. Lawrence, a fine person, and a man of influence, who was accordingly appointed. I then propos'd a lottery to defray the expense of building a battery below the town, and furnishing it with cannon. It filled expeditiously, and the battery was soon erected, the merlons being fram'd of logs and fill'd with earth. We bought some old cannon from Boston, but, these not being sufficient, we wrote to England for more, soliciting, at the same, our proprietaries for some assistance, tho' without much expectation of obtaining it.

Meanwhile, Colonel Lawrence, William Allen, Abram Taylor, Esqr., and myself were sent to New York by the associators, commission'd to borrow some cannon of Governor [George] Clinton. He at first refus'd us peremptorily; but at dinner with his council, where there was great drinking of Madeira wine, as the custom of that place then was, he softened by degrees, and said he would lend us six. After a few more bumpers he advanc'd to ten; and at length he very good-naturedly conceded eighteen. They were fine cannon, eighteen-pounders, with their carriages, which we soon transported and mounted on our battery, where the associators kept a nightly guard while the war lasted, and among the rest I regularly took my turn of duty there as a common soldier.

My activity in these operations was agreeable to the governor and council; they took me into confidence, and I was consulted by them in every measure wherein their concurrence was thought useful to the association. Calling in the aid of religion, I propos'd to them the proclaiming a fast, to promote reformation, and implore the blessing of Heaven on our undertaking.

They embrac'd the motion; but, as it was the first fast ever thought of in the province, the secretary had no precedent from which to draw the proclamation. My education in New England, where a fast is proclaimed every year, was here of some advantage: I drew it in the accustomed stile, it was translated into German, printed in both languages, and divulg'd thro' the province. This gave the clergy of the different sects an opportunity of influencing their congregations to join in the association, and it would probably have been general among all but Quakers if the peace had not soon interven'd.

It was thought by some of my friends that, by my activity in these affairs, I should offend that sect, and thereby lose my interest in the Assembly of the province, where they formed a great majority. A young gentleman who had likewise some friends in the House, and wished to succeed me as their clerk, acquainted me that it was decided to displace me at the next election; and he, therefore, in good will, advis'd me to resign, as more consistent with my honour than being turn'd out. My answer to him was, that I had read or heard of some public man who made it a rule never to ask for an office, and never to refuse one when offer'd to him. "I approve," says I, "of his rule, and will practice it with a small addition; I shall never *ask*, never *refuse*, nor ever *resign* an office. If they will have my office of clerk to dispose of to another, they shall take it from me. I will not, by giving it up, lose my right of some time or other making reprisals on my adversaries." I heard, moreover, no more of this; I was chosen again unanimously as usual at the next election. Possibly, as they dislik'd my late intimacy with the members of council, who had join'd the governors in all the disputes about military preparations, with which the House had long been harass'd, they might have been pleas'd if I would voluntarily have left them; but they did not care to displace me on account merely of my zeal for the association, and they could not well give another reason.

Indeed I had some cause to believe that the defense of the country was not disagreeable to any of them, provided they were not requir'd to assist in it. And I found that a much greater number of them than I could have imagined, tho' against offensive war, were clearly for the defensive. Many pamphlets *pro and con* were publish'd on the subject, and some by good Quakers, in favour of defense, which I believe convinc'd most of their younger people.

A transaction in our fire company gave me some insight into their prevailing sentiments. It had been propos'd that we should encourage the scheme for building a battery by laying out the present stock, then about sixty pounds, in tickets of the lottery. By our rules, no money could be dispos'd of till the next meeting after the proposal. The company consisted of thirty members, of which twenty-two were Quakers, and eight only of other persuasions. We eight punctually attended the meeting; but, tho' we thought that some of the Quakers would join us, we were by no means sure of a majority. Only one Quaker, Mr. James Morris, appear'd to oppose the measure. He expressed much sorrow that it had ever been propos'd, as he said *Friends* were all against it, and it would create such discord as might break up the company. We told him that we saw no reason for that; we were the minority, and if *Friends* were against the measure, and outvoted us, we must and should, agreeably to the usage of all societies, submit. When the hour for business arriv'd it was mov'd to put the vote; he allow'd we might then do it by the rules, but, as he could assure us that a number of members intended to be present for the purpose of opposing it, it would be but candid to allow a little time for their appearing.

While we were disputing this, a waiter came to tell me two gentlemen below desir'd to speak with me. I went down, and found they were two of our Quaker members. They told me there were eight of them assembled at a tavern just by; that they were determin'd to come and vote with us if there should be occasion, which they hop'd would not be the case, and desir'd we would not call for their assistance if we could do without it, as their voting for such a measure might embroil them with their elders and friends. Being thus secure of a majority, I went up, and after a little seeming hesitation, agreed to a delay of another hour. This Mr. Morris allow'd to be extremely fair. Not one of his opposing friends appear'd, at which he express'd great surprize; and, at the expiration of the hour, we carry'd the resolution eight to one; and as, of the twenty-two Quakers, eight were ready to vote with us, and thirteen, by their absence, manifested that they were not inclin'd to oppose the measure, I afterward estimated the proportion of Quakers sincerely against defense as one to twenty-one only; for these were all regular members of that society, and in good reputation among them, and had due notice of what was propos'd at that meeting.

The honorable and learned Mr. [James] Logan, who had always been of that sect, was one who wrote an address to them, declaring his approbation of defensive war, and supporting his opinion by many strong arguments. He put into my hands sixty pounds to be laid out in lottery tickets for the battery, with direction to apply what prizes might be drawn wholly to that service. He told me the following anecdote of his old master, William Penn, respecting defense. He came over from England, when a young man, with that proprietary, and as his secretary. It was war-time, and their ship was chas'd by an armed vessel, suppos'd to be an enemy. Their captain prepar'd for defense; but told William Penn, and his company of Quakers, that he did not expect their assistance, and they might retire into the cabin, which they did, except James Logan, who chose to stay upon deck, and was quarter'd to a gun. The suppos'd enemy prov'd a friend, so there was no fighting; but when the secretary went down to communicate the intelligence, William Penn rebuk'd him severely for staying upon deck, and undertaking to assist in defending the vessel, contrary to the principles of *Friends,* especially as it had not been required by the captain. This reproof, being before all the company, piqu'd the secretary who answer'd, *"I being thy servant, why did thee not order me to come down? But thee was willing enough that I should stay and help to fight the ship when thee thought there was danger."*

My being many years in the Assembly, the majority of which

were constantly Quakers, gave me frequent opportunities of seeing the embarrassment given them by their principle against war, whenever application was made to them, by order of the crown, to grant aids for military purposes. They were unwilling to offend government, on the one hand, by a direct refusal; and their friends, the body of the Quakers, on the other, by a compliance contrary to their principles; hence a variety of evasions to avoid complying, and modes of disguising the compliance when it became unavoidable. The common mode at last was, to grant money under the phrase of its being *"for the king's use,"* and never to inquire how it was applied.

But, if the demand was not directly from the crown, that phrase was found not so proper, and some other was to be invented. As, when powder was wanting (I think it was for the garrison at Louisburg), and the government of New England solicited a grant of some from Pennsylvania, which was much urg'd on the House by Governor Thomas, they could not grant money to buy powder, because that was an ingredient of war; but they voted an aid to New England of three thousand pounds, to be put into the hands of the governor, and appropriated it for the purchasing of bread, flour, wheat, or *other grain*. Some of the council, desirous of giving the House still further embarrassment, advis'd the governor not to accept provision, as not being the thing he had demanded; but he reply'd, "I shall take the money, for I understand very well their meaning; other grain is gunpowder," which he accordingly bought, and they never objected to it.

It was in allusion to this fact that, when in our fire company we feared the success of our proposal in favour of the lottery, and I had said to my friend Mr. Syng, one of our members, "If we fail, let us move the purchase of a fire-engine with the money; the Quakers can have no objection to that; and then, if you nominate me and I you as a committee for that purpose, we will buy a great gun, which is certainly a *fire-engine*." "I see," says he, "you have improv'd by being so long in the Assembly; your equivocal project would be just a match for their wheat or *other grain.*"

These embarrassments that the Quakers suffer'd from having establish'd and published it as one of their principles that no kind of war was lawful, and which, being once published, they could not afterwards, however they might change their minds, easily get rid of, reminds me of what I think a more prudent conduct in another sect among us, that of the Dunkers. I was acquainted with one of its founders, Michael Welfare, soon after it appear'd. He complain'd to me that they were grievously calumniated by the zealots of other persuasions, and charg'd with abominable principles and practices, to which they were utter strangers. I told him this had always been the case with new sects, and that, to put a stop to such abuse, I imagin'd it might be well to publish the articles of their belief, and the rules of their discipline. He said that it had been propos'd among them, but not agreed to, for this reason: "When we were first drawn together as a society," says he, "it had pleased God to enlighten our minds so far as to see that some doctrines, which we once esteemed truths, were errors; and that others, which we had esteemed errors, were real truths. From time to time He has been pleased to afford us farther light, and our principles have been improving, and our errors diminishing. Now we are not sure that we are arrived at the end of this progression, and at the perfection of spiritual or theological knowledge; and we fear that, if we should once print our confession of faith, we should feel ourselves as if bound and confin'd by it, and perhaps be unwilling to receive further improvement, and our successors still more so, as conceiving what we their elders and founders had done, to be something sacred, never to be departed from."

This modesty in a sect is perhaps a singular instance in the history of mankind, every other sect supposing itself in possession of all truth, and that those who differ are so far in the wrong; like a man traveling in foggy weather, those at some distance from him on the road he sees wrapped up in the fog, as well as those behind him, and also the people in the fields on each side, but near him all appears clear, tho' in truth he is as much in the fog as any of them. To avoid this kind of embarrassment, the Quakers have of late years been gradually declining the public service in the Assembly and in the magistracy, choosing rather to quit their power than their principle.

In order of time, I should have mentioned before, that having, in 1742, invented an open stove for the better warming of rooms, and at the same time saving fuel, as the fresh air admitted was warmed in entering, I made a present of the model to Mr. Robert Grace, one of my early friends, who, having an iron-furnace, found the casting of the plates for these stoves a profitable thing, as they were growing in demand. To promote that demand, I wrote and published a pamphlet, entitled *"An Account of the new-invented Pennsylvania Fireplaces; wherein their Construction and Manner of Operation is particularly explained; their Advantages above every other Method of warming Rooms demonstrated; and all Objections that have been raised against the Use of them answered and obviated,"* etc. This pamphlet had a good effect. Gov'r. Thomas was so pleas'd with the construction of this stove, as described in it, that he offered to give me a patent for the sole vending of them for a term of years; but I declin'd it from a principle which has ever weighed with me on such occasions, viz., *That, as we enjoy great advantages from the inventions of others, we should be glad of an opportunity to serve others by any invention of ours; and this we should do freely and generously.*

An ironmonger in London however, assuming a good deal of my pamphlet, and working it up into his own, and making some small changes in the machine, which rather hurt its operation, got a patent for it there, and made, as I was told, a little fortune by it. And this is not the only instance of patents taken out for my inventions by others, tho' not always with the same success, which I never contested, as having no desire of profiting by patents myself, and hating disputes. The use of these fireplaces in very many houses, both of this and the neighbouring colonies, has been, and is, a great saving of wood to the inhabitants.

Peace being concluded, and the association business therefore at an end, I turn'd my thoughts again to the affair of establishing an academy. The first step I took was to associate in the design a number of active friends, of whom the Junto furnished a good part; the next was to write and publish a pamphlet, entitled *Proposals Relating to the Education of Youth in Pennsylvania.* This I distributed among the principal inhabitants gratis; and as soon as I could suppose their minds a little prepared by the perusal of it, I set on foot a subscription for opening and supporting an academy; it was to be paid in quotas yearly for five years; by so dividing it, I judg'd the subscription might be larger, and I believed it was so, amounting to no less, if I remember right, than five thousand pounds.

In the introduction to these proposals, I stated their publication, not as an act of mine, but of some *public-spirited gentlemen,* avoiding as much as I could, according to my usual rule, the presenting myself to the public as the author of any scheme for their benefit.

The subscribers, to carry the project into immediate execution, chose out of their number twenty-four trustees, and appointed Mr. Francis, then attorney-general, and myself to draw up constitutions for the government of the academy; which being done and signed, a house was hired, masters engag'd, and the schools opened, I think, in the same year, 1749.

The scholars increasing fast, the house was soon found too small, and we were looking out for a piece of ground, properly situated, with intention to build, when Providence threw into our way a large house ready built, which, with a few alterations, might well serve our purpose. This was the building before mentioned, erected by the hearers of Mr. Whitefield, and was obtained for us in the following manner.

It is to be noted that the contributions to this building being made by people of different sects, care was taken in the nomination of trustees, in whom the building and ground was to be vested, that a predominancy should not be given to any sect, lest in time that predominancy might be a means of appropriating the whole to the use of such sect, contrary to the original intention. It was therefore that one of each sect was appointed, viz., one Church-of-England man, one Presbyterian, one Baptist, one Moravian, etc., those, in case of vacancy by death, were to fill it by election from among the contributors. The Moravian happen'd not to please his colleagues, and on his death they resolved to have no other of that sect. The difficulty then was, how to avoid having two of some other sect, by means of the new choice.

Several persons were named, and for that reason not agreed to. At length one mention'd me, with the observation that I was merely an honest man, and of no sect at all, which prevail'd with them to chuse me. The enthusiasm which existed when the house was built had long since abated, and its trustees had not been able to procure fresh contributions for paying the ground-rent, and discharging some other debts the building had occasion'd, which embarrass'd them greatly. Being now a member of both setts of trustees, that for the building and that for the academy, I had a good opportunity of negotiating with both, and brought them finally to an agreement, by which the trustees for the building were to cede it to those of the academy, the latter undertaking to discharge the debt, to keep forever open in the building a large hall for occasional preachers, according to the original intention, and maintain a free-school for the instruction of poor children. Writings were accordingly drawn, and on paying the debts the trustees of the academy were put in possession of the premises; and by dividing the great and lofty hall into stories, and different rooms above and below for the several schools, and purchasing some additional ground, the whole was soon made fit for our purpose, and the scholars remov'd into the building. The care and trouble of agreeing with the workmen, purchasing materials, and superintending the work, fell upon me; and I went thro' it the more cheerfully, as it did not then interfere with my private business, having the year before taken a very able, industrious, and honest partner, Mr. David Hall, with whose character I was well acquainted, as he had work'd for me four years. He took off my hands all care of the printing-office, paying me punctually my share of the profits. The partnership continued eighteen years, successfully for us both.

The trustees of the academy, after a while, were incorporated by a charter from the governor; their funds were increas'd by contributions in Britain and grants of land from the proprietaries, to which the Assembly has since made considerable addition; and thus was established the present University of Philadelphia. I have been continued one of its trustees from the beginning, now near forty years, and have had the very great pleasure of seeing a number of the youth who have receiv'd their education in it, distinguish'd by their improv'd abilities, serviceable in public stations, and ornaments to their country.

When I disengaged myself, as above mentioned, from private business, I flatter'd myself that, by the sufficient tho' moderate fortune I had acquir'd, I had secured leisure during the rest of my life for philosophical studies and amusements. I purchased all Dr. Spence[r]'s apparatus, who had come from England to lecture here, and I proceeded in my electrical experiments with great alacrity; but the publick, now considering me as a man of leisure, laid hold of me for their purposes, every part of our civil government, and almost at the same time, imposing some duty upon me. The governor put me into the commission of the peace; the corporation of the city chose me of the common council, and soon after an alderman; and the citizens at large chose me a burgess to represent them in Assembly. This latter station was the more agreeable to me, as I was at length tired with sitting there to hear debates, in which, as clerk, I could take no part, and which were often so unentertaining that I was induc'd to amuse myself with making magic squares or circles, or any thing to avoid weariness; and I conceiv'd my becoming a member would enlarge my power of doing good. I would not, however, insinuate that my ambition was not flatter'd by all these promotions; it certainly was; for, considering my low beginning, they were great things to me; and they were still more pleasing, as being so many spontaneous testimonies of the public good opinion, and by me entirely unsolicited.

The office of justice of the peace I try'd a little, by attending a few courts, and sitting on the bench to hear causes; but finding that more knowledge of the common law than I possess'd was necessary to act in that station with credit, I gradually withdrew from it, excusing myself by my being oblig'd to attend the higher duties of a legislator in the Assembly. My election to this trust was repeated every year for ten years, without my ever asking any elector for his vote, or signifying, either directly or indirectly, any desire of being chosen. On taking my seat in the House, my son was appointed their clerk.

The year following, a treaty being to be held with the Indians at Carlisle, the governor sent a message to the House, proposing that they should nominate some of their members, to be join'd with some members of council, as commissioners for that purpose. The House named the speaker (Mr. Norris) and myself; and, being commission'd, we went to Carlisle, and met the Indians accordingly.

As those people are extremely apt to get drunk, and, when so, are very quarrelsome and disorderly, we strictly forbad the selling of any liquor to them; and when they complain'd of this restriction, we told them that if they would continue sober during the treaty, we would give them plenty of rum when business was over. They promis'd this, and they kept their promise, because they could get no liquor, and the treaty was conducted very orderly, and concluded to mutual satisfaction. They then claim'd and receiv'd the rum; this was in the afternoon; they were near one hundred men, women, and children, and were lodg'd in temporary cabins, built in the form of a square, just without the town. In the evening, hearing a great noise among them, the commissioners walk'd out to see what was the matter. We found they had made a great bonfire in the middle of the square; they were all drunk, men and women, quarreling and fighting. Their dark-colour'd bodies, half naked, seen only by the gloomy light of the bonfire, running after and beating one another with firebrands, accompanied by their horrid yellings, form'd a scene the most resembling our ideas of hell that could well be imagin'd; there was no appeasing the tumult, and we retired to our lodging. At midnight a number of them came thundering at our door, demanding more rum, of which we took no notice.

The next day, sensible they had misbehav'd in giving us that disturbance, they sent three of their old counselors to make their apology. The orator acknowledg'd the fault, but laid it upon the rum; and then endeavored to excuse the rum by saying, *"The Great Spirit, who made all things, made every thing for some use, and whatever use he design'd any thing for, that use it should always be put to. Now, when he made rum, he said, 'Let this be for the Indians to get drunk with,' and it must be so."* And, indeed, if it be the design of Providence to extirpate these savages in order to make room for cultivators of the earth, it seems not improbable that rum may be the appointed means. It has already annihilated all the tribes who formerly inhabited the seacoast.

In 1751, Dr. Thomas Bond, a particular friend of mine, conceived the idea of establishing a hospital in Philadelphia (a very beneficent design, which has been ascrib'd to me, but was originally his), for the reception and cure of poor sick persons, whether inhabitants of the province or strangers. He was zealous and active in endeavouring to procure subscriptions for it, but the proposal being a novelty in America, and at first not well understood, he met with but small success.

At length he came to me with the compliment that he found there was no such thing as carrying a public-spirited project through without my being concern'd in it. "For," says he, "I am often ask'd by those to whom I propose subscribing, Have you consulted Franklin upon this business? And what does he think of it? And when I tell them that I have not (supposing it rather out of your line), they do not subscribe, but say they will consider of it." I enquired into the nature and probable utility of his scheme, and receiving from him a very satisfactory explanation, I not only subscrib'd to it myself, but engag'd heartily in the design of procuring subscriptions from others. Previously, however, to the solicitation, I endeavoured to prepare the minds of the people by writing on the subject in the newspapers, which was my usual custom in such cases, but which he had omitted.

The subscriptions afterwards were more free and generous; but, beginning to flag, I saw they would be insufficient without some assistance from the Assembly, and therefore propos'd to petition for it, which was done. The country members did not at first relish the project; they objected that it could only be serviceable to the city, and therefore the citizens alone should be at the expense of it; and they doubted whether the citizens themselves generally approv'd of it. My allegation on the contrary, that it met with such approbation as to leave no doubt of our being able to raise two thousand pounds by voluntary donations, they considered as a most extravagant supposition, and utterly impossible.

On this I form'd my plan; and, asking leave to bring in a bill for incorporating the contributors according to the prayer of their petition, and granting them a blank sum of money, which leave was obtained chiefly on the consideration that the House could throw the bill out if they did not like it, I drew it so as to make the important clause a conditional one, viz., "And be it enacted, by the authority aforesaid, that when the said contributors shall have met and chosen their managers and treasurer, *and shall have raised by their contributions a capital stock of —— value* (the yearly interest of which is to be applied to the accommodating of the sick poor in the said hospital, free of charge for diet, attendance, advice, and medicines), *and shall make the same appear to the satisfaction of the speaker of the Assembly for the time being,* that *then* it shall and may be lawful for the said speaker, and he is hereby required, to sign an order on the provincial treasurer for the payment of two thousand pounds, in two yearly payments, to the treasurer of the said hospital, to be applied to the founding, building, and finishing of the same."

This condition carried the bill through; for the members, who had oppos'd the grant, and now conceiv'd they might have the credit of being charitable without the expence, agreed to its passage; and then, in soliciting subscriptions among the people, we urg'd the conditional promise of the law as an additional motive to give, since every man's donation would be doubled; thus the clause work'd both ways. The subscriptions accordingly soon exceeded the requisite sum, and we claim'd and receiv'd the public gift, which enabled us to carry the design into execution. A convenient and handsome building was soon erected; the institution has by constant experience been found useful, and flourishes to this day; and I do not remember any of my political manœuvres, the success of which gave me at the time more pleasure, or wherein, after thinking of it, I more easily excus'd myself for having made some use of cunning.

It was about this time that another projector, the Rev. Gilbert Tennent, came to me with a request that I would assist him in procuring a subscription for erecting a new meeting-house. It was to be for the use of a congregation he had gathered among the Presbyterians, who were originally disciples of Mr. Whitefield. Unwilling to make myself disagreeable to my fellow-citizens by too frequently soliciting their contributions, I absolutely refus'd. He then desired I would furnish him with a list of names of persons I knew by experience to be generous and public-spirited. I thought it would be unbecoming in me, after their kind compliance with my solicitations, to mark them out to be worried by other beggars, and therefore refus'd also to give such a list. He then desir'd I would at least give him my advice. "That I will readily do," said I; "and, in the first place, I advise you to apply to all those whom you know will give something; next, to those whom you are uncertain whether they will give any thing or not, and show them the list of those who have given; and, lastly, do not neglect those who you are sure will give nothing, for in some of them you may be mistaken." He laugh'd and thank'd me, and said he would take my advice. He did so, for he ask'd of *everybody*, and he obtain'd a much larger sum than he expected, with which he erected the capacious and very elegant meeting-house that stands in Arch-street.

Our city, tho' laid out with a beautiful regularity, the streets large, strait, and crossing each other at right angles, had the disgrace of suffering those streets to remain long unpav'd, and in wet weather the wheels of heavy carriages plough'd them into a quagmire, so that it was difficult to cross them; and in dry weather the dust was offensive. I had liv'd near what was call'd the Jersey Market, and saw with pain the inhabitants wading in mud while purchasing their provisions. A strip of ground down the middle of that market was at length pav'd with brick, so that, being once in the market, they had firm footing, but were often over shoes in dirt to get there. By talking and writing on the subject, I was at length instrumental in getting the street pav'd with stone between the market and the brick'd foot-pavement, that was on each side next the houses. This, for some time, gave an easy access to the market dry-shod; but, the rest of the street not being pav'd, whenever a carriage came out of the mud upon this pavement, it shook off and left its dirt upon it, and it was soon cover'd with mire, which was not remov'd, the city as yet having no scavengers.

After some inquiry, I found a poor, industrious man, who was willing to undertake keeping the pavement clean, by sweeping it twice a week, carrying off the dirt from before all the neighbours' doors, for the sum of sixpence per month, to be paid by each house. I then wrote and printed a paper setting forth the advantages to the neighbourhood that might be obtain'd by this small expense; the greater ease in keeping our houses clean, so much dirt not being brought in by people's feet; the benefit to the shops by more custom, etc., etc., as buyers could more easily get at them; and by not having, in windy weather, the dust blown in upon their goods, etc., etc. I sent one of these papers to each house, and in a day or two went round to see who would subscribe an agreement to pay these sixpences; it was unanimously sign'd, and for a time well executed. All the inhabitants of the city were delighted with the cleanliness of the pavement that surrounded the market, it being a convenience to all, and this rais'd a general desire to have all the streets paved, and made the people more willing to submit to a tax for that purpose.

After some time I drew a bill for paving the city, and brought it into the Assembly. It was just before I went to England, in 1757, and did not pass till I was gone, and then with an alteration in the mode of assessment, which I thought not for the better, but with an additional provision for lighting as well as paving the streets, which was a great improvement. It was by a private person, the late Mr. John Clifton, his giving a sample of the utility of lamps, by placing one at his door, that the people were first impress'd with the idea of enlighting all the city. The honour of this public benefit has also been ascrib'd to me, but it belongs truly to that gentleman. I did but follow his example, and have only some merit to claim respecting the form of our lamps, as differing from the globe lamps we were at first supply'd with from London. Those we found inconvenient in these respects: they admitted no air below; the smoke, therefore, did not readily go out above, but circulated in the globe, lodg'd on its inside, and soon obstructed the light they were intended to afford; giving, besides, the daily trouble of wiping them clean; and an accidental stroke on one of them would demolish it, and render it totally useless. I therefore suggested the composing them of four flat panes, with a long funnel above to draw up the smoke, and crevices admitting air below, to facilitate the ascent of the smoke; by this means they were kept clean, and did not grow dark in a few hours, as the London lamps do, but continu'd bright till morning, and an accidental stroke would generally break but a single pane, easily repair'd.

I have sometimes wonder'd that the Londoners did not, from

the effect holes in the bottom of the globe lamps us'd at Vauxhall have in keeping them clean, learn to have such holes in their street lamps. But, these holes being made for another purpose, viz., to communicate flame more suddenly to the wick by a little flax hanging down thro' them, the other use, of letting in air, seems not to have been thought of; and therefore, after the lamps have been lit a few hours, the streets of London are very poorly illuminated.

The mention of these improvements puts me in mind of one I propos'd, when in London, to Dr. [John] Fothergill, who was among the best men I have known, and a great promoter of useful projects. I had observ'd that the streets, when dry, were never swept, and the light dust carried away; but it was suffer'd to accumulate till wet weather reduc'd it to mud, and then, after lying some days so deep on the pavement that there was no crossing but in paths kept clean by poor people with brooms, it was with great labour rak'd together and thrown up into carts open above, the sides of which suffer'd some of the slush at every jolt on the pavement to shake out and fall, sometimes to the annoyance of foot-passengers. The reason given for not sweeping the dusty streets was, that the dust would fly into the windows of shops and houses.

An accidental occurrence had instructed me how much sweeping might be done in a little time. I found at my door in Craven-street, one morning, a poor woman sweeping my pavement with a birch broom; she appeared very pale and feeble, as just come out of a fit of sickness. I ask'd who employ'd her to sweep there; she said, "Nobody, but I am very poor and in distress, and I sweeps before gentlefolkses doors, and hopes they will give me something." I bid her sweep the whole street clean, and I would give her a shilling; this was at nine o'clock; at 12 she came for the shilling. From the slowness I saw at first in her working, I could scarce believe that the work was done so soon, and sent my servant to examine it, who reported that the whole street was swept perfectly clean, and all the dust plac'd in the gutter, which was in the middle; and the next rain wash'd it quite away, so that the pavement and even the kennel were perfectly clean.

I then judg'd that, if that feeble woman could sweep such a street in three hours, a strong, active man might have done it in half the time. And here let me remark the convenience of having but one gutter in such a narrow street, running down its middle, instead of two, one on each side, near the footway; for where all the rain that falls on a street runs from the sides and meets in the middle, it forms there a current strong enough to wash away all the mud it meets with; but when divided into two channels, it is often too weak to cleanse either, and only makes the mud it finds more fluid, so that the wheels of carriages and feet of horses throw and dash it upon the foot-pavement, which is thereby rendered foul and slippery, and sometimes splash it upon those who are walking. My proposal, communicated to the good doctor, was as follows:

"For the more effectual cleaning and keeping clean the streets of London and Westminster, it is proposed that the several watchmen be contracted with to have the dust swept up in dry seasons, and the mud rak'd up at other times, each in the several streets and lanes of his round; that they be furnish'd with brooms and other proper instruments for these purposes, to be kept at their respective stands, ready to furnish the poor people they may employ in the service.

"That in the dry summer months the dust be all swept up into heaps at proper distances, before the shops and windows of houses are usually opened, when the scavengers, with close-covered carts, shall also carry it all away.

"That the mud, when rak'd up, be not left in heaps to be spread abroad again by the wheels of carriages and trampling of horses, but that the scavengers be provided with bodies of carts, not plac'd high upon wheels, but low upon sliders, with lattice bottoms, which, being cover'd with straw, will retain the mud thrown into them, and permit the water to drain from it, whereby it will become much lighter, water making the greatest parts of its weight; these bodies of carts to be plac'd at convenient distances, and the mud brought to them in wheel-barrows; they remaining where plac'd till the mud is drain'd, and then horses brought to draw them away."

I have since had doubts of the practicability of the latter part of this proposal, on account of the narrowness of some streets, and the difficulty of placing the draining-sleds so as not to en-cumber too much the passage; but I am still of opinion that the former, requiring the dust to be swept up and carry'd away before the shops are open, is very practicable in the summer, when the days are long; for, in walking thro' the Strand and Fleet-street one morning at seven o'clock, I observ'd there was not one shop open, tho' it had been daylight and the sun up above three hours; the inhabitant of London chusing volun-tarily to live much by candle-light, and sleep by sunshine, and yet often complain, a little absurdly, of the duty on candles, and the high price of tallow.

Some may think these trifling matters not worth minding or relating; but when they consider that tho' dust blown into the eyes of a single person, or into a single shop on a windy day, is but of small importance, yet the great number of the instances in a populous city, and its frequent repetitions give it weight and consequence, perhaps they will not censure very severely those who bestow some attention to affairs of this seemingly low nature. Human felicity is produc'd not so much by great pieces of good fortune that seldom happen, as by little advan-tages that occur every day. Thus, if you teach a poor young man to shave himself, and keep his razor in order, you may con-tribute more to the happiness of his life than in giving him a thousand guineas. The money may be soon spent, the regret only remaining of having foolishly consumed it; but in the other case, he escapes the frequent vexation of waiting for barbers, and of their sometimes dirty fingers, offensive breaths, and dull razors; he shaves when most convenient to him, and enjoys daily the pleasure of its being done with a good instru-ment. With these sentiments I have hazarded the few preceding pages, hoping they may afford hints which some time or other may be useful to a city I love, having lived many years in it very happily, and perhaps to some of our towns in America.

Having been for some time employed by the postmaster-general of America as his comptroller in regulating several offices, and bringing the officers to account, I was, upon his death in 1753, appointed, jointly with Mr. William Hunter, to succeed him, by a commission from the postmaster-general in England. The American office never had hitherto paid any thing to that of Britain. We were to have six hundred pounds a year between us, if we could make that sum out of the profits of the office. To do this, a variety of improvements were necessary; some of these were inevitably at first expensive, so that in the first four years the office became above nine hundred pounds in debt to us. But it soon after began to repay us; and before I was displac'd by a freak of the ministers, of which I shall speak hereafter, we had brought it to yield *three times* as much clear revenue to the crown as the postoffice of Ireland. Since that imprudent transaction, they have receiv'd from it—not one farthing!

The business of the postoffice occasion'd my taking a journey this year to New England, where the College of Cambridge [Harvard], of their own motion, presented me with the degree of Master of Arts. Yale College, in Connecticut, had before made me a similar compliment. Thus, without studying in any college, I came to partake of their honours. They were conferr'd in consideration of my improvements and discoveries in the electric branch of natural philosophy.

In 1754, war with France being again apprehended, a congress of commissioners from the different colonies was, by order of the Lords of Trade, to be assembled at Albany, there to confer with the chiefs of the Six Nations concerning the means of defending both their country and ours. Governor Hamilton, having receiv'd this order, acquainted the House with it, requesting they would furnish proper presents for the Indians, to be given on this occasion; and naming the speaker (Mr. Norris) and myself to join Mr. Thomas Penn and Mr. Secretary Peters as commissioners to act for Pennsylvania. The House approv'd the nomination, and provided the goods for the present, and tho' they did not much like treating out of the provinces; and we met the other commissioners at Albany about the middle of June.

In our way thither, I projected and drew a plan for the union of all the colonies under one government, so far as might be necessary for defense, and other important general purposes. As we pass'd thro' New York, I had there shown my project to Mr. James Alexander and Mr. Kennedy, two gentlemen of great knowledge in public affairs, and, being fortified by their approbation, I ventur'd to lay it before the Congress. It then appeared that several of the commissioners had form'd plans of the same kind. A previous question was first taken, whether a union should be established, which pass'd in the affirmative unanimously. A committee was then appointed, one member from each colony, to consider the several plans and report. Mine happen'd to be preferr'd, and, with a few amendments, was accordingly reported.

By this plan the general government was to be administered by a president-general, appointed and supported by the crown, and a grand council was to be chosen by the representatives of the people of the several colonies, met in their respective assemblies. The debates upon it in Congress went on daily, hand in hand with the Indian business. Many objections and difficulties were started, but at length they were all overcome, and the plan was unanimously agreed to, and copies ordered to be transmitted to the Board of Trade and to the assemblies of the several provinces. Its fate was singular: the assemblies did not adopt it, as they all thought there was too much *prerogative* in it, and in England it was judg'd to have too much of the *democratic*. The Board of Trade therefore did not approve of it, nor recommend it for the approbation of his majesty; but another scheme was form'd, supposed to answer the same purpose better, whereby the governors of the provinces, with some members of their respective councils, were to meet and order the raising of troops, building of forts, etc., and to draw on the treasury of Great Britain for the expense, which was afterwards to be refunded by an act of Parliament laying a tax on America. My plan, with my reasons in support of it, is to be found among my political papers that are printed.

Being the winter following in Boston, I had much conversation with Governor Shirley upon both the plans. Part of what passed between us on the occasion may also be seen among those papers. The different and contrary reasons of dislike to my plan makes me suspect that it was really the true medium; and I am still of opinion it would have been happy for both sides the water if it had been adopted. The colonies, so united, would have been sufficiently strong to have defended themselves; there would then have been no need of troops from England; of course, the subsequent pretence for taxing America, and the bloody contest it occasioned, would have been avoided. But such mistakes are not new; history is full of the errors of states and princes.

> "Look around the habitable world, how few
> Know their own good, or, knowing it, pursue!"

Those who govern, having much business on their hands, do not generally like to take the trouble of considering and carrying into execution new projects. The best public measures are therefore seldom *adopted from previous wisdom, but forc'd by the occasion.*

The Governor of Pennsylvania, in sending it down to the Assembly, express'd his approbation of the plan, "as appearing to him to be drawn up with great clearness and strength of judgment, and therefore recommended it as well worthy of their closest and most serious attention." The House, however, by the management of a certain member, took it up when I happen'd to be absent, which I thought not very fair, and reprobated it without paying any attention to it at all, to my no small mortification.

In my journey to Boston this year, I met at New York with

our new governor, Mr. Morris, just arrived there from England, with whom I had been before intimately acquainted. He brought a commission to supersede Mr. Hamilton, who, tir'd with the disputes his proprietary instructions subjected him to, had resign'd. Mr. Morris ask'd me if I thought he must expect as uncomfortable an administration. I said, "No; you may, on the contrary, have a very comfortable one, if you will only take care not to enter into any dispute with the Assembly." "My dear friend," says he, pleasantly, "how can you advise my avoiding disputes? You know I love disputing; it is one of my greatest pleasures; however, to show the regard I have for your counsel, I promise you I will, if possible, avoid them." He had some reason for loving to dispute, being eloquent, an acute sophister, and, therefore, generally successful in argumentative conversation. He had been brought up to it from a boy, his father, as I have heard, accustoming his children to dispute with one another for his diversion, while sitting at table after dinner; but I think the practice was not wise; for, in the course of my observation, these disputing, contradicting, and confuting people are generally unfortunate in their affairs. They get victory sometimes, but they never get good will, which would be of more use to them. We parted, he going to Philadelphia, and I to Boston.

In returning, I met at New York with the votes of the Assembly, by which it appear'd that, notwithstanding his promise to me, he and the House were already in high contention; and it was a continual battle between them as long as he retain'd the government. I had my share of it; for, as soon as I got back to my seat in the Assembly, I was put on every committee for answering his speeches and messages, and by the committees always desired to make the drafts. Our answers, as well as his messages, were often tart, and sometimes indecently abusive; and, as he knew I wrote for the Assembly, one might have imagined that, when we met, we could hardly avoid cutting throats; but he was so good-natur'd a man that no personal difference between him and me was occasion'd by the contest, and we often din'd together.

One afternoon, in the height of this public quarrel, we met in the street. "Franklin," says he, "you must go home with me and spend the evening; I am to have some company that you will like"; and, taking me by the arm, he led me to his house. In gay conversation, over our wine, after supper, he told us, jokingly, that he much admir'd the idea of Sancho Panza, who, when it was proposed to give him a government, requested it might be a government of *blacks,* as then, if he could not agree with his people, he might sell them. One of his friends, who sat next to me, says, "Franklin, why do you continue to side with these damn'd Quakers? Had not you better sell them? The proprietor would give you a good price." "The governor," says I, "has not yet *blacked* them enough." He, indeed, had labored hard to blacken the Assembly in all his messages, but they wip'd off his coloring as fast as he laid it on, and plac'd it, in return, thick upon his own face; so that, finding he was likely to be negrofied himself, he, as well as Mr. Hamilton, grew tir'd of the contest, and quitted the government.

These public quarrels [My acts in Morris's time, military, etc.] were all at bottom owing to the proprietaries, our hereditary governors, who, when any expense was to be incurred for the defense of their province, with incredible meanness instructed their deputies to pass no act for levying the necessary taxes, unless their vast estates were in the same act expressly excused; and they had even taken bonds of these deputies to observe such instructions. The Assemblies for three years held out against this injustice, tho' constrained to bend at last. At length Captain Denny, who was Governor Morris's successor, ventured to disobey those instructions; how that was brought about I shall show hereafter.

But I am got forward too fast with my story: there are still some transactions to be mention'd that happened during the administration of Governor Morris.

War being in a manner commenced with France, the government of Massachusetts Bay projected an attack upon Crown Point, and sent Mr. Quincy to Pennsylvania, and Mr. Pownall, afterward Governor Pownall, to New York, to solicit assistance. As I was in the Assembly, knew its temper, and was Mr. Quincy's countryman, he appli'd to me for my influence and assistance. I dictated his address to them, which was well receiv'd. They voted an aid of ten thousand pounds, to be laid out in provisions. But the governor refusing his assent to their bill (which included this with other sums granted for the use of the crown), unless a clause were inserted exempting the proprietary estate from bearing any part of the tax that would be necessary, the Assembly, tho' very desirous of making their grant to New England effectual, were at a loss how to accomplish it. Mr. Quincy labored hard with the governor to obtain his assent, but he was obstinate.

I then suggested a method of doing the business without the governor, by orders on the trustees of the Loan Office, which, by law, the Assembly had the right of drawing. There was, indeed, little or no money at that time in the office, and therefore I propos'd that the orders should be payable in a year, and to bear an interest of five per cent. With these orders I suppos'd the provisions might easily be purchas'd. The Assembly, with very little hesitation, adopted the proposal. The orders were immediately printed, and I was one of the committee directed to sign and dispose of them. The fund for paying them was the interest of all the paper currency then extant in the province upon loan, together with the revenue arising from the excise, which being known to be more than sufficient, they obtain'd instant credit, and were not only receiv'd in payment for the provisions, but many money'd people, who had cash lying by them, vested it in those orders, which they found advantageous, as they bore interest while upon hand, and might on any occasion be used as money; so that they were eagerly all bought up, and in a few weeks none of them were to be seen. Thus this important affair was by my means compleated. Mr. Quincy return'd thanks to the Assembly in a handsome memorial, went home highly pleas'd with the success of his embassy, and ever after bore for me the most cordial and affectionate friendship.

One of the earliest known portraits of Benjamin Franklin, believed to have been painted about 1750, when he was forty-four, and attributed to Robert Feke

The British government, not chusing to permit the union of the colonies as propos'd at Albany, and to trust that union with their defense, lest they should thereby grow too military, and feel their own strength, suspicions and jealousies at this time being entertain'd of them, sent over General Braddock with two regiments of regular English troops for that purpose. He landed at Alexandria, in Virginia, and thence march'd to Frederictown, in Maryland, where he halted for carriages. Our Assembly apprehending, from some information, that he had conceived violent prejudices against them, as averse to the service, wish'd me to wait upon him, not as from them, but as postmaster-general, under the guise of proposing to settle with him the mode of conducting with most celerity and certainty the despatches between him and the governors of the several provinces, with whom he must necessarily have continual correspondence, and of which they propos'd to pay the expense. My son accompanied me on this journey.

We found the general at Frederictown, waiting impatiently for the return of those he had sent thro' the back parts of Maryland and Virginia to collect waggons. I stayed with him several days, din'd with him daily, and had full opportunity of removing all his prejudices, by the information of what the Assembly had before his arrival actually done, and were still willing to do, to facilitate his operations. When I was about to depart, the returns of waggons to be obtained were brought in, by which it appear'd that they amounted only to twenty-five, and not all of those were in serviceable condition. The general and all the officers were surpris'd, declar'd the expedition was then at an end, being impossible, and exclaim'd against the ministers for ignorantly landing them in a country destitute of the means of conveying their stores, baggage, etc., not less than one hundred and fifty waggons being necessary.

I happen'd to say I thought it was pity they had not been landed rather in Pennsylvania, as in that country almost every farmer had his waggon. The general eagerly laid hold of my words, and said, "Then you, sir, who are a man of interest there, can probably procure them for us; and I beg you will undertake it." I ask'd what terms were to be offer'd the owners of the waggons; and I was desir'd to put on paper the terms that appeared to me necessary. This I did, and they were agreed to, and a commission and instructions accordingly prepar'd immediately. What those terms were will appear in the advertisement I publish'd as soon as I arriv'd at Lancaster, which being, from the great and sudden effect it produc'd, a piece of some curiosity, I shall insert it at length, as follows:

"ADVERTISEMENT.

"Lancaster, April 26, 1755.

"Whereas, one hundred and fifty waggons, with four horses to each waggon, and fifteen hundred saddle or pack horses, are wanted for the service of his majesty's forces now about to rendezvous at Will's Creek, and his excellency General Braddock having been pleased to empower me to contract for the hire of the same, I hereby give notice that I shall attend for that purpose at Lancaster from this day to next Wednesday evening, and at York from next Thursday morning till Friday evening, where I shall be ready to agree for waggons and teams, or single horses, on the following terms, viz.: 1. That there shall be paid for each waggon, with four good horses and a driver, fifteen shillings per diem; and for each able horse with a pack-saddle, or other saddle and furniture, two shillings per diem; and for each able horse without a saddle, eighteen pence per diem. 2. That the pay commence from the time of their joining the forces at Will's Creek, which must be on or before the 20th of May ensuing, and that a reasonable allowance be paid over and above for the time necessary for their travelling to Will's Creek and home again after their discharge. 3. Each waggon and team, and every saddle or pack horse, is to be valued by indifferent persons chosen between me and the owner; and in case of the loss of any waggon, team, or other horse in the service, the price according to such valuation is to be allowed and paid. 4. Seven days' pay is to be advanced and paid in hand by me to the owner of each wagon and team, or horse, at the time of contracting, if required, and the remainder to be paid by General Braddock, or by the paymaster of the army, at the time of their discharge, or from time to time, as it shall be demanded. 5. No drivers of waggons, or persons taking care of the hired horses, are on any account to be called upon to do the duty of soldiers, or be otherwise employed than in conducting or taking care of their carriages or horses. 6. All oats, Indian corn, or other forage that waggons or horses bring to the camp, more than is necessary for the subsistence of the horses, is to be taken for the use of the army, and a reasonable price paid for the same.

"Note.—My son, William Franklin, is empowered to enter into like contracts with any person in Cumberland county.

"B. Franklin."

"To the inhabitants of the Counties of Lancaster, York and Cumberland.

"Friends and Countrymen,

"Being occasionally at the camp at Frederic a few days since, I found the general and officers extremely exasperated on account of their not being supplied with horses and carriages, which had been expected from this province, as most able to furnish them; but, through the dissensions between our governor and Assembly, money had not been provided, nor any steps taken for that purpose.

"It was proposed to send an armed force immediately into these countries, to seize as many of the best carriages and horses as should be wanted, and compel as many persons into the service as would be necessary to drive and take care of them.

"I apprehended that the progress of British soldiers through these counties on such an occasion, especially considering the temper they are in, and their resentment against us, would be attended with many and great inconveniences to the inhabitants, and therefore more willingly took the trouble of trying first what might be done by fair and equitable means. The people of these back counties have lately complained to the Assembly that a sufficient currency was wanting; you have an opportunity of receiving and dividing among you a very considerable sum; for, if the service of this expedition should continue, as it is more than probable it will, for one hundred and twenty days, the hire of these waggons and horses will amount to upward of thirty thousand pounds, which will be paid you in silver and gold of the king's money.

"The service will be light and easy, for the army will scarce march above twelve miles per day, and the waggons and baggage-horses, as they carry those things that are absolutely necessary to the welfare of the army, must march with the army, and no faster; and are, for the army's sake, always placed where they can be most secure, whether in a march or in a camp.

"If you are really, as I believe you are, good and loyal subjects to his majesty, you may now do a most acceptable service, and make it easy to yourselves; for three or four of such as can not separately spare from the business of their plantations a waggon and four horses and a driver, may do it together, one furnishing the waggon, another one or two horses, and another the driver, and divide the pay proportionably between you; but if you do not this service to your king and country voluntarily, when such good pay and reasonable terms are offered to you, your loyalty will be strongly suspected. The king's business must be done; so many brave troops, come so far for your defense, must not stand idle through your backwardness to do what may be reasonably expected from you; waggons and horses must be had; violent measures will probably be used, and you will be left to seek for a recompense where you can find it, and your case, perhaps, be little pitied or regarded.

"I have no particular interest in this affair, as, except the satisfaction of endeavoring to do good, I shall have only my labour for my pains. If this method of obtaining the waggons and horses is not likely to succeed, I am obliged to send word to the general in fourteen days; and I suppose Sir John St. Clair, the hussar, with a body of soldiers, will immediately enter the province for the purpose, which I shall be sorry to hear, because I am very sincerely and truly your friend and well-wisher,

"B. Franklin."

I received of the general about eight hundred pounds, to be disbursed in advance-money to the waggon owners, etc.; but that sum being insufficient, I advanc'd upward of two hundred pounds more, and in two weeks the one hundred and fifty waggons, with two hundred and fifty-nine carrying horses, were on their march for the camp. The advertisement promised payment according to the valuation, in case any waggon or horse should be lost. The owners, however, alleging they did not know General Braddock, or what dependence might be had on his promise, insisted on my bond for the performance, which I accordingly gave them.

While I was at the camp, supping one evening with the officers of Colonel Dunbar's regiment, he represented to me his concern for the subalterns, who, he said, were generally not in affluence, and could ill afford, in this dear country, to lay in the stores that might be necessary in so long a march, thro' a wilderness, where nothing was to be purchas'd. I commiserated their case, and resolved to endeavor procuring them some relief. I said nothing, however, to him of my intention, but wrote the next morning to the committee of the Assembly, who had the disposition of some public money, warmly recommending the case of these officers to their consideration, and proposing that a present should be sent them of necessaries and refreshments. My son, who had some experience of a camp life, and of its wants, drew up a list for me, which I enclos'd in my letter. The committee approv'd, and used such diligence that, conducted by my son, the stores arrived at the camp as soon as the waggons. They consisted of twenty parcels, each containing

6 lbs. loaf sugar.
6 lbs. good Muscovado do.
1 lb. good green tea.
1 lb. good bohea do.
6 lbs. good ground coffee.
6 lbs. chocolate.
1-2 cwt. best white biscuit.
1-2 lb. pepper.
1 quart best white wine vinegar.

1 Gloucester cheese.
1 kegg containing 20 lbs. good butter.
2 doz. old Madeira wine.
2 gallons Jamaica spirits.
1 bottle flour of mustard.
2 well-cur'd hams.
1-2 dozen dry'd tongues.
6 lbs. rice.
6 lbs. raisins.

These twenty parcels, well pack'd, were placed on as many horses, each parcel, with the horse, being intended as a present for one officer. They were very thankfully receiv'd, and the kindness acknowledg'd by letters to me from the colonels of both regiments, in the most grateful terms. The general, too, was highly satisfied with my conduct in procuring him the waggons, etc., and readily paid my account of disbursements, thanking me repeatedly, and requesting my farther assistance in sending provisions after him. I undertook this also, and was busily employ'd in it till we heard of his defeat, advancing for the service of my own money, upwards of one thousand pounds sterling, of which I sent him an account. It came to his hands, luckily for me, a few days before the battle, and he return'd me immediately an order on the paymaster for the round sum of one thousand pounds, leaving the remainder to the next account. I consider this payment as good luck, having never been able to obtain that remainder, of which more hereafter.

This general was, I think, a brave man, and might probably have made a figure as a good officer in some European war. But he had too much self-confidence, too high an opinion of the validity of regular troops, and too mean a one of both Americans and Indians. George Croghan, our Indian interpreter, join'd him on his march with one hundred of those people, who might have been of great use to his army as guides, scouts, etc., if he had treated them kindly; but he slighted and neglected them, and they gradually left him.

In conversation with him one day, he was giving me some

account of his intended progress. "After taking Fort Duquesne," says he, "I am to proceed to Niagara; and, having taken that, to Frontenac, if the season will allow time; and I suppose it will, for Duquesne can hardly detain me above three or four days; and then I see nothing that can obstruct my march to Niagara." Having before revolv'd in my mind the long line his army must make in their march by a very narrow road, to be cut for them thro' the woods and bushes, and also what I had read of a former defeat of fifteen hundred French, who invaded the Iroquois country, I had conceiv'd some doubts and some fears for the event of the campaign. But I ventur'd only to say, "To be sure, sir, if you arrive well before Duquesne, with these fine troops, so well provided with artillery, that place not yet completely fortified, and as we hear with no very strong garrison, can probably make but a short resistance. The only danger I apprehend of obstruction to your march is from ambuscades of Indians, who, by constant practice, are dexterous in laying and executing them; and the slender line, near four miles long, which your army must make, may expose it to be attack'd by surprise in its flanks, and to be cut like a thread into several pieces, which, from their distance, can not come up in time to support each other."

He smil'd at my ignorance, and reply'd, "These savages may, indeed, be a formidable enemy to your raw American militia, but upon the king's regular and disciplin'd troops, sir, it is impossible they should make any impression." I was conscious of an impropriety in my disputing with a military man in matters of his profession, and said no more. The enemy, however, did not take the advantage of his army which I apprehended its long line of march expos'd it to, but let it advance without interruption till within nine miles of the place; and then, when more in a body (for it had just passed a river, where the front had halted till all were come over), and in a more open part of the woods than any it had pass'd, attack'd its advanced guard by a heavy fire from behind trees and bushes, which was the first intelligence the general had of an enemy's being near him.

This guard being disordered, the general hurried the troops up to their assistance, which was done in great confusion, thro' waggons, baggage, and cattle; and presently the fire came upon their flank: the officers, being on horseback, were more easily distinguish'd, pick'd out as marks, and fell very fast; and the soldiers were crowded together in a huddle, having or hearing no orders, and standing to be shot at till two-thirds of them were killed; and then, being seiz'd with a panick, the whole fled with precipitation.

The waggoners took each a horse out of his team and scamper'd; their example was immediately followed by others; so that all the waggons, provisions, artillery, and stores were left to the enemy. The general, being wounded, was brought off with difficulty; his secretary, Mr. Shirley, was killed by his side; and out of eighty-six officers, sixty-three were killed or wounded, and seven hundred and fourteen men killed out of eleven hundred. These eleven hundred had been picked men from the whole army; the rest had been left behind with Colonel Dunbar, who was to follow with the heavier part of the stores, provisions, and baggage. The flyers, not being pursu'd, arriv'd at Dunbar's camp, and the panick they brought with them instantly seiz'd him and all his people; and, tho' he had now above one thousand men, and the enemy who had beaten Braddock did not at most exceed four hundred Indians and French together, instead of proceeding, and endeavoring to recover some of the lost honour, he ordered all the stores, ammunition, etc., to be destroy'd, that he might have more horses to assist his flight towards the settlements, and less lumber to remove. He was there met with request from the governors of Virginia, Maryland, and Pennsylvania, that he would post his troops on the frontier, so as to afford some protection to the inhabitants; but he continu'd his hasty march thro' all the country, not thinking himself safe till he arriv'd at Philadelphia, where the inhabitants could protect him. This whole transaction gave us Americans the first suspicion that our exalted ideas of the prowess of British regulars had not been well founded.

The Philadelphia Library, founded by Franklin

In their first march, too, from their landing till they got beyond the settlements, they had plundered and stripped the inhabitants, totally ruining some poor families, besides insulting, abusing, and confining the people if they remonstrated. This was enough to put us out of conceit of such defenders, if we had really wanted any. How different was the conduct of our French friends in 1781, who, during a march thro' the most inhabited part of our country from Rhode Island to Virginia, near seven hundred miles, occasioned not the smallest complaint for the loss of a pig, a chicken, or even an apple.

Captain Orme, who was one of the general's aids-de-camp, and, being grievously wounded, was brought off with him, and continu'd with him to his death, which happen'd in a few days, told me that he was totally silent all the first day, and at night only said, *"Who would have thought it?"* That he was silent again the following day, saying only at last, *"We shall better know how to deal with them another time";* and dy'd in a few minutes after.

The secretary's papers, with all the general's orders, instructions, and correspondence, falling into the enemy's hands, they selected and translated into French a number of the articles, which they printed, to prove the hostile intentions of the British court before the declaration of war. Among these I saw some letters of the general to the ministry, speaking highly of the great service I had rendered the army, and recommending me to their notice. David Hume, too, who was some years after secretary to Lord Hertford, when minister in France, and afterward to General Conway, when secretary of state, told me he had seen among the papers in that office, letters from Braddock highly recommending me. But, the expedition having been unfortunate, my service, it seems, was not thought of much value, for those recommendations were never of any use to me.

As to rewards from himself, I ask'd only one, which was, that he would give orders to his officers not to enlist any more of our bought servants, and that he would discharge such as had been already enlisted. This he readily granted, and several were ac-

cordingly return'd to their masters, on my application. Dunbar,
when the command devolv'd on him, was not so generous. He
being at Philadelphia, on his retreat, or rather flight, I apply'd
to him for the discharge of the servants of three poor farmers
of Lancaster county that he had enlisted, reminding him of the
late general's orders on that head. He promised me that, if the
masters would come to him at Trenton, where he should be in
a few days on his march to New York, he would there deliver
their men to them. They accordingly were at the expense and
trouble of going to Trenton, and there he refus'd to perform
his promise, to their great loss and disappointment.

As soon as the loss of the waggons and horses was generally
known, all the owners came upon me for the valuation which
I had given bond to pay. Their demands gave me a great deal
of trouble, my acquainting them that the money was ready in
the paymaster's hands, but that orders for paying it must first
be obtained from General Shirley, and my assuring them that
I had apply'd to that general by letters; but, he being at a distance, an answer could not soon be receiv'd, and they must
have patience, all this was not sufficient to satisfy, and some
began to sue me. General Shirley at length relieved me from
this terrible situation by appointing commissioners to examine
the claims, and ordering payment. They amounted to near
twenty thousand pound, which to pay would have ruined me.

Before we had the news of this defeat, the two Doctors Bond
came to me with a subscription paper for raising money to
defray the expense of a grand firework, which it was intended
to exhibit at a rejoicing on receipt of the news of our taking
Fort Duquesne. I looked grave, and said it would, I thought,
be time enough to prepare for the rejoicing when we knew we
should have occasion to rejoice. They seem'd surpris'd that I
did not immediately comply with their proposal. "Why the
d—l!" says one of them, "you surely don't suppose that the fort
will not be taken?" "I don't know that it will not be taken, but
I know that the events of war are subject to great uncertainty."
I gave them the reasons of my doubting; the subscription was

dropt, and the projectors thereby missed the mortification they would have undergone if the firework had been prepared. Dr. Bond, on some other occasion afterward, said that he did not like Franklin's forebodings.

Governor Morris, who had continually worried the Assembly with message after message before the defeat of Braddock, to beat them into the making of acts to raise money for the defense of the province, without taxing, among others, the proprietary estates, and had rejected all their bills for not having such an exempting clause, now redoubled his attacks with more hope of success, the danger and necessity being greater. The Assembly, however, continu'd firm, believing they had justice on their side, and that it would be giving up an essential right if they suffered the governor to amend their money-bills. In one of the last, indeed, which was for granting fifty thousand pounds, his propos'd amendment was only of a single word. The bill express'd "that all estates, real and personal, were to be taxed, those of the proprietaries *not* excepted." His amendment was, for *not* read *only:* a small, but very material alteration. However, when the news of this disaster reached England, our friends there, whom we had taken care to furnish with all the Assembly's answers to the governor's messages, rais'd a clamor against the proprietaries for their meanness and injustice in giving their governor such instructions; some going so far as to say that, by obstructing the defense of their province, they forfeited their right to it. They were intimidated by this, and sent orders to their receiver-general to add five thousand pounds of their money to whatever sum might be given by the Assembly for such purpose.

This, being notified to the House, was accepted in lieu of their share of a general tax, and a new bill was form'd, with an exempting clause, which passed accordingly. By this act I was appointed one of the commissioners for disposing of the money, sixty thousand pounds. I had been active in modelling the bill and procuring its passage, and had, at the same time, drawn a bill for establishing and disciplining a voluntary militia, which

I carried thro' the House without much difficulty, as care was taken in it to leave the Quakers at their liberty. To promote the association necessary to form the militia, I wrote a dialogue, stating and answering all the objections I could think of to such a militia, which was printed, and had, as I thought, great effect.

While the several companies in the city and country were forming, and learning their exercise, the governor prevail'd with me to take charge of our North-western frontier, which was infested by the enemy, and provide for the defense of the inhabitants by raising troops and building a line of forts. I undertook this military business, tho' I did not conceive myself well qualified for it. He gave me a commission with full powers, and a parcel of blank commissions for officers, to be given to whom I thought fit. I had but little difficulty in raising men, having soon five hundred and sixty under my command. My son, who had in the preceding war been an officer in the army rais'd against Canada, was my aid-de-camp, and of great use to me. The Indians had burned Gnadenhut, a village settled by the Moravians, and massacred the inhabitants; but the place was thought a good situation for one of the forts.

In order to march thither, I assembled the companies at Bethlehem, the chief establishment of those people. I was surprised to find it in so good a posture of defense; the destruction of Gnadenhut had made them apprehend danger. The principal buildings were defended by a stockade; they had purchased a quantity of arms and ammunition from New York, and had even plac'd quantities of small paving stones between the windows of their high stone houses, for their women to throw down upon the heads of any Indians that should attempt to force into them. The armed brethren, too, kept watch, and reliev'd as methodically as in any garrison town. In conversation with the bishop, Spangenberg, I mention'd this my surprise; for, knowing they had obtained an act of Parliament exempting them from military duties in the colonies, I had suppos'd they were conscientiously scrupulous of bearing arms. He answer'd me that it was not one of their established principles, but that, at the time of their obtaining that act, it was thought to be a principle with many of their people. On this occasion, however, they, to their surprise, found it adopted by but a few. It seems they were either deceiv'd in themselves, or deceiv'd the Parliament; but common sense, aided by present danger, will sometimes be too strong for whimsical opinions.

It was the beginning of January when we set out upon this business of building forts. I sent one detachment toward the Minisink, with instructions to erect one for the security of that upper part of the country, and another to the lower part, with similar instructions; and I concluded to go myself with the rest of my force to Gnadenhut, where a fort was tho't more immediately necessary. The Moravians procur'd me five waggons for our tools, stores, baggage, etc.

Just before we left Bethlehem, eleven farmers, who had been driven from their plantations by the Indians, came to me requesting a supply of firearms, that they might go back and fetch off their cattle. I gave them each a gun with suitable ammunition. We had not march'd many miles before it began to rain, and it continued raining all day; there were no habitations on the road to shelter us, till we arriv'd near night at the house of a German, where, and in his barn, we were all huddled together, as wet as water could make us. It was well we were not attack'd in our march, for our arms were of the most ordinary sort, and our men could not keep their gun locks dry. The Indians are dextrous in contrivances for that purpose, which we had not. They met that day the eleven poor farmers above mentioned, and killed ten of them. The one who escap'd inform'd that his and his companions' guns would not go off, the priming being wet with the rain.

The next day being fair, we continu'd our march, and arriv'd at the desolated Gnadenhut. There was a saw-mill near, round which were left several piles of boards, with which we soon hutted ourselves; an operation the more necessary at that inclement season, as we had no tents. Our first work was to bury more effectually the dead we found there, who had been half interr'd by the country people.

The next morning our fort was plann'd and mark'd out, the circumference measuring four hundred and fifty-five feet, which would require as many palisades to be made of trees, one with another, of a foot diameter each. Our axes, of which we had seventy, were immediately set to work to cut down trees, and, our men being dextrous in the use of them, great despatch was made. Seeing the trees fall so fast, I had the curiosity to look at my watch when two men began to cut at a pine; in six minutes they had it upon the ground, and I found it of fourteen inches diameter. Each pine made three palisades of eighteen feet long, pointed at one end. While these were preparing, our other men dug a trench all round, of three feet deep, in which the palisades were to be planted; and, our waggons, the bodys being taken off, and the fore and hind wheels separated by taking out the pin which united the two parts of the perch, we had ten carriages, with two horses each, to bring the palisades from the woods to the spot. When they were set up, our carpenters built a stage of boards all round within, about six feet high, for the men to stand on when to fire thro' the loopholes. We had one swivel gun, which we mounted on one of the angles, and fir'd it as soon as fix'd, to let the Indians know, if any were within hearing, that we had such pieces; and thus our fort, if such a magnificent name may be given to so miserable a stockade, was finish'd in a week, though it rain'd so hard every other day that men could not work.

This gave me occasion to observe, that, when men are employed, they are best content'd; for on the days they worked they were good-natur'd and cheerful, and, with the consciousness of having done a good day's work, they spent the evening jollily; but on our idle days they were mutinous and quarrelsome, finding fault with their pork, the bread, etc., and in continual ill-humour, which put me in mind of a sea-captain, whose rule it was to keep his men constantly at work; and, when his mate once told him that they had done every thing, and there was nothing further to employ them about, *"Oh," says he, "make them scour the anchor."*

This kind of fort, however contemptible, is a sufficient defense against Indians, who have no cannon. Finding ourselves now posted securely, and having a place to retreat to on occasion, we ventur'd out in parties to scour the adjacent country. We met with no Indians, but we found the places on the neighboring hills where they had lain to watch our proceedings. There was an art in their contrivance of those places that seems worth mention. It being winter, a fire was necessary for them; but a common fire on the surface of the ground would by its light have discover'd their position at a distance. They had therefore dug holes in the ground about three feet diameter, and somewhat deeper; we saw where they had with their hatchets cut off the charcoal from the sides of burnt logs lying in the woods. With these coals they had made small fires in the bottom of the holes, and we observ'd among the weeds and grass the prints of their bodies, made by their laying all round, with their legs hanging down in the holes to keep their feet warm, which, with them, is an essential point. This kind of fire, so manag'd, could not discover them, either by its light, flame, sparks, or even smoke; it appear'd that their number was not great, and it seems they saw we were too many to be attacked by them with prospect of advantage.

We had for our chaplain a zealous Presbyterian minister, Mr. Beatty, who complained to me that the men did not generally attend his prayers and exhortations. When they enlisted, they were promised, besides pay and provisions, a gill of rum a day, which was punctually serv'd out to them, half in the morning, and the other half in the evening; and I observ'd they were as punctual in attending to receive it; upon which I said to Mr. Beatty, "It is, perhaps, below the dignity of your profession to act as steward of the rum, but if you were to deal it out and only just after prayers, you would have them all about you." He liked the tho't, undertook the office, and, with the help of a few hands to measure out the liquor, executed it to satisfaction, and never were prayers more generally and more punctually attended; so that I thought this method preferable to the punishment inflicted by some military laws for non-attendance on divine service.

I had hardly finish'd this business, and got my fort well stor'd with provisions, when I receiv'd a letter from the governor, acquainting me that he had call'd the Assembly, and wished my attendance there, if the posture of affairs on the frontiers was such that my remaining there was no longer necessary. My friends, too, of the Assembly, pressing me by their letters to be, if possible, at the meeting, and my three intended forts being now compleated, and the inhabitants contented to remain on their farms under that protection, I resolved to return; the more willingly, as a New England officer, Colonel Clapham, experienced in Indian war, being on a visit to our establishment, consented to accept the command. I gave him a commission, and, parading the garrison, had it read before them, and introduc'd him to them as an officer who, from his skill in military affairs, was much more fit to command them than myself; and, giving them a little exhortation, took my leave. I was escorted as far as Bethlehem, where I rested a few days to recover from the fatigue I had undergone. The first night, being in a good bed, I could hardly sleep, it was so different from my hard lodging on the floor of our hut at Gnaden wrapt only in a blanket or two.

While at Bethlehem, I inquir'd a little into the practice of the Moravians: some of them had accompanied me, and all were very kind to me. I found they work'd for a common stock, eat at common tables, and slept in common dormitories, great numbers together. In the dormitories I observed loopholes, at certain distances all along just under the ceiling, which I thought judiciously placed for change of air. I was at their church, where I was entertain'd with good musick, the organ being accompanied with violins, hautboys, flutes, clarinets, etc. I understood that their sermons were not usually preached to mixed congregations of men, women, and children, as is our common practice, but that they assembled sometimes the married men, at other times their wives, then the young men, the young women, and the little children, each division by itself. The sermon I heard was to the latter, who came in and were plac'd in rows on benches; the boys under the conduct of a young man, their tutor, and the girls conducted by a young woman. The discourse seem'd well adapted to their capacities, and was deliver'd in a pleasing, familiar manner, coaxing them, as it were, to be good. They behav'd very orderly, but looked pale and unhealthy, which made me suspect they were kept too much within doors, or not allow'd sufficient exercise.

I inquir'd concerning the Moravian marriages, whether the report was true that they were by lot. I was told that lots were us'd only in particular cases; that generally, when a young man found himself dispos'd to marry, he inform'd the elders of his class, who consulted the elder ladies that govern'd the young women. As these elders of the different sexes were well acquainted with the tempers and dispositions of their respective pupils, they could best judge what matches were suitable, and their judgments were generally acquiesc'd in; but if, for example, it should happen that two or three young women were found to be equally proper for the young man, the lot was then recurred to. I objected, if the matches are not made by the mutual choice of the parties, some of them may chance to be very unhappy. "And so they may," answer'd my informer, "if you let the parties chuse for themselves"; which, indeed, I could not deny.

Being returned to Philadelphia, I found the association went on swimmingly, the inhabitants that were not Quakers having pretty generally come into it, formed themselves into companies, and chose their captains, lieutenants, and ensigns, according to the new law. Dr. B. visited me, and gave me an account of the pains he had taken to spread a general good liking to the law, and ascribed much to those endeavors. I had had the vanity to ascribe all to my *Dialogue;* however, not knowing but that he might be in the right, I let him enjoy his opinion, which I take to be generally the best way in such cases. The

officers, meeting, chose me to be colonel of the regiment, which
I this time accepted. I forget how many companies we had, but
we paraded about twelve hundred well-looking men, with a
company of artillery, who had been furnished with six brass
field-pieces, which they had become so expert in the use of as
to fire twelve times in a minute. The first time I reviewed my
regiment they accompanied me to my house, and would salute
me with some rounds fired before my door, which shook down
and broke several glasses of my electrical apparatus. And my
new honour proved not much less brittle; for all our commissions were soon after broken by a repeal of the law in England.

During this short time of my colonelship, being about to set
out on a journey to Virginia, the officers of my regiment took it
into their heads that it would be proper for them to escort me
out of town, as far as the Lower Ferry. Just as I was getting on
horseback they came to my door, between thirty and forty,
mounted, and all in their uniforms. I had not been previously
acquainted with the project, or I should have prevented it, being naturally averse to the assuming of state on any occasion;
and I was a good deal chagrin'd at their appearance, as I could
not avoid their accompanying me. What made it worse was,
that, as soon as we began to move, they drew their swords and
rode with them naked all the way. Somebody wrote an account
of this to the proprietor, and it gave him great offense. No such
honor had been paid him when in the province, nor to any of
his governors; and he said it was only proper to princes of the
blood royal, which may be true for aught I know, who was, and
still am, ignorant of the etiquette in such cases.

This silly affair, however, greatly increased his rancour
against me, which was before not a little, on account of my conduct in the Assembly respecting the exemption of his estate
from taxation, which I had always oppos'd very warmly, and not
without severe reflections on his meanness and injustice of contending for it. He accused me to the ministry as being the great
obstacle to the king's service, preventing, by my influence in the
House, the proper form of the bills for raising money, and he

instanced this parade with my officers as a proof of my having an intention to take the government of the province out of his hands by force. He also applied to Sir Everard Fawkener, the postmaster-general, to deprive me of my office; but it had no other effect than to procure from Sir Everard a gentle admonition.

Notwithstanding the continued wrangle between the governor and the House, in which I, as a member, had so large a share, there still subsisted a civil intercourse between that gentleman and myself, and we never had any personal difference. I have sometimes since thought that his little or no resentment against me, for the answers it was known I drew up to his messages, might be the effect of professional habit, and that, being bred a lawyer, he might consider us both as merely advocates for contending clients in a suit, he for the proprietaries and I for the Assembly. He would, therefore, sometimes call in a friendly way to advise with me on difficult points, and sometimes, tho' not often, take my advice.

We acted in concert to supply Braddock's army with provisions; and, when the shocking news arrived of his defeat, the governor sent in haste for me, to consult with him on measures for preventing the desertion of the back counties. I forget now the advice I gave; but I think it was, that Dunbar should be written to, and prevail'd with, if possible, to post his troops on the frontiers for their protection, till, by re-enforcements from the colonies, he might be able to proceed on the expedition. And after my return from the frontier, he would have had me undertake the conduct of such an expedition with provincial troops, for the reduction of Fort Duquesne, Dunbar and his men being otherwise employed; and he proposed to commission me as general. I had not so good an opinion of my military abilities as he profess'd to have, and I believe his professions must have exceeded his real sentiments; but probably he might think that my popularity would facilitate the raising of the men, and my influence in Assembly, the grant of money to pay them, and that, perhaps, without taxing the proprietary estate. Finding me not so forward to engage as he had expected, the project was dropt, and he soon after left the government, being superseded by Captain Denny.

Before I proceed in relating the part I had in public affairs under this new governor's administration, it may not be amiss here to give some account of the rise and progress of my philosophical reputation.

In 1746, being at Boston, I met there with a Dr [A.] Spence[r], who was lately arrived from Scotland, and show'd me some electric experiments. They were imperfectly perform'd, as he was not very expert; but, being on a subject quite new to me, they equally surpris'd and pleased me. Soon after my return to Philadelphia, our library company receiv'd from Mr. P[eter] Collinson, Fellow of the Royal Society of London, a present of a glass tube, with some account of the use of it in making such experiments. I eagerly seized the opportunity of repeating what I had seen at Boston; and, by much practice, acquir'd great readiness in performing those, also, which we had an account of from England, adding a number of new ones. I say much practice, for my house was continually full, for some time, with people who came to see these new wonders.

To divide a little this incumbrance among our friends, I caused a number of similar tubes to be blown at our glasshouse, with which they furnish'd themselves, so that we had at length several performers. Among these, the principal was Mr. Kinnersley, an ingenious neighbor, who, being out of business, I encouraged to undertake showing the experiments for money, and drew up for him two lectures, in which the experiments were rang'd in such order, and accompanied with such explanations in such method, as that the foregoing should assist in comprehending the following. He procur'd an elegant apparatus for the purpose, in which all the little machines that I had roughly made for myself were nicely form'd by instrument-makers. His lectures were well attended, and gave great satisfaction; and after some time he went thro' the colonies, exhibiting them in every capital town, and pick'd up some money. In the West

India islands, indeed, it was with difficulty the experiments could be made, from the general moisture of the air.

Oblig'd as we were to Mr. Collinson for his present of the tube, etc., I thought it right he should be inform'd of our success in using it, and wrote him several letters containing accounts of our experiments. He got them read in the Royal Society, where they were not at first thought worth so much notice as to be printed in their Transactions. One paper, which I wrote for Mr. Kinnersley, on the sameness of lightning with electricity, I sent to Dr. Mitchel, an acquaintance of mine, and one of the members also of that society, who wrote me word that it had been read, but was laughed at by the connoisseurs. The papers, however, being shown to Dr. Fothergill, he thought them of too much value to be stifled, and advis'd the printing of them. Mr. Collinson then gave them to [Edward] *Cave* for publication in his Gentleman's Magazine; but he chose to print them separately in a pamphlet, and Dr. Fothergill wrote the preface. Cave, it seems, judged rightly for his profit, for by the additions that arrived afterward they swell'd, to a quarto volume, which has had five editions, and cost him nothing for copy-money.

It was, however, some time before those papers were much taken notice of in England. A copy of them happening to fall into the hands of the Count de Buffon, a philosopher deservedly of great reputation in France, and, indeed, all over Europe, he prevailed with M. Dalibard to translate them into French, and they were printed at Paris. The publication offended the Abbé Nollet, preceptor in Natural Philosophy to the royal family, and an able experimenter, who had form'd and publish'd a theory of electricity, which then had the general vogue. He could not at first believe that such a work came from America, and said it must have been fabricated by his enemies at Paris, to decry his system. Afterwards, having been assur'd that there really existed such a person as Franklin in Philadelphia, which he had doubted, he wrote and published a volume of Letters, chiefly address'd to me, defending his theory, and denying the verity of my experiments, and of the positions deduc'd from them.

I once purpos'd answering the abbé, and actually began the answer; but, on consideration that my writings contain'd a description of experiments which any one might repeat and verify, and if not to be verifi'd, could not be defended; or of observations offer'd as conjectures, and not delivered dogmatically, therefore not laying me under any obligation to defend them; and reflecting that a dispute between two persons, writing in different languages, might be lengthened greatly by mistranslations, and thence misconceptions of one another's meaning, much of one of the abbé's letters being founded on an error in the translation, I concluded to let my papers shift for themselves, believing it was better to spend what time I could spare from public business in making new experiments, than in disputing about those already made. I therefore never answered M. Nollet, and the event gave me no cause to repent my silence; for my friend M. le Roy, of the Royal Academy of Sciences, took up my cause and refuted him; my book was translated into the Italian, German, and Latin languages; and the doctrine it contain'd was by degrees universally adopted by the philosophers of Europe, in preference to that of the abbé; so that he lived to see himself the last of his sect, except Monsieur B———, of Paris, his *élève* and immediate disciple.

What gave my book the more sudden and general celebrity, was the success of one of its proposed experiments, made by Messrs. Dalibard and De Lor at Marly, for drawing lightning from the clouds. This engag'd the public attention every where. M. de Lor, who had an apparatus for experimental philosophy, and lectur'd in that branch of science, undertook to repeat what he called the *Philadelphia Experiments;* and, after they were performed before the king and court, all the curious of Paris flocked to see them. I will not swell this narrative with an account of that capital experiment, nor of the infinite pleasure I receiv'd in the success of a similar one I made soon after with a kite at Philadelphia, as both are to be found in the histories of electricity.

Dr. Wright, an English physician, when at Paris, wrote to a friend, who was of the Royal Society, an account of the high esteem my experiments were in among the learned abroad, and of their wonder that my writings had been so little noticed in England. The society, on this, resum'd the consideration of the letters that had been read to them; and the celebrated Dr. Watson drew up a summary account of them, and of all I had afterwards sent to England on the subject, which he accompanied with some praise of the writer. This summary was then printed in their Transactions; and some members of the society in London, particularly the very ingenious Mr. Canton, having verified the experiment of procuring lightning from the clouds by a pointed rod, and acquainting them with the success, they soon made me more than amends for the slight with which they had before treated me. Without my having made any application for that honor, they chose me a member, and voted that I should be excus'd the customary payments, which would have amounted to twenty-five guineas; and ever since have given me their Transactions gratis. They also presented me with the gold medal of Sir Godfrey Copley for the year 1753, the delivery of which was accompanied by a very handsome speech of the president, Lord Macclesfield, wherein I was highly honoured.

Our new governor, Captain Denny, brought over for me the before-mentioned medal from the Royal Society, which he presented to me at an entertainment given him by the city. He accompanied it with very polite expressions of his esteem for me, having, as he said, been long acquainted with my character. After dinner, when the company, as was customary at that time, were engag'd in drinking, he took me aside into another room, and acquainted me that he had been advis'd by his friends in England to cultivate a friendship with me, as one who was capable of giving him the best advice, and of contributing most effectually to the making his administration easy; that he therefore desired of all things to have a good understanding with me,

and he begg'd me to be assur'd of his readiness on all occasions
to render me every service that might be in his power. He said
much to me, also, of the proprietor's good disposition towards
the province, and of the advantage it might be to us all, and to
me in particular, if the opposition that had been so long continu'd to his measures was dropt, and harmony restored between
him and the people; in effecting which, it was thought no one
could be more serviceable than myself; and I might depend on
adequate acknowledgments and recompenses, etc., etc. The
drinkers, finding we did not return immediately to the table,
sent us a decanter of Madeira, which the governor made liberal
use of, and in proportion became more profuse of his solicitations and promises.

My answers were to this purpose: that my circumstances,
thanks to God, were such as to make proprietary favours unnecessary to me; and that, being a member of the Assembly, I
could not possibly accept of any; that, however, I had no personal enmity to the proprietary, and that, whenever the public
measures he propos'd should appear to be for the good of the
people, no one should espouse and forward them more zealously
than myself; my past opposition having been founded on this,
that the measures which had been urged were evidently intended to serve the proprietary interest, with great prejudice to
that of the people; that I was much obliged to him (the governor) for his professions of regard to me, and that he might
rely on every thing in my power to make his administration as
easy as possible, hoping at the same time that he had not brought
with him the same unfortunate instruction his predecessor had
been hamper'd with.

On this he did not then explain himself; but when he afterwards came to do business with the Assembly, they appear'd
again, the disputes were renewed, and I was as active as ever in
the opposition, being the penman, first, of the request to have
a communication of the instructions, and then of the remarks
upon them, which may be found in the votes of the time, and
in the Historical Review I afterward publish'd. But between

Benjamin Franklin, from a portrait by B. Wilson painted in 1759

us personally no enmity arose; we were often together; he was a man of letters, had seen much of the world, and was very entertaining and pleasing in conversation. He gave me the first information that my old friend Jas. Ralph was still alive; that he was esteem'd one of the best political writers in England; had been employ'd in the dispute between Prince Frederic and the king, and had obtain'd a pension of three hundred a year; that his reputation was indeed small as a poet, Pope having damned his poetry in the Dunciad; but his prose was thought as good as any man's.

The Assembly finally finding the proprietary obstinately persisted in manacling their deputies with instructions inconsistent not only with the privileges of the people, but with the service of the crown, resolv'd to petition the king against them, and appointed me their agent to go over to England, to present and support the petition. The House had sent up a bill to the governor, granting a sum of sixty thousand pounds for the king's use (ten thousand pounds of which was subjected to the orders of the then general, Lord Loudoun), which the governor absolutely refus'd to pass, in compliance with his instructions.

I had agreed with Captain Morris, of the paquet at New York, for my passage, and my stores were put on board, when Lord Loudoun arriv'd at Philadelphia, expressily, as he told me, to endeavor an accommodation between the governor and Assembly, that his majesty's service might not be obstructed by their dissensions. Accordingly, he desir'd the governor and myself to meet him, that he might hear what was to be said on both sides, we met and discuss'd the business. In behalf of the Assembly, I urg'd all the various arguments that may be found in the public papers of that time, which were of my writing, and are printed with the minutes of the Assembly; and the governor pleaded his instructions; the bond he had given to observe them, and his ruin if he disobey'd, yet seemed not unwilling to hazard himself if Lord Loudoun would advise it. This his lordship did not chuse to do, though I once thought I had nearly prevail'd with him to do it; but finally he rather chose to urge the compliance of the Assembly; and he entreated me to use my endeavours with them for that purpose, declaring that he would spare none of the king's troops for the defense of our frontiers, and that, if we did not continue to provide for that defense ourselves, they must remain expos'd to the enemy.

I acquainted the House with what had pass'd, and, presenting them with a set of resolutions I had drawn up, declaring our rights, and that we did not relinquish our claim to those rights, but only suspended the exercise of them on this occasion thro' *force,* against which we protested, they at length agreed to drop that bill, and frame another conformable to the proprietary instructions. This of course the governor pass'd, and I was then at liberty to proceed on my voyage. But, in the meantime, the paquet had sailed with my sea-stores, which was some loss to me, and my only recompense was his lordship's thanks for my service, all the credit of obtaining the accommodation falling to his share.

He set out for New York before me; and, as the time for dispatching the paquet-boats was at his disposition, and there were two then remaining there, one of which, he said, was to sail very soon, I requested to know the precise time, that I might not miss her by any delay of mine. His answer was, "I have given out that she is to sail on Saturday next; but I may let you know, *entre nous,* that if you are there by Monday morning, you will be in time, but do not delay longer." By some accidental hinderance at a ferry, it was Monday noon before I arrived, and I was much afraid she might have sailed, as the wind was fair; but I was soon made easy by the information that she was still in the harbor, and would not move till the next day. One would imagine that I was now on the very point of departing for Europe. I thought so; but I was not then so well acquainted with his lordship's character, of which *indecision* was one of the strongest features. I shall give some instances. It was about the beginning of April that I came to New York, and I think it was near the end of June before we sail'd. There were then two of the paquet-boats, which had been long in port, but were de-

tained for the general's letters, which were always to be ready
to-morrow. Another paquet arriv'd; she too was detain'd; and,
before we sail'd, a fourth was expected. Ours was the first to be
dispatch'd, as having been there longest. Passengers were engag'd in all, and some extremely impatient to be gone, and the
merchants uneasy about their letters, and the orders they had
given for insurance (it being war time) for fall goods; but their
anxiety avail'd nothing; his lordship's letters were not ready;
and yet whoever waited on him found him always at his desk,
pen in hand, and concluded he must needs write abundantly.

Going myself one morning to pay my respects, I found in his
antechamber one Innis, a messenger of Philadelphia, who had
come from thence express with a paquet from Governor Denny
for the General. He delivered to me some letters from my
friends there, which occasion'd my inquiring when he was to
return, and where he lodg'd, that I might send some letters by
him. He told me he was order'd to call to-morrow at nine for
the general's answer to the governor, and should set off immediately. I put my letters into his hands the same day. A fortnight after I met him again in the same place. "So, you are soon
return'd, Innis?" "*Return'd!* no, I am not *gone* yet." "How
so?" "I have called here by order every morning these two weeks
past for his lordship's letter, and it is not yet ready." "Is it possible, when he is so great a writer? for I see him constantly at
his escritoire." "Yes," says Innis, "but he is like St. George on
the signs, *always on horseback, and never rides on.*" This observation of the messenger was, it seems, well founded; for,
when in England, I understood that Mr. Pitt gave it as one
reason for removing this general, and sending Generals Amherst
and Wolfe, *that the minister never heard from him, and could
not know what he was doing.*

This daily expectation of sailing, and all the three paquets
going down to Sand Hook, to join the fleet there, the passengers
thought it best to be on board, lest by a sudden order the ships
should sail, and they be left behind. There, if I remember right,
we were about six weeks, consuming our sea-stores, and oblig'd

to procure more. At length the fleet sail'd. the General and all his army on board, bound to Louisburg, with intent to besiege and take that fortress; all the paquet-boats in company ordered to attend the General's ship, ready to receive his dispatches when they should be ready. We were out five days before we got a letter with leave to part, and then our ship quitted the fleet and steered for England. The other two paquets he still detained, carried them with him to Halifax, where he stayed some time to exercise the men in sham attacks upon sham forts, then alter'd his mind as to besieging Louisburg, and return'd to New York, with all his troops, together with the two paquets above mentioned, and all their passengers! During his absence the French and savages had taken Fort George, on the frontier of that province, and the savages had massacred many of the garrison after capitulation.

I saw afterwards in London Captain Bonnell, who commanded one of those paquets. He told me that, when he had been detain'd a month, he acquainted his lordship that his ship was grown foul, to a degree that must necessarily hinder her fast sailing, a point of consequence for a paquet-boat, and requested an allowance of time to heave her down and clean her bottom. He was asked how long time that would require. He answer'd, three days. The general replied, "If you can do it in one day, I give leave; otherwise not; for you must certainly sail the day after to-morrow." So he never obtain'd leave, though detained afterwards from day to day during full three months.

I saw also in London one of Bonnell's passengers, who was so enrag'd against his lordship for deceiving and detaining him so long at New York, and then carrying him to Halifax and back again, that he swore he would sue him for damages. Whether he did or not, I never heard; but, as he represented the injury to his affairs, it was very considerable.

On the whole, I wonder'd much how such a man came to be intrusted with so important a business as the conduct of a great army; but, having since seen more of the great world, and the means of obtaining, and motives for giving places, my wonder is diminished. General Shirley, on whom the command of the army devolved upon the death of Braddock, would, in my opinion, if continued in place, have made a much better campaign than that of Loudoun in 1757, which was frivolous, expensive, and disgraceful to our nation beyond conception; for, tho' Shirley was not a bred soldier, he was sensible and sagacious in himself, and attentive to good advice from others, capable of forming judicious plans, and quick and active in carrying them into execution. Loudoun, instead of defending the colonies with his great army, left them totally expos'd while he paraded idly at Halifax, by which means Fort George was lost, besides, he derang'd all our mercantile operations, and distress'd our trade, by a long embargo on the exportation of provisions, on pretence of keeping supplies from being obtain'd by the enemy, but in reality for beating down their price in favor of the contractors, in whose profits, it was said, perhaps from suspicion only, he had a share. And, when at length the embargo was taken off, by neglecting to send notice of it to Charlestown, the Carolina fleet was detain'd near three months longer, whereby their bottoms were so much damaged by the worm that a great part of them foundered in their passage home.

Shirley was, I believe, sincerely glad of being relieved from so burdensome a charge as the conduct of an army must be to a man unacquainted with military business. I was at the entertainment given by the city of New York to Lord Loudoun, on his taking upon him the command. Shirley, tho' thereby superseded, was present also. There was a great company of officers, citizens, and strangers, and, some chairs having been borrowed in the neighborhood, there was one among them very low, which fell to the lot of Mr. Shirley. Perceiving it as I sat by him, I said, "They have given you, sir, too low a seat." "No matter," says he, "Mr. Franklin, I find a *low seat* the easiest."

While I was, as afore mention'd, detain'd at New York, I receiv'd all the accounts of the provisions, etc., that I had furnish'd to Braddock, some of which accounts could not sooner be obtain'd from the different persons I had employ'd to assist in the business. I presented them to Lord Loudoun, desiring to be paid the balance. He caus'd them to be regularly examined by the proper officer, who, after comparing every article with its voucher, certified them to be right; and the balance due for which his lordship promis'd to give me an order on the paymaster. This was, however, put off from time to time; and, tho' I call'd often for it by appointment, I did not get it. At length, just before my departure, he told me he had, on better consideration, concluded not to mix his accounts with those of his predecessors. "And you," says he, "when in England, have only to exhibit your accounts at the treasury, and you will be paid immediately."

I mention'd, but without effect, the great and unexpected expense I had been put to by being detain'd so long at New York, as a reason for my desiring to be presently paid; and on my observing that it was not right I should be put to any further trouble or delay in obtaining the money I had advanc'd, as I charged no commission for my service, "O, Sir," says he, "you must not think of persuading us that you are no gainer; we understand better those affairs, and know that every one concerned in supplying the army finds means, in the doing it, to fill his own pockets." I assur'd him that was not my case, and that I had not pocketed a farthing; but he appear'd clearly not to believe me; and, indeed, I have since learnt that immense fortunes are often made in such employments. As to my balance, I am not paid it to this day, of which more hereafter.

Our captain of the paquet had boasted much, before we sailed, of the swiftness of his ship; unfortunately, when we came to sea, she proved the dullest of ninety-six sail, to his no small mortification. After many conjectures respecting the cause, when we were near another ship almost as dull as ours, which, however, gain'd upon us, the captain ordered all hands to come aft, and stand as near the ensign staff as possible. We were, passengers included, about forty persons. While we stood there, the ship mended her pace, and soon left her neighbour far behind, which prov'd clearly what our captain suspected, that she was loaded too much by the head. The casks of water, it seems, had been all plac'd forward; these he therefore order'd to be mov'd further aft, on which the ship recover'd her character, and proved the sailer in the fleet.

The captain said she had once gone at the rate of thirteen knots, which is accounted thirteen miles per hour. We had on board, as a passenger, Captain Kennedy, of the Navy, who contended that it was impossible, and that no ship ever sailed so fast, and that there must have been some error in the division of the log-line, or some mistake in heaving the log. A wager ensu'd between the two captains, to be decided when there should be sufficient wind. Kennedy thereupon examin'd rigorously the log-line, and, being satisfi'd with that, he determin'd to throw the log himself. Accordingly some days after, when the wind blew very fair and fresh, and the captain of the paquet, Lutwidge, said he believ'd she then went at the rate of thirteen knots, Kennedy made the experiment, and own'd his wager lost.

The above fact I give for the sake of the following observation. It has been remark'd, as an imperfection in the art of ship-building, that it can never be known, till she is tried, whether a new ship will or will not be a good sailer; for that the model of a good-sailing ship has been exactly follow'd in a new one, which has prov'd, on the contrary, remarkably dull. I apprehend that this may partly be occasion'd by the different opinions of seamen respecting the modes of lading, rigging, and sailing of a ship; each has his system; and the same vessel, laden by the judgment and orders of one captain, shall sail better or worse than when by the orders of another. Besides, it scarce ever happens that a ship is form'd, fitted for the sea, and sail'd by the same person. One man builds the hull, another rigs her, a third lades and sails her. No one of these has the advantage of knowing all the ideas and experience of the others, and, therefore, can not draw just conclusions from a combination of the whole.

Even in the simple operation of sailing when at sea, I have often observ'd different judgments in the officers who commanded the successive watches, the wind being the same. One would have the sails trimm'd sharper or flatter than another, so that they seem'd to have no certain rule to govern by. Yet I think a set of experiments might be instituted, first, to determine the most proper form of the hull for swift sailing; next, the best dimensions and properest place for the masts; then the form and quantity of sails, and their position, as the wind may be; and, lastly, the disposition of the lading. This is an age of experiments, and I think a set accurately made and combin'd would be of great use. I am persuaded, therefore, that ere long some ingenious philosopher will undertake it, to whom I wish success.

We were several times chas'd in our passage, but outsail'd every thing, and in thirty days had soundings. We had a good observation, and the captain judg'd himself so near our port, Falmouth, that, if we made a good run in the night, we might be off the mouth of that harbor in the morning, and by running in the night might escape the notice of the enemy's privateers, who often crus'd near the entrance of the channel. Accordingly, all the sail was set that we could possibly make, and the wind being very fresh and fair, we went right before it, and made great way. The captain, after his observation, shap'd his course, as he thought, so as to pass wide of the Scilly Isles; but it seems there is sometimes a strong indraught setting up St. George's Channel, which deceives seamen and caused the loss of Sir Cloudesley Shovel's squadron. This indraught was probably the cause of what happened to us.

We had a watchman plac'd in the bow, to whom they often called, *"Look well out before there,"* and he as often answered, *"Ay, ay";* but perhaps had his eyes shut, and was half asleep at the time, they sometimes answering, as it said, mechanically; for he did not see a light just before us, which had been hid by the studding-sails from the man at helm, and from the rest of the watch, but by an accidental yaw of the ship was discovered, and occasion'd a great alarm, we being very near it, the light appearing to me as big as a cart-wheel. It was midnight, and our captain fast asleep; but Captain Kennedy, jumping upon deck,

Portrait of Franklin painted in London, 1767, by David Martin

and seeing the danger, ordered the ship to wear round, all sails standing; an operation dangerous to the masts, but it carried us clear, and we escaped shipwreck, for we were running right upon the rocks on which the light-house was erected. This deliverance impressed me strongly with the utility of light-houses, and made me resolve to encourage the building more of them in America, if I should live to return there.

In the morning it was found by the soundings, etc., that we were near our port, but a thick fog hid the land from our sight. About nine o'clock the fog began to rise, and seem'd to be lifted up from the water like the curtain at a play-house, discovering underneath, the town of Falmouth, the vessels in its harbor, and the fields that surrounded it. This was a most pleasing spectacle to those who had been so long without any other prospects than the uniform view of a vacant ocean, and it gave us the more pleasure as we were now free from the anxieties which the state of war occasion'd.

I set out immediately, with my son, for London, and we only stopt a little by the way to view Stonehenge on Salisbury Plain, and Lord Pembroke's house and gardens, with his very curious antiquities at Wilton. We arrived in London the 27th of July, 1757.

As soon as I was settled in a lodging Mr. Charles had provided for me, I went to visit Dr. Fothergill, to whom I was strongly recommended, and whose counsel respecting my proceedings I was advis'd to obtain. He was against an immediate complaint to government, and thought the proprietaries should first be personally appli'd to, who might possibly be induc'd by the interposition and persuasion of some private friends, to accommodate matters amicably. I then waited on my old friend and correspondent, Mr. Peter Collinson, who told me that John Hanbury, the great Virginia merchant, had requested to be informed when I should arrive, that he might carry me to Lord Granville's, who was then President of the Council, and wished to see me as soon as possible. I agreed to go with him the next morning. Accordingly Mr. Hanbury called for me and took me in his carriage to that nobleman's, who receiv'd me with great civility; and after some questions respecting the present state of affairs in America and discourse thereupon, he said to me: "You Americans have wrong ideas of the nature of your constitution; you contend that the king's instructions to his governors are not laws, and think yourselves at liberty to regard or disregard them at your own discretion. But those instructions are not like the pocket instructions given to a minister going abroad, for regulating his conduct in some trifling point of ceremony. They are first drawn up by judges learned in the laws; they are then considered, debated, and perhaps amended in Council, after which they are signed by the king. They are then, so far as they relate to you, the *law of the land,* for the king is the LEGISLATOR OF THE COLONIES." I told his lordship this was new doctrine to me. I had always understood from our charters that our laws were to be made by our Assemblies, to be presented indeed to the king for his royal assent, but that being once given the king could not repeal or alter them. And as the Assemblies could not make permanent laws without his assent, so neither could he make a law for them without theirs. He assur'd me I was totally mistaken. I did not think so, however, and his lordship's conversation having a little alarm'd me as to what might be the sentiments of the court concerning us, I wrote it down as soon as I return'd to my lodgings. I recollected that about 20 years before, a clause in a bill brought into Parliament by the ministry had propos'd to make the king's instructions laws in the colonies, but the clause was thrown out by the Commons, for which we adored them as our friends and friends of liberty, till by their conduct towards us in 1765 it seem'd that they had refus'd that point of sovereignty to the king only that they might reserve it for themselves.

After some days, Dr. Fothergill having spoken to the proprietaries, they agreed to a meeting with me at Mr. T. Penn's house in Spring Garden. The conversation at first consisted of mutual declarations of disposition to reasonable accommodations, but I suppose each party had its own ideas of what should be meant by *reasonable*. We then went into consideration of our several points of complaint, which I enumerated. The proprietaries justify'd their conduct as well as they could, and I the Assembly's. We now appeared very wide, and so far from each other in our opinions as to discourage all hope of agreement. However, it was concluded that I should give them the heads of our complaints in writing, and they promis'd then to consider them. I did so soon after, but they put the paper into the hands of their solicitor, Ferdinand John Paris, who managed for them all their law business in their great suit with the neighbouring proprietary of Maryland, Lord Baltimore, which had subsisted 70 years, and wrote for them all their papers and messages in their dispute with the Assembly. He was a proud, angry man, and as I had occasionally in the answers of the Assembly treated his papers with some severity, they being really weak in point of argument and haughty in expression, he had conceived a mortal enmity to me, which discovering itself whenever we met, I declin'd the proprietary's proposal that he and I should discuss the heads of complaint between our two selves, and refus'd treating with any one but them. They then by his advice put the paper into the hands of the Attorney and Solicitor-General for their opinion and counsel upon it, where it lay unanswered a year wanting eight days, during which time I made frequent demands of an answer from the proprietaries, but without obtaining any other than that they had not yet received the opinion of the Attorney and Solicitor-General. What it was when they did receive it I never learnt, for they did not communicate it to me, but sent a long message to the Assembly drawn and signed by Paris, reciting my paper, complaining of its want of formality, as a rudeness on my part, and giving a flimsy justification of their conduct, adding that they should be willing to accommodate matters if the Assembly would send out *some person of candour* to treat with them for that purpose, intimating thereby that I was not such.

The want of formality or rudeness was, probably, my not having address'd the paper to them with their assum'd titles of

True and Absolute Proprietaries of the Province of Pennsylvania, which I omitted as not thinking it necessary in a paper, the intention of which was only to reduce to a certainty by writing, what in conversation I had delivered *viva voce*.

But during this delay, the Assembly having prevailed with Gov'r Denny to pass an act taxing the proprietary estate in common with the estates of the people, which was the grand point in dispute, they omitted answering the message.

When this act however came over, the proprietaries, counselled by Paris, determined to oppose its receiving the royal assent. Accordingly they petition'd the king in Council, and a hearing was appointed in which two lawyers were employ'd by them against the act, and two by me in support of it. They alleg'd that the act was intended to load the proprietary estate in order to spare those of the people, and that if it were suffer'd to continue in force, and the proprietaries who were in odium with the people, left to their mercy in proportioning the taxes, they would inevitably be ruined. We reply'd that the act had no such intention, and would have no such effect. That the assessors were honest and discreet men under an oath to assess fairly and equitably, and that any advantage each of them might expect in lessening his own tax by augmenting that of the proprietaries was too trifling to induce them to perjure themselves. This is the purport of what I remember as urged by both sides, except that we insisted strongly on the mischievous consequences that must attend a repeal, for that the money, £100,-000, being printed and given to the king's use, expended in his service, and now spread among the people, the repeal would strike it dead in their hands to the ruin of many, and the total discouragement of future grants, and the selfishness of the proprietors in soliciting such a general catastrophe, merely from a groundless fear of their estate being taxed too highly, was insisted on in the strongest terms. On this, Lord Mansfield, one of the counsel rose, and beckoning me took me into the clerk's chamber, while the lawyers were pleading, and asked me if I was really of opinion that no injury would be done the proprietary estate in the execution of the act. I said certainly. "Then," says he, "you can have little objection to enter into an engagement to assure that point." I answer'd, "None at all." He then call'd in Paris, and after some discourse, his lordship's proposition was accepted on both sides; a paper to the purpose was drawn up by the Clerk of the Council, which I sign'd with Mr. Charles, who was also an Agent of the Province for their ordinary affairs, when Lord Mansfield returned to the Council Chamber, where finally the law was allowed to pass. Some changes were however recommended and we also engaged they should be made by a subsequent law, but the Assembly did not think them necessary; for one year's tax having been levied by the act before the order of Council arrived, they appointed a committee to examine the proceedings of the assessors, and on this committee they put several particular friends of the proprietaries. After a full enquiry, they unanimously sign'd a report that they found the tax had been assess'd with perfect equity.

The Assembly looked into my entering into the first part of the engagement, as an essential service to the Province, since it secured the credit of the paper money then spread over all the country. They gave me their thanks in form when I return'd. But the proprietaries were enraged at Governor Denny for having pass'd the act, and turn'd him out with threats of suing him for breach of instructions which he had given bond to observe. He, however, having done it at the instance of the General, and for His Majesty's service, and having some powerful interest at court, despis'd the threats and they were never put in execution. . . . [Unfinished].

II. COMMENTARY ON

Poor Richard's Almanac

IN COLONIAL America there were but two pieces of printed matter in most homes—a Bible and an almanac. The latter, a paper bound, pocket-sized booklet, was a combination calendar, miniature encyclopedia, moral counselor and the source of tidbits of all kinds of miscellaneous information. It noted the holidays, the tides, the quarters of the moon, the dates of the fairs and the court sessions, and forecast the weather. In addition, Franklin's contained jokes, poems and the famous maxims.

These "Sayings of Poor Richard" probably constitute Franklin's best known literary legacy, although most of them did not originate with Franklin. In fact, there was nothing very original about the almanac. The name was based on that of one that his brother was publishing, *Poor Robin's Almanac*. The Richard Saunders who supposedly edited it was actually an English astrologer who had nothing to do with the almanac except unwittingly to lend his name.

In addition to his many other accomplishments, Franklin was a canny publicist, and America's first propagandist. To attract attention to his almanac he perpetrated one of the literary hoaxes in which he took much delight. For the first issue he wrote the preface which follows in this volume, justifying his publication by predicting the death of a rival Philadelphia almanac publisher, his "good friend and fellow student" Titan Leeds. The latter, no good friend of Franklin's, wrathfully replied that he was very much alive and intended to remain so. To keep the hoax—and the publicity—going, Franklin wrote the 1734 preface in which he assumed that the continued publication of the Almanac of the "late" Leeds must be by an impostor. His "good friend" had been too much of a gentleman to call him "a false predicter, an ignorant, a conceited scribbler, a fool, and a liar." Pennsylvanians chuckled at the feud—and bought ten thousand almanacs.

In his *Autobiography* Franklin told how he "filled all the little spaces that occurred between the remarkable days of the calendar with proverbial sentences." These became the famed *Sayings of Poor Richard*—some of the world's best known maxims. Franklin said that he found these in "the wisdom of many ages and many nations." Because age-old wisdom spoke with many tongues, Franklin taught himself to read French, Spanish, Italian, German and Latin during the early days of Poor Richard.

But Franklin did not merely copy the old proverbs. He changed them to conform to his smooth, clear, concise and vigorous style. In their original forms most would have been long since forgotten. Franklin revised them to become part of the common speech of many lands. Hardly a man is now alive who does not know that "God helps them that help themselves." It is doubtful that the proverb would have lived in the form in which Franklin found it; "Help thyself, and God will help thee."

Franklin said that writing should be "smooth, clear and short," and he whittled and pummeled the proverbs to this end. "The greatest talkers are the least doers" became, "Great talkers, little doers." "God restoreth health and the physician hath the thanks" was changed to "God heals and the doctor takes the fee." "Fresh fish and new-come guests smell, but that they are three days old" was shortened and clarified to "Fish and visitors smell in three days." Sometimes a slight change pointed up a proverb to make it more meaningful: "Many strokes fell great oaks," to "Little strokes fell great oaks." In other cases Franklin added a thought to give the original a whole new meaning, as in the proverb "The King's cheese goes half away in parings," which he changed to, "The King's cheese is half wasted in parings; but no matter, 'tis made from the people's milk."

In his *Autobiography* Franklin told how he assembled many of these proverbs into a sermon on industry and frugality in the guise of a "harangue of a wise old man to the people attending an auction." This preface to the 1757 Almanac, which follows in these pages, was reprinted under the title *The Way to Wealth*, and became an immediate best seller on both sides of the Atlantic. Particularly, the thrifty French took this sermon to heart and as a result the creator of "Bonhomme Richard" became a hero to the French middle class—a role which strengthened his position immeasurably when, twenty years later, he sought the support of their government for the struggling colonies.

Because *The Way to Wealth* was by far the most widely circulated piece of Franklin's writing it was responsible for a mistaken image of him that was handed down to posterity. It is devoted solely to a glorification of industry and frugality; and most people concluded that the writer was a priggish, parsimonious money grubber. They failed to realize that Franklin was addressing this to young people, most of them as poor as he had been, whose sole hope of moving up from a life of poverty and toil to relative security and leisure was through early hard work and thrift.

The concept of Franklin the miser based on *The Way to Wealth* is entirely false. He worked hard as a printer for twenty years and saved his money for one reason—so that he could retire to live as he pleased. For money, as such, he cared little. He could have become wealthy by patenting his inventions, which he refused to do because he believed that any discovery which benefited his fellow men should be made available for the public good. Another man gained a fortune by building Franklin's stove—with plans supplied gratis by Franklin. He continued to work hard after he retired from business because the mentality which Carl Van Doren described as "the most eminent mind that has ever existed in America," could not be idle.

As to frugality, Franklin was thrifty in his early years. He hated debt—said that the debtor was the slave to the creditor. But during the last half of his life he did not practice what he preached. He disliked ostentation in clothing and detested jewelry, but the cases of gifts that he sent from abroad to Deborah and his darling Sally belied his preachments against all luxuries. The Franklin of London and Paris lived rather well. Franklin's attitude toward money was expressed in a letter to his mother in which he wrote, "So the years roll by and the last will come, when I would rather have it said 'He lived usefully' than 'He died rich.'"

In these days of "buy now, pay later" many of Franklin's precepts may seem outmoded. But there is much truth in the comment of a more recent sage who said: "For the past two centuries, Franklin's homely aphorisms and observations have influenced more Americans than the learned wisdom of all the formal philosophers put together."

PREFACE, 1733

Courteous Reader,

I might in this place attempt to gain thy favor by declaring that I write almanacs with no other view than that of the public good; but in this I should not be sincere; and men are nowadays too wise to be deceived by pretences how specious soever. The plain truth of the matter is, I am excessive poor, and my wife, good woman, is, I tell her, excessive proud; she cannot bear, she says, to sit spinning in her shift of tow, while I do nothing but gaze at the stars; and has threatened more than once to burn all my books and rattling-traps (as she calls my instruments) if I do not make some profitable use of them for the good of my family. The printer has offered me some considerable share of the profits, and I have thus begun to comply with my dame's desire.

Indeed, this motive would have had force enough to have made me publish an almanac many years since, had it not been overpowered by my regard for my good friend and fellow student Mr. Titan Leeds, whose interest I was extremely unwilling to hurt: But this obstacle (I am far from speaking it with pleasure) is soon to be removed, since inexorable death, who was never known to respect merit, has already prepared the mortal dart, the fatal sister has already extended her destroying shears, and that ingenious man must soon be taken from us. He dies, by my calculation made at his request, on Oct. 17. 1733. 3 h. 29 m. P.M. at the very instant of the ☌ of ☉ and ☿ : by his own calculation he will survive till the 26th of the same month. This small difference between us we have disputed whenever we have met these 9 years past; but at length he is inclinable to agree with my judgment. Which of us is most exact, a little time will now deter-

187

mine. As therefore these provinces may not longer expect to see any of his performances after this year, I think myself free to take up the task, and request a share of the public encouragement, which I am the more apt to hope for on this account, that the buyer of my almanac may consider himself not only as purchasing an useful utensil, but as performing an act of charity to his poor friend and servant,

R. Saunders

PREFACE, 1734

Courteous Readers,

Your kind and charitable assistance last year, in purchasing so large an impression of my almanacs, has made my circumstances much more easy in the world and requires my grateful acknowledgment. My wife has been enabled to get a pot of her own, and is no longer obliged to borrow one from a neighbor; nor have we ever since been without something of our own to put in it. She has also got a pair of shoes, two new shifts, and a new warm petticoat; and for my part, I have bought a secondhand coat, so good that I am now not ashamed to go to town or be seen there. These things have rendered her temper so much more pacific than it used to be that I may say I have slept more and more quietly within this last year than in the three foregoing years put together. Accept my hearty thanks therefor, and my sincere wishes for your health and prosperity.

In the preface to my last almanac, I foretold the death of my dear old friend and fellow student, the learned and ingenious Mr. Titan Leeds, which was to be on the 17th of October, 1733, 3 h. 29 m. P.M. at the very instant of the ☌ of ☉ and ☿. By his own calculation he was to survive till the 26th of the same month, and expire in the time of the eclipse, near 11 o'clock

A.M. At which of these times he died, or whether he be really yet dead, I cannot at this present writing positively assure my readers; forasmuch as a disorder in my own family demanded my presence, and would not permit me, as I had intended, to be with him in his last moments, to receive his last embrace, to close his eyes, and do the duty of a friend in performing the last offices to the departed. Therefore it is that I cannot positively affirm whether he be dead or not; for the stars only show to the skillful what will happen in the natural and universal chain of causes and effects; but it is well known that the events which would otherwise certainly happen at certain times in the course of nature are sometimes set aside or postponed for wise and good reasons by the immediate particular dispositions of providence; which particular dispositions the stars can by no means discover or foreshow. There is however (and I cannot speak it without sorrow), there is the strongest probability that my dear friend is no more; for there appears in his name, as I am assured, an almanac for the year 1734, in which I am treated in a very gross and unhandsome manner; in which I am called *a false predicter, an ignorant, a conceited scribler, a fool, and a liar.* Mr. Leeds was too well bred to use any man so indecently and so scurrilously, and moreover his esteem and affection for me was extraordinary; so that it is to be feared that pamphlet may be only a contrivance of somebody or other who hopes perhaps to sell two or three year's almanacs still, by the sole force and virtue of Mr. Leeds's name; but certainly, to put words into the mouth of a gentleman and a man of letters, against his friend, which the meanest and most scandalous of the people might be ashamed to utter even in a drunken quarrel, is an unpardonable injury to his memory and an imposition upon the public.

Mr. Leeds was not only profoundly skillful in the useful science he professed, but he was a man of exemplary sobriety, a most sincere friend, and exact performer of his word. These valuable qualifications, with many others, so much endeared him to me that although it should be so that, contrary to all probability, contrary to my prediction and his own, he might possibly be yet alive, yet my loss of honor as a prognosticator cannot afford me so much mortification as his life, health and safety would give me joy and satisfaction.

      I am, courteous and kind reader,

Your poor friend and servant,

R. Saunders

Octob. 30, 1733

ADVICE TO YOUTH

January

First, let the fear of Him who formed thy frame,
Whose hand sustained thee e'er thou hadst a name,
Who brought thee into birth, with power of thought
Receptive of immortal good, be wrought
Deep in thy soul. His, not thy own, thou art;
To him resign the empire of thy heart.
His will, thy law; His service, thy employ;
His frown, thy dread, his smile be all thy joy.

February

Waked by the call of morn, on early knee,
Ere the world thrust between thy God and thee,
Let thy pure orisons, ascending, gain
His ear, and succor of his grace obtain,
In wants, in toils, in perils of the day,
And strong temptations that beset thy way.
Thy best resolves then in his strength renew
To walk in virtue's paths, and vice eschew.

March

To Him intrust thy slumbers, and prepare
The fragrant incense of thy evening prayer.
But first tread back the day, with search severe,
And *conscience*, chiding or applauding, hear.
Review each step; *Where, acting, did I err?*
Omitting, where? Guilt either way infer.
Labor this point, and while thy frailties last,
Still let each following day correct the last.

April

Life is a shelvy sea, the passage fear,
And not without a skilful pilot steer.
Distrust thy youth, experienced age implore,
And borrow all the wisdom of threescore.
But chief a father's, mother's voice revere;
'T is love that chides, 't is love that counsels here.
Thrice happy is the youth whose pliant mind
To all a parent's culture is resigned.

May

O, well begun, virtue's great work pursue,
Passions at first we may with ease subdue;
But if neglected, unrestrained too long.
Prevailing in their growth, by habit strong,
They've wrapped the mind, have fixed the stubborn bent,
And force of custom to wild nature lent;
Who then would set the crooked tree aright,
As soon may wash the tawny Indian white.

June

Industry's bounteous hand may *plenty* bring,
But wanting *frugal care,* 't will soon take wing.

Small thy supplies, and scanty in their source,
'Twixt *av'rice* and profusion steer thy course.
Av'rice is deaf to want's heart-bursting groan,
Profusion makes the beggar's rags thy own:
Close fraud and wrong from griping av'rice grow,
From rash *profusion* desperate acts and woe.

July

Honor the softer sex; with courteous style,
And gentleness of manners, win their smile;
Nor shun their virtuous converse; but when age
And circumstance consent, thy faith engage
To some discreet, well-natured, cheerful fair,
One not too stately for the household care,
One formed in person and in mind to please
To season life, and all its labors ease.

August

Gaming, the vice of knaves and fools, detest,
Miner of time, of substance and of rest;
Which, in the winning or the losing part,
Undoing or undone, will wring the heart:
Undone, self-cursed, thy madness thou wilt rue;
Undoing, curse of others will pursue
Thy hated head. A parent's, household's tear,
A neighbour's groan, and *heaven's* displeasure fear.

September

Wouldst thou extract the purest sweet of life,
Be nor ally nor principal in strife.
A mediator there, thy balsam bring,
And lenify the wound, and draw the sting;
On *hate* let *kindness* her warm embers throw,
And mold into a friend the melting foe.

The weakest foe boasts some revenging power;
The weakest friend some serviceable hour.

October

In converse be reserved, yet not morose,
In season grave, in season, too, jocose.
Shun party wranglings, mix not in debate
With bigots in religion or the state.
No arms to scandal or detraction lend,
Abhor to wound, be fervent to defend.
Aspiring still to know, a babbler scorn,
But watch where wisdom opes her golden horn.

November

In quest of gain be just: a conscience clear
Is lucre, more than thousands in a year;
Treasure no moth can touch, no rust consume;
Safe from the knave, the robber, and the tomb.
Unrighteous gain is the cursed seed of woe,
Predestined to be reaped by them who sow;
A dreadful harvest! when the avenging day
Shall like a tempest sweep the unjust away.

December

But not from wrong alone thy hand restrain,
The *appetite* of gold demands the rein.
What nature asks, what decency requires,
Be this the bound that limits thy desires:
This, and the generous godlike power to feed
The hungry, and to warm the loins of *need:*
To dry misfortune's tear, and scatter wide
Thy blessings, like the Nile's o'erflowing tide.

MAXIMS

The Good and Virtuous Life

The noblest question in the world is, "What good may I do in it?"

There is no man so bad but he secretly respects the good.

Hast thou virtue?—acquire also the graces and beauties of virtue.

You may be more happy than princes, if you will be more virtuous.

Wish not so much to live long as to live well.

> Keep conscience clear,
> Then never fear.

Be at war with your vices, at peace with your neighbors, and let every New Year find you a better man.

A good example is the best sermon.

Pardoning the bad is injuring the good.

Act uprightly and despise calumny; dirt may stick to a mud wall, but not to polished marble.

Let thy child's first lesson be obedience, and the second will be what thou wilt.

He that cannot obey cannot command.

Great good nature, without prudence, is a great misfortune.

A long life may not be good enough, but a good life is long enough.

He is ill clothed that is bare of virtue.

Sell not virtue to purchase wealth, nor liberty to purchase power.

An honest man will receive neither money nor praise that is not his due.

He that can have patience can have what he will.

Wouldst thou confound thy enemy, be good thy self.

'Tis hard (but glorious) to be poor and honest; an empty sack can hardly stand upright; but if it does, 't is a stout one.

What is more valuable than gold? Diamonds. Than diamonds? Virtue.

Though modesty is a virtue, bashfulness is a vice.

Content is the philosopher's stone that turns all it touches into gold.

Many have quarrelled about religion that never practised it.

Serving God is doing good to man, but praying is thought an easier service, and therefore more generally chosen.

Great modesty often hides great merit.

What you would seem to be, be really.

To be humble to superiors is duty, to equals courtesy, to inferiors nobleness.

Better is a little with content than too much with contention.

> Content and riches seldom meet together,
> Riches take thou, contentment I had rather.

A lie stands on one leg, truth on two.

All mankind are beholden to him that is kind to the good.

Let our fathers and grandfathers be valued for *their* goodness, ourselves for our own.

What is serving God? 'T is doing good to man.

> Work as if you were to live 100 years.
> Pray as if you were to die tomorrow.

Half the truth is often a great lie.

Observe all men; thyself most.

Blessed is he that expects nothing, for he shall never be disappointed.

Trust thyself, and another shall not betray thee.

Many a man thinks he is buying pleasure, when he is really selling himself a slave to it.

Pain wastes the body; pleasures, the understanding.

Eat to live, and not live to eat.

'T is easier to suppress the first desire than to satisfy all that follow it.

Let no pleasure tempt thee, no profit allure thee, no ambition corrupt thee, no example sway thee, no persuasion move thee, to do anything which thou knowest to be evil; so shalt thou always live jollily: for a good conscience is a continual Christmas.

There are three things extremely hard, steel, a diamond, and to know one's self.

Death takes no bribes.

Great beauty, great strength, and great riches are really and truly of no great use; a right heart exceeds all.

To lengthen thy life, lessen thy meals.

Fly pleasures, and they'll follow you.

Who pleasure gives, shall joy receive.

Content makes poor men rich; discontent makes rich men poor.

He that's content hath enough.

He that complains hath too much.

Nothing brings more pain than too much pleasure; nothing more bondage than too much liberty.

Would you live with ease, do what you ought, and not what you please.

None preaches better than the ant, and she says nothing.

Follies and Faults; Vanity and Vices

E'er you remark another's sin,
Bid your conscience look within.

Wink at small faults—remember thou hast great ones.

Vice knows she's ugly, so puts on her mask.

Search others for their virtues, thyself for thy vices.

Sin is not hurtful because it is forbidden, but it is forbidden because it is hurtful.

Fear to do ill, and you need fear nought else.

'Tis a shame that your family is an honor to you! You ought to be an honor to your family.

The proud hate pride—in others.

Let thy discontents be thy secrets;—if the world knows them, it will despise thee and increase them.

Success has ruined many a man.

A man in passion rides a mad horse.

Now I have a sheep and a cow, everybody bids me good morrow.

Tim was so learned that he could name a horse in nine languages. So ignorant, that he bought a cow to ride on.

Being ignorant is not so much a shame as being unwilling to learn.

> In other men we faults can spy,
> And blame the mote that dims their eye;
> Each little speck and blemish find;
> To our own stronger errors blind.

Suspicion may be no fault, but showing it may be a great one.

All blood is alike ancient.

Glass, china, and reputation are easily cracked, and never well mended.

The worst wheel of the cart makes the most noise.

The wolf sheds his coat once a year; his disposition, never.

Many foxes grow gray, but few grow good.

Clean your finger before you point at my spots.

Most fools think they are only ignorant.

Anger is never without a reason, but seldom with a good one.

You may sometimes be much in the wrong in owning your being in the right.

> A quiet conscience sleeps in thunder,
> But rest and guilt live far asunder.

Who has deceived thee so oft as thyself?

If passion drives, let reason hold the reins.

When prosperity was well mounted, she let go the bridle, and soon came tumbling out of the saddle.

Is there anything men take more pains about than to make themselves unhappy?

If a man could half his wishes, he would double his troubles.

Discontented minds, and fevers of the body, are not to be cured by changing beds or business.

As sore places meet most rubs, proud folks meet most affronts.

> If evils come not, then our fears are vain;
> And if they do, fear but augments the pain.

A learned blockhead is a greater blockhead than an ignorant one.

> Life with fools consists in drinking,
> With the wise man, living's thinking.

When the wine enters, out goes the truth.

> Each year one vicious habit rooted out,
> In time might make the worst man good throughout.

He is a governor that governs his passions, and he a servant that serves them.

A man is never so ridiculous by those qualities that are his own as by those that he affects to have.

What signifies your patience, if you can't find it when you want it.

Fools need advice most, but wise men only are the better for it.

He's a fool that cannot conceal his wisdom.

What's proper is becoming: See the blacksmith with his white silk apron!

Vainglory flowereth but beareth no fruit.

He that lieth down with dogs shall rise up with fleas.

Poverty wants some things, luxury many things, avarice all things.

> Fond pride of dress is sure an empty curse;
> E'er fancy you consult, consult your purse.

The second vice is lying; the first is running in debt.

Keep thou from the opportunity, and God will keep thee from the sin.

He that falls in love with himself will have no rivals.

> If what most men admire they would despise,
> 'T would look as if mankind were growing wise.

He does not possess wealth; it possesses him.

Avarice and happiness never saw each other. How then should they become acquainted?

He that drinks fast pays slow.

> A flatterer never seems absurd;
> The flattered always takes his word.

Approve not of him who commends all you say.

> Seven wealthy towns contend for Homer dead,
> Through which the living Homer begged his bread.

Tomorrow every fault is to be amended; but that tomorrow never comes.

Drink does not drown care, but waters it and makes it grow faster.

> Tomorrow you'll reform, you always cry;
> In what far country does this morrow lie,
> That 'tis so mighty long ere it arrive?
> Beyond the Indies does this morrow live?

'T is so farfetched this morrow, that I fear
'T will be both very old and very dear.
Tomorrow I'll reform, the fool does say;
Today itself's too late;—the *wise* did yesterday.

Love your enemies, for they tell you your faults.

He that never eats too much will never be lazy.

He that would travel much, should eat little.

Let thy vices die before thee.

The nearest way to come at glory is to do that for conscience which we do for glory.

When reason preaches, if you don't hear her she'll box your ears.

An ill wound, but not an ill name, may be healed.

Neglect mending a small fault, and 't will soon be a great one.

He that resolves to mend hereafter, resolves not to mend now.

On Trying to Please All

Once on a time it by chance came to pass,
That a man and his son were leading an ass.
Cries a passenger, Neighbor, you're shrewdly put to't,
To lead an ass empty, and trudge it on foot.
Nay, quoth the old fellow, if folk do so mind us
I'll e'en climb the ass, and boy mount behind us:

But as they jogged on they were laugh't and hissed,
What, two booby lubbers on one sorry beast!
This is such a figure as never was known;
'Tis a sign that the ass is none of your own.

Then down gets the boy, and walks by the side,
Till another cries, What, you old fool must you ride?

When you see the poor child that's weakly and young
Forced through thick and thin to trudge it along?

Then down gets the father, and up gets the son;
If this cannot please them we ne'er shall have done.
They had not gone far, but a woman cries out,
O you young graceless imp, you'll be hang'd, no doubt!
Must you ride an ass, and your father that's gray
E'en foot it, and pick out the best of his way?

So now to please all they but one trick lack,
And that was to carry the ass a pick pack:
But when that was tried, it appeared such a jest,
It occasioned more laughter by half than the rest.
Thus he who'd please all, and their good liking gain,
Shows a deal of good nature, but labors in vain.

Women and Marriage

There are no ugly loves, nor handsome prisons.

Happy's the wooing that's not long a doing.

Marry your son when you will, but your daughter when you can.

A house without woman and firelight is like a body without soul or sprite.

Love, cough, and a smoke, can't well be hid.

If you would be loved, love and be lovable.

Keep your eyes wide open before marriage, half shut afterwards.

He that has not got a wife, is not yet a complete man.

A ship under sail and a big-bellied woman are the handsomest two things that can be seen common.

You cannot pluck roses without fear of thorns
Nor enjoy a fair wife without danger of horns.

Let thy maidservant be faithful, strong, and homely.

Women are books, and men the readers be,
Who sometimes in those books erratas see;
Yet oft the reader's raptured with each line,
Fair print and paper, fraught with sense divine;
Though some, neglectful, seldom care to read,
And faithful wives no more than Bibles heed.
Are women books? says Hodge, then would mine were
An almanack, to change her every year.

An undutiful daughter will prove an unmanageable wife.

He that takes a wife takes care.

Ne'er take a wife till thou hast a house (and a fire) to put
her in.

Where there's marriage without love, there will be love without marriage.

Love and lordship hate companions.

She that will eat her breakfast in her bed,
And spend the morn in dressing of her head,
And sit at dinner like a maiden bride,
And talk of nothing all day but of pride;
God in his mercy may do much to save her,
But what a case is he in that shall have her.

Good wives and good plantations are made by good husbands.

When a man and woman die, as poets sung,
His heart's the last part moves,—her last, the tongue.

Wedlock, as old men note, hath likened been,
Unto a public crowd or common rout;
Where those that are without would fain get in,
And those that are within, would fain get out.

Grief often treads upon the heels of pleasure,
Married in haste, we oft repent at leisure;
Some by experience find these words misplaced,
Married at leisure, they repent in haste.

A little house well filled, a little field well tilled, and a little wife well willed, are great riches.

Good women are like stars in darkest night,
Their virtuous actions shining as a light
To guide their ignorant sex, which ofttimes fall,
And falling oft, turn diabolical.
Good women, sure, are angels on the earth:
Of those good angels we have had a dearth;
And therefore all you men that have good wives,
Respect their virtues equal with your lives.

Love and toothache have many cures, but none infallible except possession and dispossession.

Epitaph on a Talkative Old Maid

Beneath this silent stone is laid,
  A noisy, antiquated maid,
Who, from her cradle talked till death,
  And ne'er before was out of breath.
Wither she's gone we cannot tell;
  For if she talks not, she's in——!
If she's in ——, she's there unblest
  Because she hates a place of rest.

People

Mankind are very odd creatures: One half censure what they practise, the other half practise what they censure; the rest always say and do as they ought.

He that would live in peace and ease,
Must not speak all he knows, nor judge all he sees.

Men meet, mountains never.

To err is human, to repent divine; to persist devilish.

A false friend and a shadow attend only while the sun shines.

Lend money to an enemy, and thou'lt gain him; to a friend, and thou'lt lose him.

The rotten apple spoils his companion.

Love your neighbor; yet don't pull down your hedge.

The same man cannot be both friend and flatterer.

A brother may not be a friend, but a friend will always be a brother.

When you speak to a man, look on his eyes; when he speaks to thee, look on his mouth.

When you're good to others, you are best to yourself.

Don't judge of men's wealth or piety by their Sunday appearances.

It's common for men to give pretended reasons instead of one real one.

A quarrelsome man has no good neighbors.

He is not well bred that cannot bear ill-breeding in others.

Tart words make no friends: spoonful of honey will catch more flies than gallon of vinegar.

Mary's mouth costs her nothing, for she never opens it but at others expense.

The good will of the governed will be starved, if not fed by the good deeds of the governors.

Children and princes will quarrel for trifles.

Mad kings and mad bulls are not to be held by treaties and packthread.

A mob's a monster; heads enough but no brains.

To serve the public faithfully, and at the same time please it entirely, is impracticable.

War brings scars.

You may give a man an office, but you cannot give him discretion.

An innocent plowman is more worthy than a vicious prince.

A farmer once made a complaint to a judge,
My bull, if it please you, Sir, owing a grudge,
Belike to one of your good Worship's cattle,
Has slain him outright in a mortal battle:
I'm sorry at heart because of the action,
And want to know how must be made satisfaction,
Why, you must give me your bull, that's plain,
Says the judge, or pay me the price of the slain.
But I have mistaken the case, Sir, says John,
The dead bull I talk of, and please you, 's my own:
And yours is the beast that the mischief has done.
The judge soon replies with a serious face:
Say you so; then this accident *alters the case.*

A countryman between two lawyers is like a fish between two cats.

He's the best physician that knows the worthlessness of the most medicines.

If you would keep your secret from an enemy, tell it not to a friend.

Lawyers, preachers, and tomtit's eggs, there are more of them hatched than come to perfection.

The magistrate should obey the laws, the people should obey the magistrate.

Visit your aunt, but not every day; and call at your brothers, but not every night.

If you'd lose a troublesome visitor, lend him money.

Don't go to the doctor with every distemper, nor to the lawyer with every quarrel, nor to the pot for every thirst.

He's a fool that makes his doctor his heir.

Do good to thy friend to keep him, to thy enemy to gain him.

The absent are never without fault, nor the present without excuse.

Men and melons are hard to know.

Approve not of him who commends all you say.

Friendship cannot live with ceremony, nor without civility.

Write with the learned, pronounce with the vulgar.

He that has neither fools nor beggars among his kindred is the son of thundergust.

> To friend, lawyer, doctor, tell plain your whole case;
> Nor think on bad matters to put a good face:
> How can they advise, if they see but a part?
> 'Tis very ill driving black hogs in the dark.

Wit and Wisdom

The doors of wisdom are never shut.

A change of fortune hurts a wise man no more than a change of the moon.

If you have no honey in your pot, have some in your mouth.

> To whom thy secret thou dost tell,
> To him thy freedom thou dost sell.

Three may keep a secret, if two of them are dead.

All would live long, but none would be old.

Dost thou love life? Then do not squander time; for that's the stuff life is made of.

Read much, but not too many books.

He that would catch fish must venture his bait.

Courage would fight, but discretion won't let him.

The excellency of hogs is—fatness; of men—virtue.

> Some men grow mad by studying much to know,
> But who grows mad by studying good to grow?

The sting of a reproach is the truth of it.

The honest man takes pains, and then enjoys pleasures; the knave takes pleasure, and then suffers pains.

He that can compose himself is wiser than he that composes books.

There have been as great souls unknown to fame as any of the most famous.

> Doing an injury puts you below your enemy;
> Revenging one makes you but even with him;
> Forgiving it sets you above him.

By diligence and patience, the mouse bit in two the cable.

If your head is wax, don't walk in the sun.

He that's secure is not safe.

Words may show a man's wit, but actions his meaning.

Write injuries in dust, benefits in marble.

Franklin signing the Declaration of Independence. Reproduced from a painting by Charles B. Mills in the Franklin Union, Boston.

It is wise not to seek a secret and honest not to reveal it.

Learn of the skilful: He that teaches himself hath a fool for his master.

Good sense is a thing all need, few have, and none think they want.

> Those who in quarrels interpose,
> Must often wipe a bloody nose.

He that pursues two hares at once does not catch one and lets t'other go.

Men differ daily about things which are subject to sense; is it likely then they should agree about things invisible?

Fools make feasts and wise men eat them.

> If you ride a horse, sit close and tight,
> If you ride a man, sit easy and light.

For want of a nail the shoe is lost; for want of a shoe the horse is lost; for want of a horse the rider is lost.

There was never a good knife made of bad steel.

The ancients tell us what is best; but we must learn of the moderns what is fittest.

There's a time to wink as well as to see.

The wise and brave dares own that he was wrong.

Great talkers should be cropped, for they have no need of ears.

Teach your child to hold his tongue, he'll learn fast enough to speak.

> Man's tongue is soft, and bone doth lack;
> Yet a stroke therewith may break a man's back.

An old young man will be a young old man.

An old man in a house is a good sign.

Lost time is never found again.

Different sects, like different clocks, may be all near the matter, though they don't quite agree.

A full belly makes a full brain.

Hunger is the best pickle.

Caesar did not merit the triumphal car more than he that conquers himself.

Want of care does us more damage than want of knowledge.

Genius without education is like silver in the mine.

Two dry sticks will burn a green one.

Don't overload gratitude; if you do, she'll kick.

When the well's dry, we know the worth of water.

Employ thy time well, if thou meanest to gain leisure.

A child thinks twenty shillings and twenty years can scarce ever be spent.

Time is an herb that cures all diseases.

The wise understand half a word.

You may talk too much on the best of subjects.

Better slip with foot than tongue.

At twenty years of age the will reigns; at thirty the wit; at forty the judgment.

'Tis easy to see, hard to foresee.

Look before, or you'll find yourself behind.

Don't throw stones at your neighbors', if your own windows are glass.

He that scatters thorns, let him not go barefoot.

The heart of the fool is in his mouth, but the mouth of the wise man is in his heart.

Defer not thy well doing; be not like St. George, who is always a-horseback and never rides on.

Experience keeps a dear school, yet fools will learn in no other.

In the affairs of this world, men are saved not by faith but by the want of it.

Three removes is as bad as a fire.

The cat in gloves catches no mice.

Sloth and silence are a fool's virtues.

THE WAY TO WEALTH

[PREFACE TO *Poor Richard Improved,* 1758]

Courteous Reader,

I have heard that nothing gives an author so great pleasure as to find his works respectfully quoted by other learned authors. This pleasure I have seldom enjoyed; for though I have been, if I may say it without vanity, an *eminent author* of almanacs annually now a full quarter of a century, my brother authors in the same way, for what reason I know not, have ever been very sparing in their applauses, and no other author has taken the least notice of me, so that did not my writings produce me some solid pudding, the great deficiency of praise would have quite discouraged me.

I concluded at length that the people were the best judges of my merit, for they buy my works; and besides, in my rambles, where I am not personally known, I have frequently heard one or other of my adages repeated, with, "as Poor Richard says," at the end on it; this gave me some satisfaction, as it showed not only that my instructions were regarded, but discovered likewise some respect for my authority; and I own that to encourage the practice of remembering and repeating those wise sentences, I have sometimes quoted myself with great gravity.

Judge, then, how much I must have been gratified by an incident I am going to relate to you. I stopped my horse lately where a great number of people were collected at a vendue of merchant goods. The hour of sale not being come, they were conversing on the badness of the times, and one of the company called to a plain clean old man, with white locks, "Pray, Father Abraham, what think you of the times? Won't these heavy taxes quite ruin the country? How shall we be ever able to pay them? What would you advise us to?" Father Abraham stood up, and replied, "If you'd have my advice, I'll give it you in short, for *A word to the wise is enough*, and *many words won't fill a bushel*, as Poor Richard says." They joined in desiring him to speak his mind, and gathering round him, he proceeded as follows:

"Friends," says he, and neighbors, "the taxes are indeed very heavy, and if those laid on by the government were the only ones we had to pay, we might more easily discharge them; but we have many others, and much more grievous to some of us. We are taxed twice as much by our idleness, three times as much by our pride, and four times as much by our folly; and from these taxes the commissioners cannot ease or deliver us by allowing an abatement. However, let us hearken to good advice, and something may be done for us; *God helps them that help themselves*, as Poor Richard says in his Almanac of 1733.

"It would be thought a hard government that should tax its people one-tenth part of their time, to be employed in its service. But idleness taxes many of us much more, if we reckon all that is spent in absolute sloth, or doing of nothing, with that which is spent in idle employments or amusements that amount to nothing. Sloth, by bringing on diseases, absolutely shortens life. *Sloth, like rust, consumes faster than labor wears; while the used key is always bright,* as Poor Richard says. *But dost thou love life, then do not squander time, for that's the stuff life is made of,* as Poor Richard says. How much more than is necessary do we spend in sleep, forgetting that *The sleeping fox catches no poultry,* and that *There will be sleeping enough in the grave,* as Poor Richard says.

"If *Time be of all things the most precious, wasting time must be,* as Poor Richard says, *the greatest prodigality;* since, as he elsewhere tells us, *Lost time is never found again; and what we call time enough, always proves little enough.* Let us then up and be doing, and doing to the purpose; so by diligence shall we do more with less perplexity. *Sloth makes all things difficult, but industry all easy,* as Poor Richard says; and *He that riseth late must trot all day, and shall scarce overtake his business at night,* while *Laziness travels so slowly that poverty soon overtakes him,* as we read in Poor Richard, who adds, *Drive thy Business, let not that drive thee;* and *Early to bed, and early to rise, makes a man healthy, wealthy, and wise.*

"So what signifies wishing and hoping for better times? We may make these times better, if we bestir ourselves. *Industry need not wish,* as Poor Richard says, *and he that lives upon hope will die fasting. There are no gains without pains; then help hands, for I have no lands,* or if I have, they are smartly taxed. And, as Poor Richard likewise observes, *He that hath a trade hath an estate; and he that hath a calling, hath an office of profit and honor;* but then the trade must be worked at, and the calling well followed, or neither the estate nor the office will enable us to pay our taxes. If we are industrious, we shall never starve; for, as Poor Richard says, *At the working-man's house hunger looks in, but dares not enter.* Nor will the bailiff or the constable enter, for *Industry pays debts, while despair encreaseth them,* says Poor Richard. What though you have found no treasure, nor has any rich relation left you a legacy, *Diligence is the mother of good luck,* as Poor Richard says, *and God gives all things to industry. Then plough deep, while sluggards sleep, and you shall have corn to sell and to keep,* says Poor Dick. Work while it is called today, for you know not how much you may be hindered tomorrow, which makes Poor Richard say, *One today is worth two tomorrows,* and farther, *Have you somewhat to do tomorrow, do it today.* If you were a servant, would you not be ashamed that a good master should catch you idle? Are you then your own master, *be ashamed to catch yourself idle,* as Poor Dick says. When there is so much to be done for yourself, your family, your country, and your gracious king, be up by peep of day; *Let not the sun look down and say, Inglorious here he lies.* Handle your tools without mittens; remember that *The cat in gloves catches no mice,* as Poor Richard says. 'Tis true there is much to be done, and perhaps you are weak-handed; but stick to it steadily, and you will see great effects, for *Constant dropping wears away stones,* and *by diligence and patience the mouse ate in two the cable;* and *Little strokes fell great oaks,* as Poor Richard says in his Almanac, the year I cannot just now remember.

"Methinks I hear some of you say, *'Must a man afford himself no leisure?'* I will tell thee, my friend, what Poor Richard says, *Employ thy time well, if thou meanest to gain leisure; and, since thou art not sure of a minute, throw not away an hour.* Leisure is time for doing something useful; this leisure the diligent man will obtain, but the lazy man never; so that, as Poor Richard says, *A life of leisure and a life of laziness are two things.* Do you imagine that sloth will afford you more comfort than labor? No, for as Poor Richard says, *Trouble springs from idleness, and grievous toil from needless ease. Many without labor would live by their wits only, but they break for want of stock.* Whereas industry gives comfort, and plenty, and respect: *Fly pleasures, and they'll follow you. The diligent spinner has a large shift; and now I have a sheep and a cow, everybody bids me good morrow;* all of which is well said by Poor Richard.

"But with our industry, we must likewise be steady, settled, and careful, and oversee our own affairs with our own eyes, and not trust too much to others; for, as Poor Richard says,

> *I never saw an oft-removed tree,*
> *Nor yet an oft-removed family,*
> *That throve so well as those that settled be.*

And again, *Three removes is as bad as a fire;* and again, *Keep thy shop, and thy shop will keep thee;* and again, *If you would have your business done, go; if not, send.* And again,

> *He that by the plough would thrive,*
> *Himself must either hold or drive.*

And again, *The eye of a master will do more work than both his hands;* and again, *Want of care does us more damage than want of knowledge;* and again, *Not to oversee workmen, is to leave them your purse open.* Trusting too much to others' care is the ruin of many; for, as the Almanac says, *In the affairs of this world, men are saved, not by faith, but by the want of it;* but a man's own care is profitable; for, saith Poor Dick, *Learning is to the studious, and riches to the careful, as well as power to the bold, and heaven to the virtuous,* and farther, *If you would have a faithful servant, and one that you like, serve yourself.* And again, he adviseth to circumspection and care, even in the smallest matters, because sometimes *A little neglect may breed great mischief;* adding, *for want of a nail the shoe was lost; for want of a shoe the horse was lost; and for want of a horse the rider was lost, being overtaken and slain by the enemy; all for want of care about a horse-shoe nail.*

"So much for industry, my friends, and attention to one's own business; but to these we must add frugality, if we would make our industry more certainly successful. A man may, if he knows not how to save as he gets, keep his nose all his life to the grindstone, and die not worth a groat at last. *A fat kitchen makes a lean will,* as Poor Richard says; and

> *Many estates are spent in the getting,*
> *Since women for tea forsook spinning and knitting,*
> *And men for punch forsook hewing and splitting.*

If you would be wealthy, says he, in another Almanac, *think of saving as well as of getting: The Indies have not made Spain rich, because her outgoes are greater than her incomes.*

"Away then with your expensive follies, and you will not then have so much cause to complain of hard times, heavy taxes, and chargeable families; for, as Poor Dick says,

> *Women and wine, game and deceit,*
> *Make the wealth small and the wants great.*

And farther, *What maintains one vice, would bring up two children.* You may think, perhaps, that a little tea, or a little punch now and then, diet a little more costly, clothes a little finer, and a little entertainment now and then, can be no great matter; but remember what Poor Richard says, *Many a little makes a mickle;* and farther, *Beware of little expenses; a small leak will sink a great ship;* and again, *Who dainties love, shall beggars prove;* and moreover, *Fools make feasts, and wise men eat them.*

"Here you are all got together at this vendue of fineries and knicknacks. You call them *goods;* but if you do not take care, they will prove evils to some of you. You expect they will be sold cheap, and perhaps they may for less than they cost; but if you have no occasion for them, they must be dear to you. Remember what Poor Richard says; *Buy what thou hast no need of, and ere long thou shalt sell thy necessaries.* And again, *At a great pennyworth pause a while.* He means that perhaps the cheapness is apparent only, and not real; or the bargain, by straitening thee in thy business, may do thee more harm than good. For in another place he says, *Many have been ruined by buying good pennyworths.* Again, Poor Richard says, *'tis foolish to lay out money in a purchase of repentance;* and yet this folly is practised every day at vendues, for want of minding the Almanac. *Wise Men,* as Poor Dick says, *learn by others' harms, fools scarcely by their own; but felix quem faciunt aliena pericula cautum.* Many a one, for the sake of finery on the back, have gone with a hungry belly, and half-starved their

Drawing of Franklin by C. N. Cochin, 1777, with a facsimile of his signature

Families. *Silks and satins, scarlet and velvets,* as Poor Richard says, *put out the kitchen fire.*

"These are not the necessaries of life; they can scarcely be called the conveniences; and yet only because they look pretty, how many want to have them! The artificial wants of mankind thus become more numerous than the natural; and, as Poor Dick says, *for one poor person, there are an hundred indigent.* By these, and other extravagancies, the genteel are reduced to poverty and forced to borrow of those whom they formerly despised, but who through industry and frugality have maintained their standing; in which case it appears plainly that *A ploughman on his legs is higher than a gentleman on his knees,* as Poor Richard says. Perhaps they have had a small estate left them, which they knew not the getting of; they think, *'tis day, and will never be night;* that a little to be spent out of so much, is not worth minding; *A child and a fool,* as Poor Richard says, *imagine twenty shillings and twenty years can never be spent* but, *always taking out of the meal tub, and never putting in, soon comes to the bottom;* as Poor Dick says, *When the well's dry, they know the worth of water.* But this they might have known before, if they had taken his advice; *If you would know the value of money, go and try to borrow some; for, he that goes a borrowing goes a sorrowing;* and indeed so does he that lends to such people, when he goes to get it in again. Poor Dick farther advises, and says,

> *Fond pride of dress is sure a very curse;*
> *E'er fancy you consult, consult your purse.*

And again, *Pride is as loud a beggar as Want, and a great deal more saucy.* When you have bought one fine thing, you must buy ten more, that your appearance may be all of a piece; but Poor Dick says, *'Tis easier to suppress the first desire than to satisfy all that follow it.* And 'tis as truly folly for the poor to ape the rich, as for the frog to swell, in order to equal the ox.

> *Great Estates may venture more,*
> *But little boats should keep near shore.*

'Tis, however, a folly soon punished; for *Pride that dines on vanity, sups on contempt,* as Poor Richard says. And in another Place, *Pride breakfasted with Plenty, dined with Poverty, and supped with Infamy.* And after all, of what use is this pride of appearance, for which so much is risked, so much is suffered? It cannot promote health, or ease pain; it makes no increase of merit in the person; it creates envy, it hastens misfortune.

> *What is a butterflly? At best*
> *He's but a caterpillar drest*
> *The gaudy fop's his picture just,*

as Poor Richard says.

"But what madness must it be to run in debt for these super-fluities! We are offered, by the terms of this vendue, six months' credit; and that perhaps has induced some of us to attend it, because we cannot spare the ready money, and hope now to be fine without it. But, ah, think what you do when you run in debt; you give to another power over your liberty. If you can-not pay at the time, you will be ashamed to see your creditor; you will be in fear when you speak to him; you will make poor pitiful sneaking excuses, and by degrees come to lose your veracity, and sink into base downright lying; for, as Poor Rich-ard says, *The second vice is lying, the first is running in debt.* And again, to the same purpose, *Lying rides upon Debt's Back.* Whereas a free-born Englishman ought not to be ashamed or afraid to see or speak to any man living. But poverty often de-prives a man of all spirit and virtue: *'Tis hard for an empty bag to stand upright,* as Poor Richard truly says.

"What would you think of that prince, or that government, who should issue an edict forbidding you to dress like a gentle-man or a gentlewoman, on pain of imprisonment or servitude? Would you not say that you were free, have a right to dress as you please, and that such an edict would be a breach of your privileges, and such a government tyrannical? And yet you are about to put yourself under that tyranny when you run in debt for such dress! Your creditor has authority at his pleasure to deprive you of your liberty by confining you in gaol for life, or to sell you for a servant, if you should not be able to pay him! When you have got your bargain, you may, perhaps, think little of payment; but *Creditors,* Poor Richard tells us, *have better memories than debtors;* and in another place says, *Creditors are a superstitious sect, great observers of set days and times.* The day comes round before you are aware, and the demand is made before you are prepared to satisfy it. Or if you bear your debt in mind, the term which at first seemed so long will, as it lessens, appear extremely short. Time will seem to have added wings to his heels as well as shoulders. *Those have a short Lent,* saith Poor Richard, *who owe money to be paid at Easter.* Then since, as he says, *The borrower is a slave to the lender, and the debtor to the creditor,* disdain the chain, preserve your freedom, and maintain your independency. Be industrious and free; be frugal and free. At present, perhaps, you may think yourself in thriving circumstances, and that you can bear a little extravagance without injury; but,

> *For age and want, save while you may;*
> *No morning sun lasts a whole day,*

as Poor Richard says. Gain may be temporary and uncertain, but ever, while you live, expense is constant and certain; and *'tis easier to build two chimneys than to keep one in fuel,* as Poor Richard says. So, *Rather go to bed supperless than rise in debt.*

> *Get what you can, and what you get hold;*
> *'Tis the stone that will turn all your lead into gold,*

as Poor Richard says. And when you have got the philosopher's stone, sure you will no longer complain of bad times or the difficulty of paying taxes.

"This doctrine, my friends, is reason and wisdom; but after all, do not depend too much upon your own industry, and frugality and prudence, though excellent things, for they may all be blasted without the blessing of heaven; and therefore, ask that blessing humbly, and be not uncharitable to those that at present seem to want it, but comfort and help them. Remember, Job suffered, and was afterwards prosperous.

"And now to conclude, *Experience keeps a dear school, but fools will learn in no other, and scarce in that;* for it is true, *we may give advice, but we cannot give conduct,* as Poor Richard says. However, remember this, *They that won't be counselled, can't be helped,* as Poor Richard says: and farther that, *if you will not hear Reason, she'll surely rap your knuckles."*

Thus the old gentleman ended his harangue. The people heard it, and approved the doctrine, and immediately practiced the contrary, just as if it had been a common sermon; for the vendue opened, and they began to buy extravagantly, notwithstanding his cautions and their own fear of taxes. I found the good man had thoroughly studied my Almanacs, and digested all I had dropped on these topics during the course of five and twenty years. The frequent mention he made of me must have tired anyone else, but my vanity was wonderfully delighted with it, though I was conscious that not a tenth part of the wisdom was my own, which he ascribed to me, but rather the gleanings I had made of the sense of all ages and nations. However, I resolved to be the better for the echo of it; and though I had at first determined to buy stuff for a new coat, I went away resolved to wear my old one a little longer. Reader, if thou wilt do the same, thy profit will be as great as mine. I am, as ever, thine to serve thee,

Richard Saunders

July 7, 1757

III. COMMENTARY ON THE

Junto

In his *Autobiography* Franklin describes how he organized his "ingenious acquaintances into a club of mutual improvement," which he called the Junto. Actually, the Junto was much more than this. It was a combination debating society, forum, social group, business service club and Junior Chamber of Commerce. At first it was commonly called the Leather Apron Club.

Franklin was twenty-one years old when he organized it. Most of his friends were somewhat older, but they were all inconspicuous artisans or tradesmen who were struggling for intellectual as well as financial advancement. The club helped in both directions and, in addition, gave root to some of Franklin's most important public services. There is nothing unusual about young men organizing a club, but this one was unusual in that it lasted thirty years and its members gave birth to such things as the first public circulating library, the American Philosophical Society and the University of Pennsylvania.

Franklin probably borrowed the idea for the Junto from, of all people, Cotton Mather. At least, Mather had organized somewhat similar mutual benefit societies in Boston, one for each church. The rules for the Junto, which follow, include a list of questions to be proposed at each meeting. Several of these are almost identical with the ten questions that opened the meetings in Mather's clubs. In Boston there was a pause after each question—presumably for meditation. In Philadelphia there was a similar pause—long enough to drink a glass of wine.

There is no previously published collection of Franklin writings relating to the Junto. In fact, it is not known that he wrote much specifically for use at the club with the exception of some drinking songs, one of which is included herein, and one or two of his more earthy pieces. The Junto was a stag club, and Franklin was a lusty man, despite his historical reputation as a paragon of virtue whose life would serve as a model for all small boys. In general it would; but he was not the prig that history would make him. He did leave some notes as to questions which he raised at the Junto, together with some answers, and these follow the Rules in this volume.

The Dialogues Between Philocles and Horatio, included herein, were originally written to be read at the Junto and later published in his newspaper. These Socratic dialogues dramatize two aspects of Franklin. The speakers are Horatio, the man of pleasure, and Philocles, the man of reason. After his pleasure Horatio goes to Philocles, for "moral rearmament," only to be told that he has paid too high a price for his pleasure.

There is nothing to connect *Reflections on Courtship and Marriage* directly with the Junto. Franklin first published it in pamphlet form in 1746, and it was the first of his booklets to be published in Europe. It is presented in the form of two letters to a friend (Franklin being both writer and friend) which stemmed from a discussion among a group of men. It is very likely that some such discussion took place at the Junto, for these inquiring male minds must have speculated on that most fascinating subject—women. Franklin's defense of women was in the nature of a minor crusade. He mentions in his *Autobiography* that one of his earliest disputations had to do with education for women, which he supported; and throughout his life he was an advocate, in a mild and often humorous way, for women's rights.

Franklin mentions in his *Autobiography* that discussions in the Junto led to his writing *The Nature and Necessity of a Paper Currency,* which he first published as a pamphlet in 1729, when he was twenty-three. Paper currency was beneficial to the little man, and Franklin, then a small tradesman, became their spokesman. His idea that gold and silver were merely commodities was a radical concept to old-line economists; and his theory of labor as a standard of value was one for which the famed economist Adam Smith received plaudits when he propounded it in *The Wealth of Nations* forty-six years after Franklin wrote his pamphlet.

It is said that Franklin was the first American economist, and through the years he wrote much on money, wages, national wealth, credit, population movements and other economic subjects. He had, perhaps, one fault in common with many mid-twentieth-century economists in that he often considered economics as the handmaiden of political expediency. He was a statesman before he was an economist.

The American Philosophical Society stemmed directly from the Junto; was, in effect, an intercolonial Junto. At least half of the original Philadelphia members came from the Junto. Franklin started this with a form letter, *A Proposal for Promoting Useful Knowledge,* which he sent in May 1743 to whatever men of learning he had heard of in the colonies. The result was America's first scientific society, with headquarters at the midway point in Philadelphia. For a time Franklin was dissatisfied with the activity of the Society. He wrote, "The members . . . here are very idle. They will take no pains." But, though the original members did not live up to the expectations of their leader, the Society flourished, and is still going strong in Philadelphia two hundred and twenty years later.

The last piece of writing in this volume connected with the Junto is the *Proposals Relating to the Education of Youth in Pennsylvania.* Franklin said that the Junto furnished "a good part" of the friends who were associated in this venture to found the Academy which subsequently became the University of Pennsylvania and of which Franklin was the first President of the Board of the Trustees. This is a good example of one of Franklin's public proposals—a combination promotional piece and prospectus which progresses from an exposition of the need for such an institution to a description of its proposed curriculum, physical facilities and other details which will make it a *fait accompli*. Franklin presented the idea as coming from some "public spirited gentleman" to avoid "as much as I could, according to my usual rule, the presenting myself to the public as the author of any scheme for their benefit."

RULES FOR A CLUB ESTABLISHED
FOR MUTUAL IMPROVEMENT [1728]

Previous Question, to Be Answered
at Every Meeting

Have you read over these queries this morning, in order to consider what you might have to offer the Junto touching any one of them? viz.,

1. Have you met with any thing, in the author you last read, remarkable or suitable to be communicated to the Junto, particularly in history, morality, poetry, physic, travels, mechanic arts, or other parts of knowledge?

2. What new story have you lately heard agreeable for telling in conversation?

3. Has any citizen in your knowledge failed in his business lately, and what have you heard of the cause?

4. Have you lately heard of any citizen's thriving well, and by what means?

5. Have you lately heard how any present rich man, here or elsewhere, got his estate?

6. Do you know of a fellow citizen who has lately done a worthy action, deserving praise and imitation; or who has lately committed an error, proper for us to be warned against and avoid?

7. What unhappy effects of intemperance have you lately observed or heard; of imprudence, of passion, or of any other vice or folly?

8. What happy effects of temperance, of prudence, of moderation, or of any other virtue?

9. Have you or any of your acquaintance been lately sick or wounded? If so, what remedies were used, and what were their effects?

10. Whom do you know that are shortly going [on] voyages or journeys, if one should have occasion to send by them?

11. Do you think of any thing at present in which the Junto may be serviceable to mankind, to their country, to their friends, or to themselves?

12. Hath any deserving stranger arrived in town since last meeting that you have heard of? And what have you heard or observed of his character or merits? And whether, think you, it lies in the power of the Junto to oblige him, or encourage him as he deserves?

13. Do you know of any deserving young beginner lately set up, whom it lies in the power of the Junto any way to encourage?

14. Have you lately observed any defect in the laws of your country of which it would be proper to move the legislature for an amendment? Or do you know of any beneficial law that is wanting?

15. Have you lately observed any encroachment on the just liberties of the people?

16. Hath any body attacked your reputation lately? And what can the Junto do toward securing it?

17. Is there any man whose friendship you want, and which the Junto, or any of them, can procure for you?

18. Have you lately heard any member's character attacked, and how have you defended it?

19. Hath any man injured you, from whom it is in the power of the Junto to procure redress?

20. In what manner can the Junto, or any of them, assist you in any of your honorable designs?

21. Have you any weighty affair on hand in which you think the advice of the Junto may be of service?

22. What benefits have you lately received from any man not present?

23. Is there any difficulty in matters of opinion, of justice and injustice, which you would gladly have discussed at this time?

24. Do you see any thing amiss in the present customs or proceedings of the Junto which might be amended?

Any person, to be qualified, [is] to stand up and lay his hand upon his breast and be asked these questions, viz.:

1. Have you any particular disrespect to any present members? *Answer.* I have not.

2. Do you sincerely declare that you love mankind in general, of what profession or religion soever? *Answer.* I do.

3. Do you think any person ought to be harmed in his body, name, or goods, for mere speculative opinions, or his external way of worship? *Answer.* No.

4. Do you love truth for truth's sake, and will you endeavor impartially to find and receive it yourself, and communicate it to others? *Answer.* Yes.

QUERIES ASKED BY FRANKLIN
OF THE *JUNTO*

How shall we judge of the goodness of a writing? Or what qualities should a writing have to be good and perfect in its kind?

Answer. To be good, it ought to have a tendency to benefit the reader, by improving his virtue or his knowledge. But, not regarding the intention of the author, the method should be just; that is, it should proceed regularly from things known to things unknown, distinctly and clearly without confusion. The words used should be the most expressive that the language affords, provided that they are the most generally understood. Nothing should be expressed in two words that can be as well expressed in one; that is, no synonymes should be used, or very rarely, but the whole should be as short as possible, consistent with clearness. The words should be so placed as to be agreeable to the ear in reading; summarily, it should be *smooth, clear,* and *short.* For the contrary qualities are displeasing.

But, taking the query otherwise, an ill man may write an ill thing well; that is, having an ill design, he may use the properest style and arguments (considering who are to be readers) to attain his ends. In this sense, that is best wrote, which is best adapted for obtaining the end of the writer.

Can a man arrive at perfection in this life, as some believe; or is it impossible, as others believe?

Answer. Perhaps they differ in the meaning of the word *perfection.* I suppose the perfection of any thing to be only the greatest the nature of the thing is capable of. Different things have different degrees of perfection, and the same thing at different times. Thus, a horse is more perfect than an oyster, yet the oyster may be a perfect oyster, as well as the horse a perfect horse. And an egg is not so perfect as a chicken, nor a chicken as a hen; for the hen has more strength than the chicken, and the chicken more life than the egg; yet it may be a perfect egg, chicken, and hen.

If they mean a man cannot in this life be so perfect as an angel, it may be true; for an angel, by being incorporeal, is allowed some perfections we are at present incapable of, and less liable to some imperfections than we are liable to. If they mean a man is not capable of being as perfect here as he is capable of being in heaven, that may be true likewise. But that a man is not capable of being so perfect here, as he is capable of being here, is not sense; it is as if I should say, a chicken, in the state of a chicken, is not capable of being so perfect as a chicken is capable of being in that state.

In the above sense, there may be a perfect oyster, a perfect horse, a perfect ship; why not a perfect man? That is, as perfect as his present nature and circumstances admit.

Question. Wherein consists the happiness of a rational creature?

Answer. In having a sound mind and a healthy body, a sufficiency of the necessaries and conveniences of life, together with the favor of God and the love of mankind.

Q. What do you mean by a sound mind?

A. A faculty of reasoning justly and truly in searching after such truths as relate to my happiness. This faculty is the gift of God, capable of being improved by experience and instruction into wisdom.

Q. What is wisdom?

A. The knowledge of what will be best for us on all occasions, and the best ways of attaining it.

Q. Is any man wise at all times and in all things?

A. No, but some are more frequently wise than others.

Q. What do you mean by the necessaries of life?

A. Having wholesome food and drink wherewith to satisfy hunger and thirst, clothing, and a place of habitation fit to secure against the inclemencies of the weather.

Q. What do you mean by the conveniences of life?

A. Such a plenty . . . . .

Whether it is worth a rational man's while to forego the pleasure arising from the present luxury of the age, in eating and drinking, and artful cookery, studying to gratify the appetite, for the sake of enjoying a healthy old age, a sound mind, and a sound body, which are the advantages reasonably to be expected from a more simple and temperate diet?

Whether those meats and drinks are not the best, that contain nothing in their natural taste, nor have any thing added by art, so pleasing as to induce us to eat or drink when we are not thirsty or hungry, or after thirst and hunger are satisfied; water, for instance, for drink, and bread or the like for meat?

Is there any difference between knowledge and prudence? If there is any, which of the two is most eligible?

Is it justifiable to put private men to death for the sake of public safety or tranquillity, who have committed no crime? As, in the case of the plague, to stop infection?

If the sovereign power attempts to deprive a subject of his right, (or, which is the same thing, of what he thinks is right,) is it justifiable in him to resist, if he is able?

What general conduct of life is most suitable for men in such circumstances as most of the members of the Junto are? Or, of the many schemes of living which are in our power to pursue, which will be most probably conducive to our happiness?

Which is best, to make a friend of a wise and good man that is poor, or of a rich man that is neither wise nor good?

Which of the two is the greatest loss to a country if they both die?

Which of the two is happiest in life?

Does it not, in a general way, require great study and intense application for a poor man to become rich and powerful, if he would do it without the forfeiture of his honesty?

Does it not require as much pains, study, and application, to become truly wise and strictly virtuous, as to become rich?

Can a man of common capacity pursue both views with success, at the same time?

If not, which of the two is it best for him to make his whole application to?

Whence comes the dew, that stands on the outside of a tankard that has cold water in it in the summer time?

A DIALOGUE BETWEEN PHILOCLES AND HORATIO, MEETING ACCIDENTALLY IN THE FIELDS, CONCERNING VIRTUE AND PLEASURE

[The Pennsylvania Gazette, June 23, 1730]

PHILOCLES. My friend Horatio! I am very glad to see you; prithee, how came such a man alone? And musing too? What misfortune in your pleasures has sent you to philosophy for relief?

HORATIO. You guess very right, my dear Philocles! We pleasure-hunters are never without them; and yet, so enchanting is the game, we can't quit the chase! How calm and undisturbed is your life! How free from present embarrassments and future cares! I know you love me, and look with compassion upon my conduct; show me then the path which leads up to that constant and invariable good, which I have heard you so beautifully describe, and which you seem so fully to possess.

PHIL. There are few men in the world I value more than you, Horatio! for, amidst all your foibles and painful pursuits of pleasure, I have oft observed in you an honest heart, and a mind strongly bent toward virtue. I wish, from my soul, I could assist you in acting steadily the part of a reasonable creature; for, if you would not think it a paradox, I should tell you I love you better than you do yourself.

HOR. A paradox indeed! Better than I do myself! When I love my dear self so well that I love everything else for my own sake.

PHIL. He only loves himself well, who rightly and judiciously loves himself.

HOR. What do you mean by that, Philocles! You men of reason and virtue are always dealing in mysteries, though you laugh at them when the church makes them. I think he loves himself very well and very judiciously too, as you call it, who allows himself to do whatever he pleases.

PHIL. What, though it be to the ruin and destruction of that very self which he loves so well! That man alone loves himself rightly, who procures the greatest possible good to himself through the whole of his existence; and so pursues pleasure as not to give for it more than 'tis worth.

HOR. That depends all upon opinion. Who shall judge what the pleasure is worth? Supposing a pleasing form of the fair kind strikes me so much that I can enjoy nothing without the enjoyment of that one object. Or, that pleasure in general is so favorite a mistress that I will take her as men do their wives, for better, for worse; mind no consequences, nor regarding what's to come. Why should I not do it?

PHIL. Suppose, Horatio, that a friend of yours entered into the world, about two-and-twenty, with a healthful vigorous body, and a fair plentiful estate of about five hundred pounds a year; and yet, before he had reached thirty, should, by following his pleasures, and not, as you say, duly regarding consequences, have run out of his estate, and disabled his body to that degree that he had neither the means nor capacity of enjoyment left, nor anything else to do but wisely shoot himself through the head to be at rest; what would you say to this unfortunate man's conduct? Is it wrong by opinion or fancy only? Or is there really a right and wrong in the case? Is not one opinion of life and action juster than another? Or, one sort of conduct preferable to another? Or, does that miserable son of pleasure appear as reasonable and lovely a being in your eyes, as a man who, by prudently and rightly gratifying his natural passions, had preserved his body in full health, and his estate entire, and enjoyed both to a good old age, and then died with a thankful heart for the good things he had received, and with an entire submission to the will of him who first called him into being? Say, Horatio! are these men equally wise and happy? And is everything to be measured by a mere fancy and opinion, without considering whether that fancy or opinion be right?

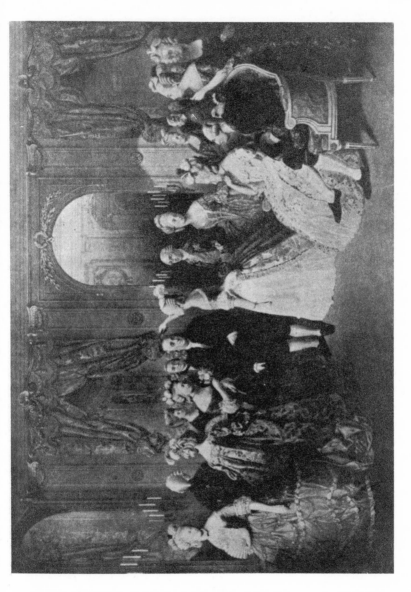

Franklin at the court of France, 1778, with Louis XVI and Marie Antoinette seated at right

HOR. Hardly so neither, I think; yet sure the wise and good author of nature could never make us to plague us. He could never give us passions, on purpose to subdue and conquer them; nor produce this self of mine, or any other self, only that it may be denied; for that is denying the works of the great Creator himself. Self-denial, then, which is what I suppose you mean by prudence, seems to me not only absurd, but very dishonorable to that Supreme wisdom and goodness, which is supposed to make so ridiculous and contradictious a creature, that must be always fighting with himself in order to be at rest, and undergo voluntary hardships in order to be happy. Are we created sick, only to be commanded to be sound? Are we born under one law, our passions, and yet bound to another, that of reason? Answer me, Philocles, for I am warmly concerned for the honor of nature, the Mother of us all.

PHIL. I find, Horatio, my two characters have affrighted you; so that you decline the trial of what is good, by reason: And had rather make a bold attack upon Providence; the usual way of you gentlemen of fashion, who, when by living in defiance of the eternal rules of reason, you have plunged yourselves into a thousand difficulties, endeavor to make yourselves easy by throwing the burden upon nature. You are, Horatio, in a very miserable condition indeed; for you say you can't be happy if you control your passions; and you feel yourself miserable by an unrestrained gratification of them; so that here's evil, irremediable evil, either way.

HOR. That is very true, at least it appears so to me. Pray, what have you to say, Philocles, in honor of nature or providence? Methinks I'm in pain for her. How do you rescue her poor lady!

PHIL. This, my dear Horatio, I have to say: that what you find fault with and clamor against, as the most terrible evil in the world, self-denial, is really the greatest good, and the highest self-gratification: if, indeed, you use the word in the sense of some weak sour moralists, and how much weaker Divines, you'll have just reason to laugh at it; but if you take it, as understood by philosophers and men of sense, you will presently see her charms, and fly to her embraces, notwithstanding her demure looks, as absolutely necessary to produce even your own darling sole good, pleasure: for, self-denial is never a duty, or a reasonable action, but as it is a natural means of procuring more pleasure than you can taste without it so that this grave, saintlike guide to happiness, as rough and dreadful as she has been made to appear, is in truth the kindest and most beautiful mistress in the world.

HOR. Prithee, Philocles! do not wrap yourself in allegory and metaphor. Why do you tease me thus? I long to be satisfied, what this philosophical self-denial is; the necessity and reason of it; I'm impatient, and all on fire; explain, therefore, in your beautiful, natural easy way of reasoning, what I'm to understand by this grave lady of yours, with so forbidding, downcast looks, and yet so absolutely necessary to my pleasures. I stand ready to embrace her; for you know, pleasure I court under all shapes and forms.

PHIL. Attend then, and you'll see the reason of this philosophical self-denial. There can be no absolute perfection in any creature; because every creature is derived, and dependent. No created being can be all-wise, all-good, and all-powerful, because his powers and capacities are finite and limited; consequently, whatever is created must in its own nature be subject to error, irregularity, excess, and disorder. All intelligent, rational agents find in themselves a power of judging what kind of beings they are; what actions are proper to preserve them, and what consequences will generally attend them, what pleasures they are formed for, and to what degree their natures are capable of receiving them. All we have to do then, Horatio, is to consider, when we are surprised with a new object, and passionately desire to enjoy it, whether gratifying that passion be consistent with the gratifying other passions and appetites, equal if not more necessary to us. And whether it consists with our happiness tomorrow, next week, or next year; for, as we all wish to live, we are obliged by reason to take as much care for our future as our present happiness, and not build one upon the ruins of the other. But if, through the strength and power of a present passion, and through want of attending to consequences, we have erred and exceeded the bounds which nature or reason have set us, we are then, for our own sakes, to refrain, or deny ourselves a present momentary pleasure for a future, constant, and durable one: so that this philosophical self-denial is only refusing to do an action which you strongly desire, because it is inconsistent with your health, fortunes, or circumstances in the world; or, in other words, because it would cost you more than it was worth. You would lose by it, as a man of pleasure. Thus you see, Horatio! that self-denial is not only the most reasonable, but the most pleasant, thing in the world.

HOR. We are just coming into town, so that we can't pursue this argument any further at present; you have said a great deal for nature, providence, and reason: Happy are they who can follow such divine guides.

PHIL. Horatio! good night; I wish you wise in your pleasures.

HOR. I wish, Philocles! I could be as wise in my pleasures as you are pleasantly wise; your wisdom is agreeable, your virtue is amiable, and your philosophy the highest luxury. Adieu! thou enchanting reasoner!

A SECOND DIALOGUE BETWEEN PHILO-CLES AND HORATIO, CONCERNING VIRTUE AND PLEASURE

[*The Pennsylvania Gazette,* July 9, 1730]

PHILOCLES. Dear Horatio! where hast thou been these three or four months? What new adventures have you fallen upon since I met you in these delightful, all-inspiring fields, and wondered how such a pleasure-hunter as you could bear being alone?

HORATIO. O Philocles, thou best of friends, because a friend to reason and virtue, I am very glad to see you. Don't you remember, I told you then that some misfortunes in my pleasures had sent me to philosophy for relief? But now I do assure you, I can, without a sigh, leave other pleasures for those of philosophy; I can hear the word *Reason* mentioned, and virtue praised, without laughing. Don't I bid fair for conversion, think you?

PHIL. Very fair, Horatio! for I remember the time when reason, virtue, and pleasure, were the same thing with you: when you counted nothing good but what pleased, nor any thing reasonable but what you got by; when you made a jest of a mind, and the pleasures of reflection, and elegantly placed your sole happiness, like the rest of the animal creation, in the gratifications of sense.

HOR. I did so. But in our last conversation, when walking upon the brow of this hill, and looking down on that broad, rapid river, and yon widely extended beautifully varied plain, you taught me another doctrine. You showed me that self-denial, which above all things I abhorred, was really the greatest good, and the highest self-gratification, and absolutely necessary to produce even my own darling sole good, pleasure.

PHIL. True, I told you that self-denial was never a duty but when it was a natural means of procuring more pleasure than we could taste without it; that as we all strongly desire to live, and to live only to enjoy, we should take as much care about our future as our present happiness, and not build one upon the ruins of the other; that we should look to the end, and regard consequences; and if, through want of attention, we had erred, and exceeded the bounds which nature had set us, we were then obliged, for our own sakes, to refrain or deny ourselves a present momentary pleasure for a future, constant, and durable good.

HOR. You have shown, Philocles, that self-denial, which weak or interested men have rendered the most forbidding, is really the most delightful and amiable, the most reasonable and pleasant thing in the world. In a word, if I understand you aright, self-denial is in truth, self-recognising, self-acknowledging, or self-owning. But now, my friend! you are to perform another promise, and show me the path which leads up to that constant, durable, and invariable good, which I have heard you so beautifully describe, and which you seem so fully to possess: Is not this good of yours a mere chimera? Can anything be constant in a world which is eternally changing and which appears to exist by an everlasting revolution of one thing into another, and where everything without us, and everything within us, is in perpetual motion? What is this constant, durable good, then, of yours? Prithee, satisfy my soul, for I'm all on fire and impatient to enjoy her. Produce this eternal blooming Goddess with never-fading charms, and see whether I won't embrace her with as much eagerness and rapture as you.

PHIL. You seem enthusiastically warm, Horatio; I will wait till you are cool enough to attend to the sober, dispassionate voice of reason.

HOR. You mistake me, my dear Philocles! my warmth is not so great as to run away with my reason; it is only just raised enough to open my faculties and fit them to receive those eternal truths, and that durable good, which you so triumphantly boasted of. Begin, then; I'm prepared.

PHIL. I will. I believe, Horatio, with all your skepticism about you, you will allow that good to be constant which is never absent from you, and that to be durable, which never ends but with your being.

HOR. Yes, go on.

PHIL. That can never be the good of a creature, which, when present, the creature may be miserable, and when absent, is certainly so.

HOR. I think not; but pray explain what you mean; for I am not much used to this abstract way of reasoning.

PHIL. I mean all the pleasures of sense. The good of man

cannot consist in the mere pleasures of sense; because, when any one of those objects which you love is absent, or can't be come at, you are certainly miserable; and if the faculty be impaired, though the object be present, you can't enjoy it. So that this sensual good depends upon a thousand things without and within you, and all out of your power. Can this then be the good of man? Say, Horatio! what think you, Is not this a chequered, fleeting, fantastical good? Can that, in any propriety of speech, be called the good of man which even, while he is tasting, he may be miserable, and which, when he cannot taste, he is necessarily so? Can that be our good, which costs us a great deal of pains to obtain; which cloys in possessing; for which we must wait the return of appetite before we can enjoy again? Or, is that our good which we can come at without difficulty; which is heightened by possession; which never ends in weariness and disappointment; and which, the more we enjoy, the better qualified we are to enjoy on?

HOR. The latter, I think; but why do you torment me thus? Philocles! show me this good immediately.

PHIL. I have showed you what it is not; it is not sensual, but it is rational and moral good. It is doing all the good we can to others, by acts of humanity, friendship, generosity, and benevolence. This is that constant and durable good, which will afford contentment and satisfaction always alike, without variation or diminution. I speak to your experience now, Horatio! did you ever find yourself weary of relieving the miserable, or of raising the distressed into life or happiness? Or rather, don't you find the pleasure grow upon you by repetition, and that it is greater in the reflection than in the act itself? Is there a pleasure upon earth to be compared with that which arises from the sense of making others happy? Can this pleasure ever be absent, or ever end but with your being? Does it not always accompany you? Doth not it lie down and rise with you, live as long as you live, give you consolation in the article of death, and remain with you in that gloomy hour when all other things are going to forsake you, or you them?

HOR. How glowingly you paint, Philocles! Methinks Horatio is amongst the enthusiasts. I feel the passion: I am enchantingly convinced, but I don't know why; overborn by something stronger than reason. Sure some Divinity speaks within me; but prithee, Philocles, give me cooly the cause, why this rational and moral good so infinitely excels the mere natural or sensual.

PHIL. I think, Horatio, that I have clearly shown you the difference between merely natural or sensual good, and rational or moral good. Natural or sensual pleasure continues no longer than the action itself; but this divine or moral pleasure continues when the action is over, and swells and grows upon your hand by reflection. The one is inconstant, unsatisfying, of short duration, and attended with numberless ills; the other is constant, yields full satisfaction, is durable, and no evils preceding, accompanying, or following it. But, if you enquire further into the cause of this difference, and would know why the moral pleasures are greater than the sensual, perhaps the reason is the same as in all other creatures, that their happiness or chief good consists in acting up to their chief faculty, or that faculty which distinguishes them from all creatures of a different species. The chief faculty in a man is his reason; and consequently his chief good, or that which may be justly called his good, consists not merely in action, but in reasonable action. By reasonable actions, we understand those actions which are preservative of the human kind, and naturally tend to produce real and unmixed happiness; and these actions, by way of distinction, we call actions morally good.

HOR. You speak very clearly, Philocles; but, that no difficulty may remain upon my mind, pray tell me what is the real difference between natural good and ill, and moral good and ill, for I know several people who use the terms without ideas.

PHIL. That may be. The difference lies only in this: that natural good and ill is pleasure and pain; moral good and ill is pleasure or pain produced with intention and design; for it is the intention only that makes the agent morally good or bad.

HOR. But may not a man, with a very good intention, do an ill action?

PHIL. Yes, but, then he errs in his judgment, though his design be good. If his error is inevitable, or such as, all things considered, he could not help, he is inculpable; but if it arose through want of diligence in forming his judgment about the nature of human actions, he is immoral and culpable.

HOR. I find, then, that in order to please ourselves rightly, or to do good to others morally, we should take great care of our opinions.

PHIL. Nothing concerns you more; for, as the happiness or real good of men consists in right action, and right action cannot be produced without right opinion, it behooves us, above all things in this world, to take care that our opinions of things be according to the nature of things. The foundation of all virtue and happiness is thinking rightly. He who sees an action is right, that is, naturally tending to good, and does it because of that tendency, he only is a moral man; and he alone is capable of that constant, durable, and invariable good, which has been the subject of this conversation.

HOR. How, my dear philosophical guide, shall I be able to know, and determine certainly, what is right and wrong in life?

PHIL. As easily as you distinguish a circle from a square, or light from darkness. Look, Horatio, into the sacred book of nature; read your own nature, and view the relation which other men stand in to you, and you to them; and you'll immediately see what constitutes human happiness, and conse- quently what is right.

HOR. We are just coming into town, and can say no more at present. You are my good genius, Philocles. You have shown me what is good. You have redeemed me from the slavery and misery of folly and vice, and made me a free and happy being.

PHIL. Then I am the happiest man in the world. Be steady, Horatio! Never depart from reason and virtue.

HOR. Sooner will I lose my existence. Good night, Philocles.

PHIL. Adieu! dear Horatio!

A close-up of Houdon's bust of Franklin

SONG SUNG AT THE JUNTO

Of their Chloes and Phyllises poets may prate,
   I sing my plain country Joan,
These twelve years my wife, still the joy of my life;
   Blest day that I made her my own.

Not a word of her face, of her shape, of her air,
   Or of flames or of darts you shall hear;
I beauty admire but virtue I prize,
   That fades not in seventy years.

Am I loaded with care, she takes off a large share,
   That the burden ne'er makes me to reel;
Does good fortune arrive, the joy of my wife
   Quite doubles the pleasure I feel. . . .

Some faults have we all, and so has my Joan,
   But then they're exceedingly small;
And now I'm grown used to them, so like my own,
   I scarcely can see them at all. . . .

REFLECTIONS ON COURTSHIP AND MARRIAGE:

In Two Letters to a Friend. Wherein a Practicable Plan is Laid Down for Obtaining and Securing Conjugal Felicity

Philadelphia, 1746

ADVERTISEMENT

Gentlemen and Ladies,

It is judged proper to acquaint you, that the ensuing Sheets were convey'd to the Press, thro' a Channel whose original Source is concealed from our Knowledge. You will find the Author did not intend it for Publick View, for indeed there are such evident Marks of a Dishabille, and such a careless Negligence of Dress, that tho' it may be allowed to pay a *Morning Visit* to an intimate Friend, it was not dressed by the Writer *to entertain Company,* but stole by a *private way, unshaved and unshifted,* to the *Closet* of his Friend. Whether by the *Death* of its Author, or his Friend, or by *what other fortuitous Turns,* it at length arrived to the Press, and now presents itself to publick Observation, we cannot inform you; but that the Author is ignorant of its Publication, as we are ignorant of him or her, and that *no dishonourable Breach of Confidence* has been made, there are many concurring Circumstances to persuade us of.

Let it therefore be considered (tho' the Press now gives it a Publick Relation) as *really a private Entertainment* in its Design, originally given behind the Curtain of a very intimate Friendship; but *Death,* or *some other* Incidents have drawn up that Curtain, and exhibited to *publick Light* this *private Scene*

of Friendly Intercourse; *Where* the Mind gives a Vent to its
Feelings, without any studious elaborate Preparation; *where*
the Sentiments flow like *a natural Cascade,* rudely beautiful,
tho' not regularly charming, with more native Impetuosity than
methodical Harmony.

It is nevertheless apprehended, tho' these REFLECTIONS were
designed only for *private Entertainment and Use,* the Publication of them may yield Pleasure and Utility to the younger Part
of each Sex; and may, perhaps, tend to discountenance the false,
unnatural, and insolent Ridicule, that frequently endeavours to
bespatter and affront the *Conjugal Tie; which* is, and has ever
been, the sacred Cement of all Societies; and *which* has had the
Approval and Veneration of the best and wisest Minds in all
Ages: The Common-place Witticisms against this amiable and
desirable Union, are indeed such low, wretched Stuff, as to be
with Indignation excluded from all polite Conversations.

The Author of the following *Reflections,* endeavours to lay
a practicable Plan, by the Execution of which, the matrimonial
State may produce such a Crop of Felicity, as to make it highly
worthy the Pursuit of every reasonable and virtuous Mind. Had
he wrote for publick View, he would probably have appeared
in a more full and regular Dress,—but that has already been
apologized for. We shall only therefore declare our Opinion,
that his Plan carries Reason and Conviction with it; and might
perhaps more fully have done so, had he consider'd his Subject
by Way of *Contrast,* as forcibly as he has in the Abstract: For
whoever has observ'd the declining Days of old Batchelors in
general, may see their unconnected, unrelative State in Society,
tottering to their Graves in a gloomy Solitude, or, at best, only
attended by a few artful rapacious Vultures, who impatiently
wait for their *Prey.* No tender affectionate Companion, of similar Mind and Manners, whose *constant* Sunshine of Love,
warm'd the Spring and Summer of his Days, and now with an
unalterable Friendship and Fellow-feeling, accompanies him
Arm-in-Arm thro' the dreary Wilds of his Winter, with the
Guard of a Son or Sons, whose filial Piety and manly Vigour,

is ever ready to protect him from the Insolence of others, or to defend him from those Calamities to which our feeble Age exposes us; surrounded with a prattling Offspring fondly caressing their hoary Grandsire, and blooming a Prospect of future Honour and Virtue. What exquisite Sensations this Patriarchal Breast must feel! What heavenly Raptures his Soul must glow with! MATRIMONY may, upon our Author's Plan, acquaint us with them.—But these divine Supports are as little to be expected by an *Old Batchelor,* as in our Power to describe.

Our Author's *Reflections* may furthermore convince the Fair Sex, that tho' Fortune may buy them a mercenary Tyrant; tho' Beauty may provoke their Ruin, or attract some Fop or Coxcomb; yet, *Good Sense,* and *real* Merit only, will touch the *Heart* of, and maintain their *Influence* over, Men of true Worth and Knowledge: *That* the Charms of Judgment, Discretion and good Temper, are the only *lasting* Foundations upon which matrimonial Felicity can be built: *That* the Cultivation of their Minds is absolutely necessary to the Production of their Happiness: that Love will soon starve without Friendship; and finally, that the Standard of human Felicity in general, is the PRACTICE OF WISDOM AND VIRTUE so also of the Conjugal Union in particular.

Letter I

You tell me the Dispute which was carried on in our Company the other Day, has rather made you a *Sceptick to both,* than a *Convert to either* Side of the Question: And you desire my deliberate Sentiments on the Subject of that Afternoon's Argument.

YOU have an unquestionable Right to ask me: I wish my Answer may prove satisfactory.

MARRIAGE, you know, was the Topick of our Conversation, and the Subject of our Dispute. We were all Batchelors, and each declared he had no Schemes of that kind on his Hands; and was therefore so far unbiassed.

YOU may remember many sprightly Things were said against that Scene of Life; some very plausible Ones.

IT was alledged, on the one Hand, that the Education of Women, in general, must naturally give them a strong Biass to *Dissembling* and *Affectation,* the Turn of Thinking, which, for the most Part, they *early* imbibe; the too much *Attention,* and *Artifice* they are taught to bestow on their *Persons;* the trifling, and often ill-judged Accomplishments, by which their Ambition is excited, and in which, for the most Part, they so studiously endeavour to excel.

By this Method of Management they are polished to a *superficial Lustre,* dazle our Sight, and work up our Passions. But, for that End, the *substantial* Culture of their *Minds* is grossly neglected; *true* good Sense, and *sound* Judgment; the inestimable Perfections of a *generous, an open,* and *noble* Mind, are but little considered in their Educations.

HEREBY are they quite unfitted for the *delicate Pleasures* of a *rational Esteem,* and the Godlike Joys of a manly Friendship.

NOT having therefore the requisite Fund of substantial Worth to raise the Thought, and touch the Heart; to be an agreeable Companion, and a steady Friend; and only striking the Springs of *Passion* and *Appetite;* when *those* are deaden'd, as they naturally will be by Possession, the Joys of Wedlock grow *dull* and *insipid,* sicken and die away, leaving us in their Room, a vain and capricious, an empty and insignificant Companion, with perhaps a helpless Infant or two, to increase our Care and Vexation.

Is there, was it asked, any thing so engaging, so eligible in this social Scheme of Life, as to induce a Man of Sense and Judgment to embrace it; to quit for it, the free, the easy and independent Pleasures of a single Life; where, cool and unmolested, he exalts and improves his Understanding in the Treasures of ancient and modern Learning; unshackled from the Cares of a Family; unclogg'd by that perplexing Chain, a petulant, or a weak, or a fantastick Wife; relaxes himself with the agreeable Conversation of polite, chearful, and witty Companions.

Is there, was it added, any Comparison between the two Scenes of Life?

IT was observed by the Advocates on this Side of the Question, that a debauched, dissolute Life, was not pleaded for; but that there was a *justifiable Mean* betwixt both Extreams, more choice-worthy than *either,* and which a Man of Prudence and Discretion might hit upon.

AND here, you may remember, a Gentleman in Company, spoke to the following Purpose:

'THE Description which has been given of the Education of our Modern young Ladies, and its *malignant Influence,* is, I must confess, but too just, and too general. And tho' many, in Pictures of this kind, often discover too much Coarseness in their Paint, yet, I think, this has been touched as becomes the Hand of a Gentleman, and one that desires to reason, not inveigh.

'THE Inferences which throw themselves on us by the Questions asked, have great Plausibility, and, generally considered, carry with them a Weight, near, and almost, to Conviction.

'BUT, Gentlemen, I wou'd Beg Leave to observe, that tho' the common Education of young Ladies is chiefly extended no farther than to *superficial* and *exterior* Accomplishments; and that their Behaviour is rather owing to a Sort of mechanical Influence, than to Sentiments from Reason and Judgment; that *Reading,* and *Reflection* are too much neglected by them, or ill regulated; that their Taste of *real Worth* and *Merit* in Men and Things, is thereby render'd very defective, and often shows itself to be mighty ridiculous; that their Passions are rather kept under Restraint by the common Rules of Decorum, than by any rational Conviction of a *real beautiful,* and *deformed* in

Characters, independant on *who sees,* or *who knows;* that they aim more to catch the Eyes, than penetrate the Heart, to blow up the Passions, than to secure the Understandings of their Admirers; that Esteem and Friendship are more remote from their Attention, than frothy Compliments and foppish Rant.

'NOTWITHSTANDING all this, I conceive, Gentlemen, where the Dispositions of a young Lady are not of a bad Turn by Nature, whatever little Weeds may be sprung or springing up from the unhappy Influence of her Education, are to be cleared; her Mind and Temper still capable of such Cultivation by a skilful Address, as to render her very worthy Esteem and Friendship to a Man of Sense, worthy his Choice, as a Companion for Life.

'I am persuaded no one in this Company will assert, Women are by Nature constituted incapable of Friendship, or any social Charms which our Sex possesses. Every Person here is better versed in History and human Nature.

'WHAT then should obstruct their shining in so exalted a Light?—Why Education, the trifling and narrow Extent of Thinking which that accustoms them to, &c. &c.

'BUT in young Minds, for of such only I speak, where there are common, docile and pliable, dispositions, Is it an insuperable Task to raise in them an Ambition for good Sense, and a judicious Taste? There are many Passions to work upon, which a *nice* and *gentle* Hand may manage to his Purpose; there are the Seeds of Reflection, and tho' they may lie under Rubbish, 'tis to be cleared away; they may be sown in good Ground, and by minding Times and Seasons, and dealing tenderly with them, they will bring forth a Crop of happy and useful Reflections.

'BUT suffer me, Gentlemen, to go yet farther. Allowing what we have said on the Education of young Ladies to be all true; do not our Sex too often compleat what that has begun? do we not in general flatter them with a Heap of bombast Stuff, and then laugh at them for seeming pleased with it? Do we not blow up their Vanity and Conceit, with Notions of that Merit to which they have no just Title? And gloss over their silly Airs and Follies with false Applause, and Epithets of Approbation? Do we not generally converse with them in a Language of Rhodomontade and Nonsense?

'How then, is it possible for them to improve; How to discern *real* from *false* Excellence, who seldom hear a Word of Sense, and less of Truth? 'Tis this Sort of Treatment young Ladies meet with in common Life, and too much of this Kind we carry with us when we make our matrimonial Addresses; to which and our subsequent Imprudences after Marriage, I cannot but ascribe the many just Satires that are thrown out against it.

'BUT wou'd we'—Here the Discourse was interrupted by a Circumstance which I doubt not you well remember.

HAD the Gentlemen proceeded, your Opinion might possibly have been determined, and prevented me an Attempt, for which I fear I am not sufficiently qualified.—However I will not add to the Trouble of your Perusal any further Apologies, which are in general the Effects more of Vanity than Modesty.

I am then of that Gentleman's Opinion, whose Discourse was broke upon:

THAT unhappy Matches are often occasioned by mere *mercenary Views* in *one* or *both* of the Parties; or by the *headstrong* Motives of *ill conducted Passion*.

THAT by a *prudent* and *judicious* Proceeding, in our Addresses to a young Lady of a good natural Temper, a probable Foundation may be laid for making her an agreeable Companion, a steady Friend, and a good Wife.

AND that after Marriage, by continuing in the Road of *Prudence* and *Judgment,* we may erect a Superstructure of as much real Felicity, and as refined an Enjoyment of Life, to its latest Period, as any other Scheme can justly lay claim to.

I shall give you my deliberate Thoughts on these four Particulars; the *first, second* and *third,* will be the Subject of *this,* the *fourth* that of *another Letter;* and, to be the less confused, I shall put them under a Sort of Method.

Sect. I. Many unhappy Matches are occasioned by mercenary Views in one or both of the Parties.

THAT Luxury, and an expensive Manner of Life, is not less the Attention than the Ambition of most People in their several Classes; and that such a Turn of Mind must naturally and necessarily carry with it a violent and insatiable Thirst for Riches; to any Person of Observation and Reflection, is as obvious, on the one Hand, as 'tis consequential on the other.

'TIS as certain, that a Passion so prevalent, will, of course, weigh down and stifle every noble, generous, and disinterested Sentiment.

WE see but too often, like a destructive Torrent, it hurries away all the Principles of Humanity, Friendship and Honour.

In short—whenever *Luxury,* and an Ambition for *Show* and *Grandeur,* becomes our *ruling Passion,* the *Love of Money,* as being the necessary Means for attaining the other, will be proportionably strong: And whatever be our *ruling Passion,* it will swallow up all the rest, and be the *governing Principle* of our Actions.

A great Philosopher, and a Poet, that has, I think, no Equal in our Language, tell us,

> *The ruling Passion, be it what it will,*
> *The ruling Passion conquers Reason still.*[1]

EVERY Man of Observation and Thought does, I believe, find, that *exterior Show,* and the Possession of Wealth, is become the common Standard of Merit; that a *slavish Obsequiousness* is paid to it, at the Expence of all that is *truly Great and Manly.*

THE same *little, sneaking,* and *selfish* Spirit, is crept into our matrimonial Pursuits; and not, I think, less with the Fair than our own Sex.

WHAT abominable *Prostitutions* of Persons and Minds are daily to be seen in many of our Marriages! How little a Share

[1] Pope's Epist. to Lord *Bathurst.*

has *real Friendship* and *Esteem* in most of them! How many *play the Harlot,* for a good Settlement, under the *legal Title* of a Wife! And how many the *Stallion,* to repair a broken Fortune, or to gain one.

ARE these *Muckworms* to expect any *social Happiness* with each other? shall their *wretched Experience* be quoted as Instances to prove Matrimony unworthy our Choice?

As well two Mountains of Peru might meet,
And mix their Dross, to make a Bondage sweet.[2]

The real Felicity of Marriage does undoubtedly consist in a *Union of Minds,* and a *Sympathy of Affections;* in a *mutual Esteem and Friendship* for each other in the highest Degree possible. But in that Alliance, where Interest and Fortune *only* is considered, those refined and tender Sentiments are neither felt or known. And what are they exchanged for? Why, to make a glare in the Eyes of the little and great Vulgar; to be hurried thro' Scenes of ridiculous and treacherous Ceremony; to raise Envy in the weak and silly Part of the World, Pity and Contempt in the Wise and Judicious.

AND what are the Consequences to the Parties themselves? Why, at best a *cold, flat,* and *insipid* Intercourse; void of the exquisite Relish of a sincere Esteem, and the divine Pleasures of a reasonable and honourable Friendship.—But more frequently the *Iniquity* of their *interested* Views, in one or both appears undisguised, is succeeded by Contempt and Disdain, and throws such a Fire of Contention and Uneasiness between them, as gives too just a Cause for that direful Simile, *a Hell upon Earth.*

IF the Happiness of a married Life does, as it most certainly *must,* arise from an *unfeigned Esteem,* and *sincere Friendship* for each other; how is it possible for such *godlike Effects* to flow from such *diabolical Causes,* as *Avaricious, mercenary,* and *self-ish* Views? Do such Dispositions, and can such *dirty Souls,* ever feel the *pure* and *delicate* Flame of a *sincere Love?* Of that *mys-*

2 Watts *(a Memoria)*

terious Affection which *swells* the Heart, and *overflows* in the *gentle Streams* of an *anxious Fondness?* Can interested Designs, can those *Slaves* to *Dross* be animated with the *Spirit* of a *generous,* an *elevated* and *inflexible Friendship?* 'Tis inconsistent and repugnant to Reason and Nature: *Gold* is their *Idol,* 'tis that they wed.

To conclude, 'tis a Truth of the plainest Demonstration, that *Slaves to Fortune,* or the Gratification of their own selfish Passions, who center their Views in Life within themselves, independant on the Feelings of others, are *incapable* of a sincere and steady Friendship; nor can their Hearts *glow* with the *warm Benevolence* of a *tender Affection.*

DOES it not then very evidently appear, that Marriages which are made on the meer motives of Interest, will naturally turn out, insipid, unhappy, and *fatal* Situations.

IF there can be found any Instances to the contrary, they must be owing to a happy Chance; those who in so important an Engagement will trust to a *Fors Fortuna* for their Happiness, are not worth reasoning with. 'Tis true, we cannot arrive to Certainty in human Contingencies, but when Reason, and the greatest Degree of Probability are against us, 'tis Madness, 'tis egregious Folly, to act in Contradiction to them.

IT must not be inferred from the foregoing, that Prudence and Discretion with regard to Fortune, are to be banish'd from our Consideration. That wou'd be an Extream, on the other Hand, equally, or more subversive of our Happiness.

To talk of a Competence, is, in Effect, saying Nothing at all; what may be so to one Man, is not so to another. But this is certain: The nearer we bring our Desires of Living, and our Relishes of Pleasure, to the Necessities of our Nature, the more easy and certain will our Happiness be: And undoubtedly Splendor and Magnificence, are more *imaginary* than *real* and *necessary* Ingredients to human Felicity.

How much, or *how little* a Fortune will content us, depends chiefly on our own Way of Thinking. Be this as it will, it should seem very proper before all Marriages, for both Parties to know

truly and fairly, what they have to *expect* on this Head, and
seriously to consider with themselves, whether it will be sufficient so far to answer their Desires, as to prevent future Mur-
murings and Anxieties, and prudently allow them to enjoy
Life as they intend. All *Deceit* herein should be *carefully
avoided,* we may otherwise impose on our selves, and ruin all
our future Felicity.

Sect. II. Unhappy Marriages are often occasioned from the Headstrong Motives of ungoverned Passion.

THE cool and considerate Views of *Interest,* have taken so
deep a Root even in very young Minds, that those *feverish
Marriages* are not very common; and we are, I think, now a
days, more liable to them in our Dotage than our Bloom.

An amorous Complexion, a lively Imagination, and a generous Temper, are so apt to be charm'd with an agreeable Person, the insinuating Accomplishments of Musick and Dancing,
un bon Grace, and a *Gaietè de Coeur,* that it is instantly transported, sighs, languishes, dies for Possession. In this *distempered*
Condition, and *amorous Fit* of Madness, his sanguine and
heated Imagination paints her out to him, in all the romantick
Lights of an *Arcadian Princess,* an *Angel Form,* and a *heavenly
Mind,* the *Pride of Nature,* and the *Joy of Man,* a Source of
immortal Pleasures, Raptures that will *never satiate, Bliss uninterrupted,* and *Transports too big for Expression.*—Bloated
with all these nonsensical Ideas or *Chimeras,* worked up to a
raging Fit of Enthusiasm, he falls down and worships this *Idol*
of his own intoxicated Brain, runs to her, talks Fustian and
Tragedy by wholesale. Miss blushes, looks down, admires his
Eloquence, pities the dying Swain, catches the Infection, and
consents, if *Papa* and *Mamma* will give theirs.

THE old People strike the *Bargain;* the young Ones are mad
and light-headed with those ravishing Scenes their warm Constitutions and distempered Fancies present to their View.

WELL, they are married, and have taken their Full of Love.

The young Spark's Rant is over, he finds his imaginary Goddess *meer Flesh and Blood* with the Addition of a *vain, affected, silly Girl;* and when his Theatrical Dress is off, she finds he was a *lying hot-brain'd Coxcomb.*

THUS come to their Senses, and the Mask thrown off, they look at one another like utter Strangers, and Persons just come out of a Trance; he finds by Experience he fell in Love with his own [no] Ideas, and she with her own Vanity. Thus pluckt from the soaring Heights of their warm and irregular Passions, they are vext at, and ashamed of themselves *first,* and heartily hate each other *afterwards.* From hence arise *Reproaches, Contradictions,* &c. Thus all their *fantastick Bliss* ends in *Shame* and *Repentance.*

IN serious Truth how can it be otherwise?

PASSIONS are extreamely transient and unsteady, and *Love,* with no other Support, will ever be short liv'd and fleeting. 'Tis a *Fire* that is *soon extinguished,* and where there is no solid Esteem and well cemented Friendship to *blow it up,* it rarely *lights* again, but from some accidental Impulses, by no Means to be depended on; which a Contrariety of Tempers, the Fatalities of Sickness, or the Frowns of Fortune, may, for ever, prevent, as Age most certainly will.

BESIDES, in Marriages of this Kind, there is neither *Time* nor *Coolness* sufficient, for fixing an Esteem and Friendship; and therefore the very *Foundations* for its *lasting* Happiness are wanting. May they follow, do you think? Alas how uncertain is that! and so many Probabilities on the contrary Side, that none surely but the most daring and *inconsiderate* People would run the Risque.

WHAT has been observed seems to point out, that a *blind,* a sudden and *intoxicating* Passion, has a natural Tendency, under its own Direction, to occasion *unhappy Marriages,* and produce Scenes of *Grief* and *Repentance.*

LET us, on the contrary, proceed with Deliberation and Circumspection. Let *Reason* and *Thought* be summoned before we engage in the Courtship of a Lady. Endeavour as much as possible, to stifle all those passionate and amorous Emotions, that wou'd *cloud* and *bribe* our Judgments. Let us *seriously* reflect, that Engagements of this Kind, are of the *greatest* Moment and Import to our future Happiness in Life. That Courtship brings on Marriage, and that makes all the Peace and Welfare of our Lives dependant on the Behaviour and Disposition of another; a Matter of the *utmost* Consequence, and of which we cannot well think too long or too much. Let not therefore our *Eyes* or *Passions* prevail with us, to barter away all that is truly valuable in our Existence for their Gratification.

SOME Women have infinite Art, being early bred to disguise and dissemble; yet by a skilful Attention, Calmness, and Impartiality, we may form a Judgment of their Characters in the main: Which we should endeavour to do, and compare them fairly with our own; see how they will *correspond:* Be rationally convinced of a Similitude in our Ways of Thinking, a *Harmony* in our Minds and Tempers, before we venture to change the Name of Mistress into that of Wife.

THUS let us deliberate, thus let us proceed, and thus arm our selves with Reason and Reflection in this great Affair. Lest by too much *Warmth* and *Precipitancy,* we draw those Miseries on our selves, which Repentance will neither assuage or remove.

HAVING now drove the *mercenary Herd* to their native Mines, and made evident their Unfitness for breathing the pure and generous Air of matrimonial Felicity; left the *Inamoratoes* to float in their Fool's Paradise with Novels and Romances; let us endeavour to fix our selves on the *true Basis* of conjugal Happiness, and see if we can hit upon the Path wherein an agreeable Companion, a steady Friend, and a good Wife, may be found.

AND this we must enter upon by a *prudent and judicious Courtship,* which as 'twas before observed, is laying the Foundation of *a happy Marriage.*

> *Sect. III. In our Addresses, let our Conduct be sincere, and Tempers undisguised; let us use no Arti-*

fices to cover or conceal our natural Frailties and
Imperfections; but be outwardly, what we really are
within, and appear such as we design stedfastly to
continue.

IN the gay Time of Courtship, it seems to be a general Practice with both Sexes, to conceal all personal Defects by every
Artifice of Dress, &c.

THIS is not so politick; and may be attended with future
Consequences very prejudicial. By so intimate an Union as that
of Marriage, all bodily Defects will soon be discovered; and as
Hypocrisy in the minutest Matters amongst Friends, is extreamly odious, those Defects will carry a Sting and Guilt with
them, to which perhaps we may be never reconciled. Whereas
had no Art been used for their Concealment, they might have
caused little or no Concern.

NOTHING to a generous Mind is more ungrateful, than any
Sort of *Imposition* from a Friend.

LOVE and Friendship are of so *nice* and *delicate* a Texture,
that *Disingenuity* in the smallest Matters should be avoided.

THESE Remarks may appear but of little Importance, to
People of a coarse and unpolished Taste, but I am persuaded
they will have their Weight with those of a contrary Turn.

FOR my own Part, I wou'd, if any thing, be rather *less* careful and exact in my personal Appearance, *before* than *after*
Marriage, because the difficulty of *raising* an Affection, is not
so great, as that of *preserving* it; as every little personal Em-
bellishment may be serviceable in the former Case, so it undoubtedly will in the latter.—But the Care of our Persons, will
come under a more particular Observation in my second Letter;
and tho' 'tis seldom neglected *before,* yet 'tis often so notori-
ously *after* Marriage, that I believe many unhappy Ones are
caused by it.

HOWEVER it be as to the Spruceness and Decoration of
our *Persons,* I must affirm it a most dangerous Folly, an Imposition highly culpable, to mask our *Tempers,* and appear what

we really are not; to exhibit a *forged Draught* of our Minds and Dispositions in order to win the Affections.

I am really at a Loss to judge, whether the Absurdity or Iniquity of such a Scheme be the greatest.

Is this Courtship? Is this laying a Foundation for our future Happiness? Monstrous! But this is sometimes, too often the Case with both Sexes. 'Tis really amazing how People can be so *preposterously* wicked, in a Correspondence of the most *sacred* and tender Kind, in the Consequences of which, all the future Happiness of their Lives may depend. How *stupid,* thus to study our own Ruin, by the infamous Deception of One, we choose for the Partner of our Joys and our Cares, the Companion of our Days and our Nights! How *shocking* to set out with Fraud, and proceed with Deceit in such solemn Engagements! How *shallow* is the Cunning of such inconsiderate Minds! Must not all the Pleasures of Marriage be unanimous and inseparable? Do they not flow from *real* and *unaffected* Loveliness? Can we think the Cheat will lie long concealed in a Society so intimate? When Time and Experience unmasks our *assumed* Appearances, shows us in our *native Colours,* and *exposes* that Reality we have so industriously laboured to *cover;* can we expect Love and Esteem from any One whom we have so *shamefully over-reached* and ensnared? Surely *no.* On the contrary we shall entail on our selves, *certain* Indignation, and *lasting* Contempt.

We have raised and supported an Affection by *false Appearances;* when those are seen thro', as most certainly they will be, what Title have we to Love or Friendship? NONE, and consequently no Prospect of social Happiness.

LET us, my Friend, on the contrary, observe a *religious Sincerity,* appear in our *Native Characters,* undisguised and unaffected. If under those we gain Esteem and Friendship, our Prospects of maintaining them, are as secure, as our own Minds and Dispositions may be lasting.—Let us be *outwardly,* what we really are *within,* and appear in such a Character as we stedfastly design to continue. Hereby we shall lay a strong Foundation for our future Happiness in Marriage.

Sect. IV. Let our Manner of conversing with a Mistress be void of fulsome Flattery, and the ridiculous Bombast of Novels and Romances.

IT was an Objection, you may remember, made against Matrimony; that the Education of young Ladies, gave such a trifling Turn to their Tempers, and Manner of Thinking, as rendred them unfit for the rational Pleasures of Society and Conversation.

ALLOWING this to be true, and in general but too true it really is, how prejudicial and fatal must *Flattery* be to such? And how completely must that Foppish Rant, called *Gallantry,* poison their understandings, and tend to destroy the Possibility of inspiring them with Sentiments of Reason and good Sense.

BY such a Proceeding, a Man naturally forms a young Creature, for a *vain* and *insipid Companion;* and if by that Means, he finds Matrimony to be an irksome and disagreeable Scene, what Wonder, and where does the Blame lye?

NOTHING more naturally carries us beyond our selves, and puffs us up with an over-rating Opinion of our own Merit; swells every Appearance of Desert; so strongly intrenches our Frailties and Imperfections, that Reason and Reflection are too much enervated to dislodge them; nothing more effectually spoils our Tempers, and corrupts our Judgments, than FLATTERY: It renders us positive in our Ignorance, and impatient of Contradiction.

THEN that Hodge-Podge of Nonsense, which many call *Making Love,* is using a Woman to such intemperate and frothy Sallies of Fancy, such romantick and unmeaning Impressions; that sober Thought, and plain good sense, are foreign to her Taste; and an Entertainment, to which being not used, she has no *Goût* or Relish.

WHAT an agreeable and pretty Sort of a Companion, what

a comfortable Wife do we hereby contrive for our selves? And how ingeniously do we thus labour to make her a positive and empty, a conceited and fantastical Simpleton? thus modelled, we soon come to despise her, and curse our Marriage.

BUT some say this is the most certain and expeditious Way to gain the Affections of a young Lady, and that a Man would make but a dull and heavy Figure in their Eyes without it, and finds his Attacks very unsuccessful.

This may be true with some, and 'tis no less a Mark of *Merit,* than a Point of great *good Fortune,* to meet with Insensibility from them.—

BUT 'tis far from being so with all; there are young Ladies, and many with whom I am persuaded a Man would find himself more acceptable and successful by a contrary Method: And to such only should every Man apply himself, for the valuable and lasting Felicities of a Conjugal Life.

If we allow a Man may make a more speedy Conquest by Fustian and Flattery, yet whoever, methinks, reflects on the Consequences, should be convinced, that it must be fatal to the future Repose and Tranquility of his Life.—Let Coxcombs boast of such Triumphs, but Men of Sense will ever despise and shun them.

> *Sect. V. Let us my Friend, on the contrary, use her we design for a Wife and Companion, to the Conversations of sober Reason and good Sense: Endeavour by every probable Method, to inspire her with the Sentiments of a rational Esteem, a generous and stedfast Friendship for us.—*

HEREBY we have great Probability, and well grounded Expectations of securing to our selves an agreeable and entertaining Companion.

BY seasonably introducing into Conversation useful Subjects on human Life and Characters; by making solid and practical Reflections thereon, and engaging the Attention by a polite, an easy and lively Manner; we shall correct and strengthen the Judgment, enlarge the Faculties of the Mind, and raise the Soul to a free and generous Way of Thinking; drive out and extirpate, that childish, that little narrow-spirited Way of Thinking, that mean and injudicious Distrust; those low and pitiful Artifices, and that lurking Sort of Cunning, which is too much the Characteristick of many Women, is the Detestation of every great Mind, and the Abhorrence of all ingenuous Spirits.

THERE is no Friendship or Confidence to be had with such *dirty, tricking, low Minds;* they are an utter Privation to all social Happiness, and when carried into a married Life, are insuperable Obstacles to its Welfare.

MANY proper Opportunities may likewise be found, for recommending the Perusal of elegant and improving Books, which by a good Choice and a judicious Taste, will have a very beneficial Effect on the Mind and Understanding.

BUT in all this, great Delicacy and a good judgment is very essential; to distinguish nicely and to manage with Discretion, are highly necessary. We should be careful to cover our good Intentions with so engaging an Artifice, as by no Means to shock the Passions; render every Thing as a Matter rather of Choice and Taste than Prescription.

YOU will not, I am persuaded, so greatly misapprehend my Meaning, under these Reflections, as to imagine I am pleading up for what is commonly understood by a *learned* and *bookish Character* in a young Lady; such a One as Mr. *Pope* points out, a

> "Wise Fool! with Pleasures too refin'd to please,
> "With too much Thinking to have common Thought."

I am far from designing any such ridiculous Extreams. Nothing in Nature is, I think, more odious and contemptible than a *female Pedant,* a formal, a conceited and affected Wit; whose Brain is loaded with a Heap of indigested Stuff, and is eternally throwing up her confused Nonsense, in hard Words ill pronounced, jumbled Quotations misapplyed, and a Jargon of

Common-Places; in order to let you know she is a Woman of Reading; whereby she convinces you, she has taken a great deal of Pains to render herself a Fool of the first Class, and of the most irreclaimable Kind.

—THE Barking of a Lap-dog is not more grating to the Ear, than the Gibberish of their impertinent Clacks; and the Chatter of a Parrot infinitely more entertaining. In short, such Women are the Mountebanks of their own, the Dread and Contempt of our Sex.

BUT must these jingling Pretenders to Wit and Sense, exclude us from the delightful Harmony, the amiable Conversation of a modest and unaffected Fair One, in whom a good Understanding is joined with a good Mind.

HOW engaging are the Graces of such a Character! How insinuating are its Charms! How imperceptibly does it win on the Mind! What a Flow of tender Sentiments, it diffuses thro' the Heart! Calms each rougher Passion, and swells the Breast with those exquisite Emotions that rise above all Description.

THUS to imitate, and if possible to equal this Character it is, that I wou'd have Conversation and Books tend. And I cannot but think, if thus adapted and directed, they wou'd have a great Efficacy towards it.

HOW great a Prospect, and what reasonable Hopes of Happiness, there must be with such a Companion, requires surely no Arguments to prove.

But the Truth is, we are either actuated by other Motives than a Regard to and Desire of social Happiness, or that we are hurried thro' Courtship, by an intemperate and unthinking Warmth: Hereby our Conversation is rendred either Designing or Ridiculous.

NOR is it less necessary to inspire our Mistress with the Sentiments of a rational Esteem, of a stedfast and generous Friendship.

IT has been already observed, that Love considered meerly as a Passion, will naturally have but a short Duration; like all other Passions 'tis changeable, transient and accidental. But

Friendship and Esteem are derived from Principles of Reason and Thought, and when once truly fixed in the Mind, are lasting Securities of an Attachment to our Persons and Fortunes; participate with, and refine all our Joys; simpathize with, and blunt the Edge of every adverse Occurrence.—In vain should I endeavour to make an Elogium on true *Friendship,* in any Measure equal to its sublime and exalted Value: There is no Good in Life comparable to it; neither are any, or all of its other Enjoyments worth desiring without it. 'Tis the Crown to all our Felicities; the Glory, and I think, the Perfection of our Natures. Life's a Wilderness without a Friend, and all its gilded Scenes but barren and tasteless.

HERE have I a copious Subject, to reflect on the many false Friendships there are in the World!—How few real and sincere ones!—How much talk'd of, how little meant, and less understood! No *generous* and *disinterested* Feelings of Mind, (the Essence of Friendship) can possibly display themselves, whilst *mercenary* Views, and *selfish Designs* are the Principles of Action. But this is a Digression:

HOWEVER it be in *common Life,* there cannot certainly be any steady or lasting Happiness in a *married One,* where a mutual Esteem and Friendship, of the strongest and noblest Kind, does not subsist. Let it therefore be the sacred Business of our Courtship to cultivate One, and on no Account engage our selves in Wedlock without it.

I know of no Method, more likely to promote and secure it, than by being prepossessed with it our selves.

THERE is a Sort of attractive Force in similar Minds, as there is in Matter.

> *Great Minds by Instinct to each other turn,*
> *Demand Alliance, and in Friendship burn*
> *Mr.* Addison's *Campaign.*

'TIS a common Saying, that *Love begets Love;* that is not always true. But where there is any Similitude of Minds, *Sentiments of Friendship, will beget Friendship.*

LET us then take every Opportunity of testifying our Esteem and Friendship: Court the Understanding, the Principles of Thought, and conciliate them to our own.

HEREBY we shall as it were enter into the Soul, and take Possession of all its Powers; this should be the Ground-work of Love, this will be a vital Principal to that, and make our Concord as lasting as our Minds are unchangeable.

THIS Subject should be often that of our Conversation; and we should particularly endeavour to fix *right* and *just* Notions concerning it. To inspire a certain Greatness of Mind, that *scorns the least Falshood* or *Treachery;* which no Distress can possibly shake, and which no Prosperity can ever relax. We should endeavour to *fire the Soul* (if you will allow me the Expression) with a Sort of *heroick Enthusiasm,* that no *Decoys* of Pleasure, no *Terrors* of Pain should ever be capable of extinguishing, and rather to dare *Matrydom* than *Apostacy.*

THUS should we fortify the Principles of Friendship, in her we choose for a Wife, and, by every possible Method in our Power, fix the Root deep in her Soul. For unless both Minds *burn* with this *noble* and *essential Flame,* our Happiness in Marriage will have but a weak Basis, and a very slender Tye; every little Flurry of Humour, every little Blast of Adversity, will go near to overset the Bark of our Felicity: We shall at best toss about without a Rudder and without a Compass.

BUT a fix'd Principle of Friendship will steady and secure us, and we shall glide o'er the Waves of Life, with Serenity and Confidence; prepared for Rocks and Quicksands, with unshaken Courage, and an equal Mind.—Thus chearful, happy, and resigned, steer a virtuous and invariable Course of Affection, 'till the Port of Mortality puts an End to our Voyage, having already anticipated that Heaven in each other's Love and Friendship, which we then go more fully to possess.

THUS, Sir, I have given you my Sentiments, in the first Place, on the *Motives* of *Interest* and of *Passion,* which when they become the leading and prevailing Ones in our matrimonial Schemes, whatever other Ends we may gain by them, appear to me (considered as the ruling Principles of Action) so unlikely to produce the real Felicity of that *Union,* as rather to be subversive of, and destructive to every social Pleasure, and the essential Foundation of *conjugal Tranquility.*

I have in the next Place *attempted* to lay before you, such a general Plan for our Conduct in Courtship, as will, I apprehend, if judiciously and honestly pursued, fix so reasonable and probable a Prospect of Happiness in Marriage, as to render that Scene of Life by no Means unworthy the Approbation and Choice of a wife and thinking Man.

NOR, on Examination, do I perceive any Thing in my Scheme too refined, or any ways impracticable, to a Man that unites in himself a *good Head* with a *good Heart;* a Character, under which an improving and grateful Experience has testified you to my Acquaintance and Friendship.

VICIOUS Minds and coarse Understandings, might, perhaps, laugh at these Things as chimerical, and too fine spun for Practice. Whatever your Opinion may be, I rest assured, that neither Goodness of Judgment, nor Delicacy of Taste will be wanting to direct it.

YOU will consider it as the private Testimony of one Friend, to the Request of another. The Privacy and Indulgence therefore of a friendly Correspondence, will secure me from any of those severe or ill-natured Criticisms, to which publick Writers are always exposed. My Vanity does as little prompt me to seek *Fame* in that way, as my Capacity unfits me for it.

BE this Declaration sufficient.

I shall only add, that in my present Way of thinking, whenever I am inclined to pay my Courtship to any Lady, it will be very much in the Way I have mentioned: I say, in some such Manner.

IF I am unsuccessful, I shall have the Consolation to think, there was not a requisite *Harmony* in our Minds and Tempers

for a mutual Affection: If successful, I shall willingly and joy-
fully build the future Happiness of my Life on this *Basis*.

  I am, &c.

Postscript

You may perhaps think me guilty of an Omission in the foregoing Reflections, in having said nothing with regard to the
Consent of Parents. I shall therefore deliver you my Opinion in
relation thereto as concisely as possible.

THAT there is a certain *Authority* lodged in Parents over
their Children, and in consequence thereof, a certain *Obedience*
due from Children to their Parents, are Truths derived from
Nature, and founded in Reason, and have had the Concurrence
of all Ages and all Nations.

History gives us Instances of this Obedience paid to Parents,
in some of the most illustrious Characters of Antiquity; and
even in respect of Marriage, as you may remember in the Life
of Cyrus the Great.

WE have likewise many past and living Examples, where the
Authority of Parents over their Children in Marriages, has been
most tyrannically and fatally exerted.

WITHOUT entering into a Train of Reasoning, I may venture to take it for granted;

THAT no parental Authority, that is *repugnant* to the Dictates of *Reason* and *Virtue,* or (which is the same Thing) the
moral Happiness of our Natures, is any ways binding on Children.

To marry without a *Union of Minds,* a Sympathy of Affections, a mutual Esteem and Friendship for each other, is
contrary to Reason and Virtue, the Moral Happiness of our
Natures.

IT follows therefore that no parental Authority, thus to make
ourselves unhappy by marrying, is any ways binding on Children.

TO marry with a Union of Minds, &c. being therefore agreeable to Reason and Virtue, and the Moral Happiness of our Natures; 'tis evident that Parents have no Authority, founded in Truth or Nature, to hinder their Children from so doing.

THO' these Propositions, and the Inferences drawn from them, are, I believe, just and true; yet Children should undoubtedly be *extreamly tender* in thwarting the Wills of their Parents: Should be *very careful,* that their *Passions* do not *blind,* or their *Caprice mislead* them: Should with great Calmness and Impartiality reason with themselves: Appeal to their Parents, with great Deference and Humility: Consult with some wise and unbiassed Friend: Desire their Interposition. In short, do every Thing in their Power to convince and persuade: and nothing but a manifest and conscious Violation of Reason and their real Happiness, should force them to oppose or disobey the Will of their Parents; especially to such as have ever behaved kindly, carefully and friendly to them: They have the *greatest Authority* over Children, that one Mortal *can have* over another.

How far it may be our *Interest* to obey or not, is another Consideration. What has been said on the Article of mercenary Views, may serve to determine us.

I conclude with the Lines of an anonymous Author,

> *Let no dire Threats, no kind Entreaties move,*
> *To give thy Person where thou canst not love.*

Letter II

Having laid out for our selves a general Plan of Conduct in *Courtship,* and considered it as the Foundation of our Happiness in *Marriage;* it now remains for us to erect the Superstructure of our Felicity in that State which we shall endeavour to do by the following Method of Behaviour therein.

Sect. I. Prerogative and Dominion in Marriage, are often Matters of Dispute in Conversations; but more frequently the Causes of Animosity and Uneasiness to the Parties themselves.

The Customs of different Nations have carried, and the Sentiments of many People do carry these Points *much too high*, and with a Severity as unreasonable as unjustifiable.

WHATEVER *tyrannick* and *arbitrary Power* the Laws of a Country may give a Man over his Wife, or should they do the reverse, there is no such Kind of Dominion derived from *Reason* or *Nature*.

MARRIAGE, in my Sense of it, is a certain voluntary and mutual Contract between the Sexes, the End or Design of which is, or should be, their joint Happiness.

'Tis therefore absurd and ridiculous to suppose or conclude, that either Party do thereby consent or bind themselves over to an *imperious* or *tyrannical sway*.

It follows therefore that Marriage, does neither by the Laws of Nature or Reason, give either Party a tyrannick and arbitrary Power over the other; and that the Exercise of such a Power, is contrary to the Will and Happiness of any rational Being; and must in consequence render a matrimonial Life uncomfortable and miserable.

To me there seems no other Standard of Obedience, than REASON and PRUDENCE; in which I am supported by the learned and judicious Mr. *Woolaston*,[3] who says, "I would have them live so far upon the Level, as (according to my constant Lesson) to be governed *both* by *Reason*. If the Man's Reason be the stronger, his Knowledge and Experience greater, (as it is commonly supposed to be) the Woman will be obliged on that Score to pay a Deference, and submit to him."

This certainly is to put the Affair on a right Footing.

Now the foregoing Observations on Courtship presuppose, and indeed plainly determine, a superior Degree of Knowledge

[3] Rel. of Nat. Delin.

and Understanding in the Man: Consequently derives to him that Deference and Submission which is assigned by Mr. *Woolaston.*

REALLY *Nature* and the Circumstances of human Life, seem to design for Man that Superiority, and to invest him with a directing Power in the more difficult and important Affairs of Life.

WHERE this superior Capacity is not fixt in the Man, and that incumbent Subordination made a Rule of Conduct by the Woman, I should greatly mistrust the Happiness of their Condition. It must certainly break in upon our Scheme of Felicity, which supposes the former, and prepares the most probable Means for the latter, by fixing a Friendship and Esteem in the Woman, for the Mind and Understanding of the Man.

This will naturally give a Veneration for his Sentiments, and a persuasive Force to his Arguments: For where we esteem, and know we are esteemed, we are easily won and prone to Submission; more especially where we have a good Opinion, and a Sort of Reverence for the Understanding and Good Sense of the Person who calmly and kindly Reasons with us, and who we are convinced, makes our Welfare his supream and ruling Concern; this, by my Scheme, the Female must of course be conscious to before Marriage, and will be so after, if we continue in the same Road of friendly and affectionate Behaviour to her; if we are tender in opposing her Inclinations; if we reason with Delicacy, Coolness and Temper, supported by a Solidity and Strength of Judgment.

ALL this is no less the *Duty,* than the *Prudence* of a married Man.

If on the contrary, he is puffed up with extravagant and rediculous Notions of his Prerogative; fond of showing and exerting on every little Occasion a formal and magisterial Authority, to which *little Minds* are very subject: No wonder then, if Contention and Animosity are often their matrimonial Entertainment.

A Man of Sense and Breeding, will be as it were superior, without seeming to know it; and support his Influence with so great a Delicacy, that his Wife shall ever seem to be his Equal, make use of a thousand polite Methods even to elevate her Character. What an amiable and engaging Scene must such a Couple exhibit! How *firm* their *Union!* And how *harmonious* their Lives!

BUT how often where Courtship has been ill managed, and Marriage worse directed, do we see the *Reverse* of that *lovely Scene?*

WHAT *Embroils* about *Trifles!* What *rude* and *shocking* Expressions to each other! What *impertinent* and *silly* Disputes about Prerogatives! till they are in such a Ferment, as to be ready to cuff each other. In short, for want of Delicacy, Judgment and Temper, 'tis the constant Struggle of their Lives, to try, as the Vulgar Proverb has it, *who shall wear the Breeches*.

To conclude: Let us, who aim at being *truly Happy* in Marriage, take the proper Steps in our Courtship for convincing the Lady, that we are best capable of directing and judging in the important Concerns of Life; and after Marriage, use the proper Methods to ascertain that Privilege.

Sect. II. All litigious Wranglings, and capricious Contentions, should be carefully avoided.

A LITTLE Observation and Reflection on the common Scenes of Matrimony, may supply us with many Instances, to show how much these trivial Jarrings spoil the Harmony, and interrupt the Felicities of it.

WHAT Fermentations and Heats often arise from breaking of China, disordering a Room, Dinner not being ready at a precise Hour, and a Thousand other such impertinent *Bagatelles*. I should also desire all the Train of fretful Aspirations, as *Pshaw, Pho,* &c, to be discarded. Give up Trifles, and not carry our Disputes on them too far. ——It would be endless to enumerate these insignificant Fopperies of Contention; my Meaning may be easily conceived from the few I have mentioned.

BUT trifling as these Things may be in themselves, 'tis too notorious, they often occasion such *Feuds* and feverish *Animosities* amongst married People, as frequently give a *bitter Tincture* to, and discompose many Hours of their Lives; and are sometimes of so bad a Consequence, as to inflame their Minds with such *Spleen* and *Distaste,* that *irreparable* Breaches are thereby opened.

THE reproving each other before Company, and *sparring* as it were together, is mighty wrong, and very unpolite; it irritates themselves, and makes their Company very uneasy.

THESE SORT of matrimonial Squabbles, put one in Mind of a little venomous Insect they have in the *West-Indies,* like a Gnat, who, when they bite, create a great Itching, which if much scratched, raises an Inflammation so malignant, that a Leg has been lost by it, and sometimes, Mortifications ensue, that have been attended with Death.

THUS it often fares with these little Tumors in Matrimony; if we scratch and work them up with *Wranglings* and *Capriciousness,* they may come to that *Malignancy,* as to cut off many of our Pleasures, and at last give a *mortal Wound* to our Felicity.

LET us therefore determine to shun these whimsical Follies, and guard our selves with Prudence and Temper, so as not to be surprised or unhinged by them; follow Mr. *Pope's* Advice on another Subject.

> *At every Trifle scorn to take Offence,*
> *It always shows great* Pride, *or little* Sense.[4]

People of low Education and mean Understandings, conceive not the unamiableness of these rude Indiscretions: They rub on thro' thick and thin, with a mechanical Sort of Enjoyment, insensible to those Delicacies, which have a material Influence on Persons of good Breeding, and superior Sense.

4 Essay on Criticism

> *Sect. III. We should on the contrary, cultivate Dispositions of reciprocal Condescension, and such a Uniformity in our Tempers, that the Pleasures of One, may be the Pleasures of Both.*

COMPLACENCY of Mind, an Ambition to please each other, and oblige by all the little Turns of Behaviour, that so frequently will occur to a polite and well disposed Inclination, must have a wonderful good Effect to support our Affections, secure mutual Esteem and Friendship. Minds of any refined Cast, have an exquisite Relish for these soothing and expressive Marks of Tenderness and they can't fail of meeting with a most grateful Reception.

WE should make it our mutual Study, to render our selves agreeable and amiable, by all the *innocent Arts* of Invention, and every laudable Stratagem of Conduct: Remembering that wise and comprehensive Remark of old *Ben. Johnson's, "That Love comes by Chance, but is kept by Art."* Which should be wrote with indelible Characters on the Memory of every married Person.

THE Thought is very wittily expressed by the ingenious Dr. *Swift,* in Regard to the Ladies: *That they lay Traps to catch Men's Hearts, but make no Cages to keep them.*

I must add another Quotation, from that valuable Author, last named, 'tis so very *a propos* to the Subject we are on.

> *"Let Prudence with good Nature strive,*
> *"To keep the Flame of Love alive;*
> *"Then, come old Age whene'er it will,*
> *"Your Friendship shall continue still:*
> *"Thus a mutual, gentle Fire,*
> *"Shall never but with Life expire."* [5]

THE little Oversights and Sallies of Frailty, to which human Nature is ever liable, and from which the most perfect Characters are not exempt, should be passed over and die un-noticed.

[5] *Strephon* and *Chloe*

WE should be ready to plead in Favour of each other in such Cases, and throw a Veil of Kindness and good humoured Condescension over them.

NOR is it of less Consequence to our Peace and Contentment, that there should be such a *Uniformity* in our Tempers, that the *Pleasures of one,* may be the *Pleasures of Both.*

How often do we see the Reverse of this create great Uneasiness amongst married People? The Husband despises and ridicules the Tastes of his Wife: She abominates and censures his. Indeed, but too frequently both are culpable. Be that as it will, 'tis a bad Sign, and gives a shrewd Suspicion, they cannot be very happy with each other.

AMONGST those who have a real Esteem and Friendship for one another, there will, strictly speaking, be no Separation of Pleasures: For tho' one Party does not actually share in the others' Pleasure; yet they will in Effect do it by the Force of Benevolence, and be pleased, because the other is so, whether they relish the particular Cause or not.

IN such Pleasures as 'tis proper and prudent for both to share, they should, I think, endeavour to unite their tastes.

THE more unexceptionably that People in a married Life make the Pleasures of One become the Pleasures of Both, the more uniform and compleat will their joint Happiness be.

THIS alone seems to me a very full and sufficient Reason, for our Regard to the Precept laid down.

Sect. IV. Modesty and Decency in our Conduct and Persons, both in Publick and in Private, should most strictly be observed.

I DON'T know any Thing in the matrimonial Life, more *essentially necessary* towards its Happiness and Welfare, than a *punctual* and *invariable* Conformity to this important Regulation of our Conduct: To the Neglect and counteracting whereof, I impute more unhappy Marriages, than to any other Fault or Folly whatsoever.

A Mind insensible to the sacred Charms of *unaffected Modesty,* and the elegant Pleasures of *Decency,* must surely be lost to every worthy, every noble, and every honourable Sentiment; must be *brutalized* to the greatest Degree, and have thrown off all that is truly lovely in the human Character.

THERE is a certain *Purity* and *Decorum* to be preserved in our most retired Pleasures. 'Tis no extraordinary Paradox, that a Man may himself debauch his own Wife; and a Woman harlotize with her own Husband. —But this Subject must be touched with great Nicety; therefore I shall only add, that even our *most unobserved* Behaviour should carry with it such a Spirit of Refinement, as to prevent that vulgar and libidinous Degeneracy, which will infallibly blunt the Edge of our Joys, and in the End pall our Relish.

WE should likewise behave with a *modest Delicacy* in publick.

IN the *really well-bred Part* of the World, a great *Elegancy,* and a *polished Neatness* of Conduct, in married People towards each other, is *inviolably* preserved. Nothing is a more evident Mark of a rustick and coarse Education, than a Want of this Discernment and polite Carriage.

ALL frothy Tendernesses and amorous Boilings-over, are Insults on and Afronts to Company. What Entertainment is our Love, and are our Passions, to People who do not feel the one, nor are to gratify the other? What a preposterous Regale are our Dalliances to such?

We may put down these cooing Doves for ill-bred Fools, and very much suspect their Sincerity and Happiness.

TRUE Love, and a well settled Affection, has none of this *luscious* and *nauseous Treacle* in it. 'Tis a fine, pure Balsamick, that softens the Heart, and flows with an imperceptible Tide of silent and interior Movements.

LET then all these doating and luxurious Follies be banished from our Behaviour, and in their Room be substituted, a *decent,* a *genteel,* and *easy Carriage,* towards each other.

Franklin's grave in Christ Church graveyard, Philadelphia

BESIDES all this, a Decency and Care of our Persons is to be added.

'Tis surprizing, tho' but too common to see (amongst both Sexes) many, who before Marriage were very assiduous, in the Adorning and Neatness of their Persons, that afterwards grow negligent and highly culpable by the Reverse: Which Inattention and Remissness, I verily believe, is often one of the first and most effectual Methods to cool the Affections, and estrange the Hearts of many a Couple. And herein, according to the most impartial Observations I have made, the Ladies are most blameable.

THAT just Remark (in page 35) of Ben. Johnson's, and Dean Swift's witty Saying, which I quoted under the former Section, are very applicable here.

MANY more judicious Authorities I might add, to impress the great Prudence and Necessity of this Oeconomy and Cleanliness of Person and Dress after Marriage; for which, the inimitable SPECTATORS, TATLERS, and GUARDIANS, are among others great and zealous Patrons. There is an admirable Letter of the very ingenious Dean *Swift's*, to a new married young Lady, in which this very Thing is warmly recommended: The whole of it is wrote with so much judgment, good Sense, and fine Spirit, and so well adapted to my Design, that I shall give you a Copy of it at the Close.

To a Man of any Delicacy, and even Moderate Neatness, nothing certainly is more odious and ungrateful, than a *slatternly* and *uncleanly* Woman: 'Tis enough to quell his strongest Passions, and damp every fond and tender Emotion: 'Tis vastly more so in a Wife, than a Stranger, (for as to *meer Person,* the Keenness of Inclination is (I suppose) generally less *after* than *before* full Possession). Therefore a *slovenly* and *unfragrant* One, in a Wife, must naturally run a great Risque of weakening, if not extinguishing Desire. Besides 'tis an Insult upon a Man's Taste, an Affront to his Senses, and bullying him to his Nose.

THIS Negligence and Dirtiness of Person, (if we expect or desire a Man to love us at the same time) is taxing him with the

Want of his Senses, with the Taste and Appetite of a Hog, whose Joy is Filth.

LET us survey the Morning Dress of some Women.

DOWN Stairs they come, pulling up their ungarter'd, dirty Stockings—Slip-shod, with naked Heels peeping out—No Stays or other decent Conveniency, but all *Flip Flop*—A Sort of a Clout thrown about the Neck, without Form or Decency—A tumbled, discoloured Mob, or Night Cap, half on, and half off, with the frowsy Hair, hanging in sweaty Ringlets, staring like *Medusa* with her Serpents—Shrugging up her Petticoats, that are sweeping the Ground, and scarce ty'd on,—Hands unwashed —Teeth furr'd—and Eyes crusted:—But I beg your Pardon, I'll go no farther with this sluttish Picture, which I am afraid has already turned your Stomach. If the *Copy*, and but an Imperfect one it is, be so shocking to us, what think you must the *Original* be to the poor Wretch her Husband, who, perhaps, for some Hours every Day in the Week, has the comfortable Sight and Odour of this Tatterdemalion. God help his Stomach! This is the real Pourtrait of many married Women, and the piteous Case of many a poor Soul of a husband; unless when happily some Stranger is expected, then Madam takes care to appear clean, and thereby convinces her Husband, she is more anxious to please a Stranger than the Man who has chosen her as his Companion for Life.

EXCUSE my Prolixity and Warmth on this unsavoury Article: I know your Temper, and my own corresponds with it. I am convinced this want of Decency and Cleanliness, is the original Source of many Peoples Unhappiness in Marriage.

A constant Care and Study to preserve the *OEconomy* and *Sweetness* of Dress and Person, must be of great Service to support Love and Esteem in Wedlock.

I don't hereby intend or mean Foppery or Finery, but that Neatness and Cleanliness, which neither is nor ought to be ashamed of seeing or being seen by any Body.

A Wife that is desirous of maintaining herself in the Affections of a Man of Sense and Spirit, should take as much Care of the Neatness of her Person, as if she was to be every Day a Bride; and whoever neglects this Conduct, must blame themselves, if their Husbands grow cool and indifferent; for it has a natural Tendency to make a Man so. It debases the Character of a Wife, and renders her cheap and unlovely.

SUFFER me yet to detain you with some Extracts from Dean Swift's Poem, intitled, *Strephon* and *Chloe;* whose judicious and sprightly Sentiments will in some Measure make you Amends for the Heaviness of mine. He says,

> *Fair* Decency, *celestial Maid*
> *Descend from Heav'n to Beauty's Aid.*
> *Tho' Beauty may beget Desire,*
> *'Tis* thou *must fan the Lover's Fire.*
> *For Beauty, like supream Dominion,*
> *Is best supported by Opinion:*
> *If* Decency *brings no Supplies,*
> Opinion *falls and* Beauty *dies.*
> *Authorities both old and recent,*
> *Direct that Women should be decent,*
> *And from their Spouse each Blemish hide,*
> *More than from all the World beside.*
> *Unjustly all our Nymphs complain,*
> *Their Empire holds so short a Reign,*
> *Is after Marriage lost so soon,*
> *It hardly holds the Honey Moon:*
> *For if they keep not what they caught,*
> *It is entirely their own Fault;*
> *They take Possession of the Crown,*
> *And then throw all their Weapons down.*
> *Though by the Politicians Scheme,*
> *Whoe'er arrives at Pow'r supream,*
> *Those Arts by which at first they gain it,*
> *They still must practise to maintain it.*

To conclude, let us at all Times avoid every Thing that is really uncomely; and let not our Familiarities run into the Extreams of a vulgar Rudeness and an unpolite Behaviour: Be as far removed from a stiff Formality, as an irregular Looseness of Conduct.

THUS we shall support that Dignity in our own Characters, and that Respect for each other, as will derive to us both Honour and Happiness.

> *Sect. V. Each Person should be so duly attentive to their respective Province of Management, as to conduct it with the utmost Prudence and Discretion in their Power.*

MARRIAGE, or an Union of the Sexes, tho' it be in it self one of the smallest Societies, is the original Fountain from whence the greatest and most extensive Governments have derived their Beings.

'Tis a monarchical one, having Reason for its Legislator and Prince: An Authority more noble and sublime than any other State can boast of.

THIS Maxim, which reaches all Governments and Societies, is not less relative to the matrimonial One; to wit, *That the Good of the Whole is maintained by a Harmony and Correspondence of its several Parts to their respective Ends and Relations.*

From this Comparison many demonstrative Arguments might be drawn, to illustrate and enforce what has been advanced in the first Section of this Letter.

THAT as Prince *Reason* (to carry on the Similitude) must act by a Sort of Vicegerency or Deputation, and that Honour, by the Rules of Justice, and for the Good of the Whole, ought undoubtedly to fall on the most capable and experienced, which by our Scheme the Man will be— All Rebellion against this Vicegerent, whilst he acts in the Character of his Prince *Reason,* is extreamly wrong and undutiful; has a fatal Tendency to subvert the Tranquility and Order of the matrimonial State:— But we will leave these Politicks, and come to the Subject in hand.

We just now observed, that the Well-being of Marriage, as of all other Societies, arose from a Harmony and Correspondence of its several Parts to their respective Ends and Relations.

THIS fundamental Truth has been hitherto considered chiefly as it relates to the *internal Characters* of the Conjugates: We shall now apply it to those practical ones which arise from the Management of *Interest* or *Fortune,* and what is called *Housewifery.*

THAT Part of Management which belongs to the preserving our Interest, or improving our Fortune, usually falls, and very properly, on the Man. And 'tis unquestionably incumbent on him, if he be a Man of Estate, and independant on any Business, to regulate his Equipage, his private and family Expences, according to the Income of his Fortune; and 'tis certainly a Point of Prudence not to live *quite up* to *that;* but to lay up a Fund, to which he may have recourse in any of those adverse Occurrences to which the most exalted Stations are liable, as also to provide for younger Children which he has, or may have. He should not confide too much in Stewards or Agents, but inspect his property so much at least, as to be able to judge of their Conduct.—He should not be indolently content with the formal Delivery of Accounts, but examine them, know why and wherefore he pays, and for what he is paid.

How fatal the contrary to all this has been to many Gentlemen of Fortune, and their Families, is so unhappily attested by many tragical Examples, as should, I think, be prevailing Arguments to enforce what has been said.

IF our Fortunes are thrown out in any Schemes of Business for Improvement, our Expences and Manner of Living should be proportionable to our Fund and Prospects of Success: And as the latter most commonly depend on Attention and Prudence, we should constantly govern our selves by them to the best of our Abilities. Avoid being engaged in any such precarious Schemes as by being abortive may utterly ruin us. As the Merchants say, we should not venture all on one Bottom, so as that the common Accidents of Winds and Weather may totally sink our Fortune. All our Engagements should be preceded by

Fore-thought and Discretion; And in very important Ones 'twou'd be but just and prudent to inform and consult a Wife, whose intimate Concern therein does, I think, demand it; she may be capable of giving us Advice that may be very serviceable; it will at least prepare her to bear, with us, any unfortunate Consequences that may attend us; and that is a very good Reason for her being informed.

To conclude, No Ridiculous Vanity or foolish Ambition should suffer the Husband or Wife, in their Dress, Furniture, or whole Way of Life, to exceed their Income or Fortune.

Their Appearance and Expences, should neither degenerate into *Sordidness,* nor run into a *Wild Extravagance.*

THAT particular Part of Management called Housewifery, belongs to the Woman, and we shall comprise it under these three Divisions.

A PRUDENT FRUGALITY,

NEATNESS,

AND A HARMONIOUS OECONOMY.

SHE should observe in the first Place a *prudent Frugality*—

BY our former Doctrine a Wife will have a general Notion of her Husband's Circumstances; she should therefore in those Affairs which fall under her Inspection and Management, be so governed by the said Circumstances, as to regulate her Household Expences by that just Proportion which his Fortune will afford.

AND as on the one Hand *Discretion* must prevent her from running into any *lavish Extravagances,* so on the other should a *generous Temper* make her *scorn* any Thing that is *mean* and *pitiful.* 'Tis the happy and judicious *Medium* between these *two Extremes,* that constitutes a *prudent Frugality,* and the true Excellency of Housewifery. 'Tis one of the most amiable Lights a Wife can show her self in to publick Observation. It throws a Glory round her, which is not less to be reverenced than admired; does Honour to her Husband, and renders the Entertainment of her Guests elegant and Pleasing. For as an *imprudent Ostentation* gives Pain and Ridicule; so any thing *meanly penurious,* raises Indignation and Contempt.

WOMEN often want Judgment to direct, and Souls to execute this skilful and lovely Medium of *prudent Frugality,* and thereby are either profuse or scandalously narrow.

'Tis therefore a Lesson highly necessary for them to learn; that all *Vanity* and *Ambition* of *exceeding* their Circumstances in this Part of Housewifery, is very *ridiculous,* and with all People of good Sense creates *Pity* for their *silly Extravagance,* and *Contempt* of their *weak Understandings.*

AND, on the other Hand, that every thing which is *niggardly* and *stingy,* or *beneath* what may *justly* be afforded, is the Mark of a *little, grovelling, dirty Soul,* and exposes us to the jests and Laughter of all Observers—The next Thing is

NEATNESS AND CLEANLINESS.

How necessary this is to the Comfort and Enjoyment of Life, and how *detestable* a *sluttish, nasty Management,* must be, are Things so very obvious, that little need be said to enforce it. But I must just mention one or two Faults in the Execution of this Part of Housewifery, which many Women are guilty of, and that I wou'd have avoided in our Scheme.

The one is the *ill timing* of *Cleanliness,* and the carrying it to such *Extreams,* that a Man's House is made an uneasy, and almost *useless,* Habitation to him. Some Women have such amphibious Dispositions, that one would think they chose to be half of their Lives in Water; there's such a Clatter of Pails and Brushes, such Inundations in every Room, that a Man can't find a dry Place for the Sole of his Foot; so that what should tend to make a Man's House an agreeable and wholesome Dwelling, become so *dangerous* and *unpleasant,* that the *Desire* of *Health* and *Peace* drives him out of it. And these Overflowings of Neatness are often so *ill timed,* that a Man's Business is interrupted, and his Meals made uncomfortable by 'em. These *Fish-wives* have generally a great Fund of ill Nature or a small one of good Sense.

ANOTHER Fault is that *Bigotry* and *Passion* for Neatness,

which makes a Woman fretful and uneasy at every accidental or unavoidable Speck of Dirt, or the least Disordering of her Furniture: You must rub your Shoes till the Bottoms of your Feet are almost sore, before you are permitted to enter a Room. Then so many nonsensical Exhortations and impertinent Questions are propos'd, that one might enter a Garrison Town in War-time with less ado. Such as, *Pray don't meddle with that,* and *Pray don't put this out of its Place,* that one would think there was a Spell on all the Furniture, or a Man was going to run away with Part of it.

THESE are all *idle* and *childish Extreams:* A prudent Housewife should so *time* her Neatness and Cleanliness, that it may be as little inconvenient and troublesome to a Man as possible, and support it with a graceful Ease, and a good-natured Sort of Indifference: The contrary has more of the *Servant-Maid* than the *well bred Woman* in it, and generally accompanies a *low* and *mean Education.*

THE third Thing in the Character of a good Housewife, is A HARMONIOUS OEconomy.

By which is meant, the maintaining *Order, Peace* and *Tranquility,* in her House; avoiding all noisy and turbulent Scolding, for which many pretended Housewifes are greatly blameable, make their Husbands, their own, and their Servant's Lives, uneasy.

MANY Ladies are apt to mistake this *bustling* and *vociferous* Turn for *good Management;* 'tis a great Mistake, and rather shows a Want of Skill and Temper.

WHERE the Mistress of a Family understands her Business, carries her Authority with *Resolution,* and at the same time with *good Nature* and *Humanity,* Servants will naturally be obedient and diligent.

BUT where Ignorance is joined with a tyrannick and insolent Temper, there are generally Blunders and Remissness in Servants, Hatred of their Mistress, a constant *Din* and *Contention* between them. A man had better live in a Paper-Mill, or a Fish-woman's Stall, than in such a House.

THESE Scenes are mighty unpleasant, very shocking, and highly prejudicial to the Tranquility of a married Life; are sure Signs of a brutal Temper, and a very vulgar Education.

WHEREAS a Woman of Judgment, an *even Mind,* and a polite Taste, will be *obeyed* and *beloved* by her Servants: All Things will go on *smooth* and *quiet:* Her Government will be *mild, calm* and *harmonious:* Her House the Habitation of *Peace, Joy* and *Contentment!*

'Tis a Truth, I believe, with very few Exceptions, that *a good Mistress makes good Servants.*

PEOPLE of that Class are not without Gratitude, and a Sense of Merit.

WHERE Women are ever complaining of *their Servants,* it carries a strong Suspicion of *their own* Capacities and Temper.

WHEN a Mistress of a House is giving Orders to Servants, or talking to them, 'tis often done in such an *imperious, bawling* Manner, that she is heard from every Corner. This is very unpolite, and shows a *little Mind,* so *swelled* with Power, that 'tis unable to support it with Decency and Temper.

THESE Cattle are such domestick Evils, that one had better live in a *Dutch* Dram-Cellar, than with their horrid Clangor.

ON the whole, a Mistress of a Family should carry on her Administration in a *mild* and *pacifick Manner,* and if she has any Disputes with her Servants, conceal them from the Ears of a Husband and Company, as much as possible: Have every Thing done quietly, and in order.

IF Servants won't be thus governed, *discard* them *at once,* and not suffer her own and her Husband's Peace to be destroyed by their Incorrigibleness.

THIS will make Home comfortable and agreeable; whereas the Want of this *harmonious Oeconomy* sours the Temper of a Woman, drives a Man out of his own House, makes Home his Aversion and destroys that Serenity which is so very essential to the Felicity of all Society.

AND now let us stop and survey a Wife thus *wisely* and discreetly filling her Sphere of Action.

WHAT *Veneration!* What *Praise!* What *Love* and *Esteem,* can sufficiently equal her *Merit.*

THE Character of a Wife, can scarcely shine in a more exalted Point of Light, nor do a more publick Honour to herself and her Husband. Whoever possesses such a One *Joy* will *sparkle* in his Eye, and *Pleasure* fill his Breast.

CAN the *flashy* and *superficial Glare* of Dress and Equipage, give a title to such *solid Excellence* and *substantial Worth?* Positively NOT. The twinkling Lustre of a Chrystal, may as well equal the august Splendor of a royal Diamond.

ON the whole, each Party thus supporting their respective Administration with Prudence and Discretion, will fix a Crown of Triumph on their Union, be a lasting Cement to their Tranquility and Happiness.

AND now my friend, your Task of Patience is drawing to a Conclusion.

CONFORMABLE to your Request, I have thrown before you my private Sentiments on the Subject of that Afternoon's Debate, which, you say, threw you into a Sort of Scepticism —Whether my rough Thoughts may in any wise tend to determine your Opinion, I know not. If they give you any Amusement, to atone for the Trouble of Reading them, I shall be well pleased.—But if neither one nor the other, you must blame your Influence over me for their Impertinence.

For my own Part, I confess, to think it *possible* for a Man of *Sense,* of *Honour* and *Virtue,* to find a Woman, in whose Society he may lay as probable a Foundation for the Enjoyment and Happiness of his Life by Marriage, and to superstruct as reasonable a Prospect of continuing his Felicity in that Union, as any other Scheme of Life can lay claim to.

'TIS a Truth as universally experienced as owned, that no State of Life is exempt from the Alternatives of Pleasure and Pain, the bitter and sweet; and that a Perfection of Happiness is not the Lot of Humanity.

IF this be the Case with human Life in general, and its proper

Character, MARRIAGE is not less worth your Choice, because it may have, or has, Inconveniencies and Alloys.—

IF those Inconveniencies and Alloys are necessarily greater, (without a proportionable Superiority of Pleasures) in a conjugal than a single Life, the latter is undoubtedly to be preferred.— But I believe they cannot be proved *necessarily* so, only *circumstantially*.— Well, the Question then is, Whether these *circumstantial* Impediments, which are, or may be, alledged against the Choice of a married Life, cannot, by a *proper Conduct, in the Time* of Courtship, and *after,* be removed.

'TIS thought they may; and the Design of these Papers is to propose *how,* and *by what Methods.*

AND we conceive, the Observations made, and the Methods proposed, may be effectual, and are not impracticable, to put the married State not only on an Equality of probable Happiness with a single One, but to give it a Prospect of superior Felicity.

HOWEVER *unskilfully* this Argument may have been handled by me, and of how little Advantage soever my *weak Attempts* may have been to serve it; the Truth of the Propositions remain *in Force.*

FIRST. *That unhappy Matches are often occasion'd by meer mercenary Views, in one or both of the Parties: Or by the headstrong Motives of ill-conducted Passion.*

SECONDLY, *That by a prudent and judicious Proceeding in our Addresses to a young Lady of a good natural Temper, we may lay a very good Foundation for making her an agreeable Companion, a steady Friend, and a good Wife.*

AND Thirdly, *That after Marriage, by continuing in the Road of Prudence and Judgment, we may make the nuptial State as happy as we can promise our selves from any other.*

To conclude, Sir, whenever I am inclined for a *matrimonial Voyage,* I shall endeavour thus to *steer my Course,* and if I cannot *gain the Port* by this Manner of Courtship and Conduct, I will rest content with my present Condition.

If, on the other Hand, I should *thereby* gain the Inclinations and Consent of a Lady, I shall endeavour to support my Happiness in some such Manner as I have herein intimated.

I *am,* &c.,

FINIS

A MODEST ENQUIRY INTO THE NATURE AND NECESSITY OF A PAPER CURRENCY

Quid asper
Utile nummus habet; patriae charisq, propinquis
Quantum elargiri deceat.

—PERS.

Philadelphia:—
Printed and sold at the new Printing-
Office, near the Market, 1729.　　(P.H.S.)

There is no Science, the Study of which is more useful and commendable than the Knowledge of the true Interest of one's Country; and perhaps there is no Kind of Learning more abstruse and intricate, more difficult to acquire in any Degree of Perfection than This, and therefore none more generally neglected. Hence it is, that we every Day find Men in Conversation contending warmly on some Point in Politicks, which, altho' it may nearly concern them both, neither of them understand any more than they do each other.

Thus much by way of Apology for this present *Enquiry into the Nature and Necessity of a Paper Currency.* And if any Thing I shall say, may be a Means of fixing a Subject, that is now the chief Concern of my Countrymen, in a clearer Light, I shall have the Satisfaction of thinking my Time and Pains well employed.

To proceed, then,

There is a certain proportionate Quantity of Money requisite to carry on the Trade of a Country freely and currently; More than which would be of no Advantage in Trade, and Less, if much less, exceedingly detrimental to it.

This leads us to the following general Considerations.

First. *A great Want of Money, in any Trading Country, occasions Interest to be at a very high Rate.* And here it may be observed, that it is impossible by any Laws to restrain Men from giving and receiving exorbitant Interest, where Money is suitably scarce: For he that wants Money will find out Ways to give 10 *per cent,* when he cannot have it for less, altho' the Law forbids to take more than 6 *per cent.* Now the Interest of Money being high is prejudicial to a Country several Ways: It makes Land bear a low Price, because few Men will lay out their Money in Land, when they can make a much greater Profit by lending it out upon Interest. And much less will Men be inclined to venture their Money at Sea, when they can, without Risque or Hazard, have a great and certain Profit by keeping it at home; thus Trade is discouraged. And if in two Neighbouring Countries the Traders of one, by Reason of a greater Plenty of Money, can borrow it to trade with at a lower Rate than the Traders of the other, they will infallibly have the Advantage, and get the greatest Part of that Trade into their own Hands; For he that trades with Money he hath borrowed at 8 or 10 *per cent,* cannot hold Market with him that borrows his money at 6 or 4. On the contrary, *a plentiful Currency will occasion Interest to be low:* And this will be an Inducement to many to lay out their Money in Lands, rather than put it out to Use, by which means Land will begin to rise in Value and bear a better Price. And at the same Time it will tend to enliven Trade exceedingly, because People will find more Profit in employing their Money that Way than in Usury; and many that understand Business very well, but have not a Stock sufficient of their own, will be encouraged to borrow Money to trade with, when they can have it at moderate Interest.

Secondly. *Want of Money in a Country reduces the Price of that Part of its Produce which is used in Trade:* Because, Trade being discouraged by it as above, there is a much less Demand for that Produce. And this is another Reason why Land in such a Case will be low, especially where the Staple Commodity of the Country is the immediate Produce of the Land; because, that Produce being low, fewer people find an Advantage in Husbandry, or the Improvement of Land. On the contrary, *a Plentiful Currency will occasion the Trading Produce to bear a good Price;* because, Trade being encouraged and advanced by it, there will be a much greater Demand for that Produce; which will be a great Encouragement of Husbandry and Tillage, and consequently make Land more valuable, for that many People would apply themselves to Husbandry, who probably might otherwise have sought some more profitable Employment.

As we have already experienced how much the Increase of our Currency, by what Paper Money has been made, has encouraged our Trade, particularly to instance only in one Article, *Ship-Building,* it may not be amiss to observe under this Head, what a great Advantage it must be to us as a Trading Country, that has Workmen and all the Materials proper for that Business within itself, to have Ship-Building as much as possible advanced: for every Ship, that is built here for the *English* merchants, gains the Province her clear Value in Gold and Silver, which must otherwise have been sent Home for Returns in her Stead; and likewise, every Ship, built in and belonging to the Province, not only saves the Province her first Cost, but all the Freight, Wages, and Provisions she ever makes or requires as long as she lasts; provided Care is taken to make This her *Pay-Port,* and that she always takes Provisions with her for the whole Voyage, which may easily be done. And how considerable an Article this is yearly in our Favour, every one, the least acquainted with mercantile Affairs, must needs be sensible; for, if we could not Build ourselves, we must either purchase so many Vessels as we want from other Countries, or else Hire them to carry our Produce to Market, which would be more expensive than Purchasing, and on many other Accounts exceedingly to our Loss. Now as Trade in general will decline where there is not a plentiful Currency, so Ship-Building must certainly of Consequence decline where Trade is declining.

Thirdly. *Want of Money in a Country discourages Labouring and Handicrafts Men (which are the chief Strength and Support of a People) from coming to settle in it, and induces many that were settled to leave the Country, and seek Entertainment and Employment in other Places, where they can be better paid.* For what can be more disheartning to an industrious labouring Man than this, that, after he hath earned his Bread with the Sweat of his Brows, he must spend as much Time, and have near as much Fatigue in getting it, as he had to earn it? *And nothing makes more bad Paymasters than a general Scarcity of Money.* And here again is a Third Reason for Land's bearing a low Price in such a Country, because Land always increases in Value in Proportion with the Increase of the People settling on it, there being so many more Buyers; and its Value will infallibly be diminished, if the Number of its Inhabitants diminish. On the contrary, *a Plentiful Currency will encourage great Numbers of labouring and Handicrafts Men to come and Settle in the Country,* by the same Reason that a Want of it will discourage and drive them out. Now the more Inhabitants, the Greater Demand for Land (as is said above), upon which it must necessarily rise in Value, and bear a better Price. The same may be said of the Value of House-Rent, which will be advanced for the same Reasons; and, by the Increase of Trade and Riches, People will be enabled to pay greater Rents. Now the Value of House-Rent rising, and Interest becoming low, many that in a Scarcity of Money practised Usury, will probably be more inclined to Building; which will likewise sensibly enliven Business in any Place; it being an Advantage not only to *Brickmakers, Bricklayers, Masons, Carpenters, Joiners, Glaziers,* and several other Trades immediately employed by Building, but likewise to *Farmers, Brewers, Bakers, Taylors, Shoemakers, Shopkeepers,* and, in short, to every one that they lay their Money out with.

Fourthly.   *Want of Money in such a Country as ours, occasions a Greater Consumption of English and European Goods, in Proportion to the Number of the People, than there would otherwise be.* Because Merchants and Traders, by whom abundance of Artificers and labouring Men are employed, finding their other Affairs require what Money they can get into their hands, oblige those who work for them to take one half or perhaps two-thirds Goods in Pay. By this Means a greater Quantity of Goods are disposed of, and to a greater Value; because Working-Men and their Families are thereby induced to be more profuse and extravagant in fine Apparel and the like, than they would be if they were obliged to pay ready Money for such Things after they had earn'd and received it, or if such Goods were not imposed upon them, of which they can make no other Use. For such People cannot send the Goods they are paid with to a Foreign Market, without losing considerably by having them sold for less than they stand 'em in here; neither can they easily dispose of them at Home, because their Neighbours are generally supplied in the same Manner. But how unreasonable would it be, if some of those very Men who *have been a Means* of thus forcing People into unnecessary Expense, should be the first and most earnest in accusing them of *Pride and Prodigality.* Now, tho' this extraordinary Consumption of Foreign Commodities may be a Profit to particular Men, yet the Country in general grows poorer by it apace. On the contrary, As *a Plentiful Currency will occasion a less consumption of European Goods, in proportion to the Number of the People,* so it will be a means of making the Balance of our Trade more equal than it now is, if it does not give it in our Favour; because our own Produce will be encouraged at the same Time. And it is to be observed, that, tho' less Foreign Commodities are consumed in Proportion to the Number of People, yet this will be no Disadvantage to the Merchant, because the Number of People increasing, will occasion an increasing Demand of more Foreign Goods in the Whole.

Thus we have seen some of the many heavy Disadvantages a Country (especially such a Country as ours) must labour under, when it has not a sufficient Stock of running Cash to manage its Trade currently. And we have likewise seen some of the Advantages which accrue from having Money sufficient, or a Plentiful Currency.

The foregoing Paragraphs being well considered, we shall naturally be led to draw the following Conclusions with Regard to what Persons will probably be for or against Emitting a large Additional Sum of Paper Bills in this Province.

1. Since Men will always be powerfully influenced in their Opinions and Actions by what appears to be their particular Interest: Therefore all those, who, wanting Courage to venture in Trade, now practise Lending Money on Security for exorbitant Interest, which, in a Scarcity of Money will be done, notwithstanding the Law, I say all such will probably be against a large Addition to our present Stock of Paper Money; because a plentiful Currency will lower Interest, and make it common to lend on less Security.

2. All those who are Possessors of large Sums of Money, and are disposed to purchase Land, which is attended with a great and sure Advantage in a growing Country as this is; I say, the Interest of all such Men will encline them to oppose a large Addition to our Money. Because their Wealth is now continually increasing by the large Interest they receive, which will enable them (if they can keep Land from rising) to purchase More some time hence than they can at present; and in the mean time all Trade being discouraged, not only those who borrow of them, but the Common People in general will be impoverished, and consequently obliged to sell More Land for less Money than they will do at present. And yet, after such Men are possessed of as much Land as they can purchase, it will then be their Interest to have Money made plentiful, because that will immediately make Land rise in Value in *their* Hands. Now

it ought not to be wonder'd at, if People from the Knowledge of a Man's Interest do sometimes make a true Guess at his Designs; for *Interest, they say, will not Lie.*

3. Lawyers, and others concerned in Court Business, will probably many of them be against a plentiful Currency; because People in that Case will have less Occasion to run in Debt, and consequently less Occasion to go to Law and Sue one another for their Debts. Tho' I know some even among these Gentlemen, that regard the Publick Good before their own apparent private Interest.

4. All those who are any way Dependants on such Persons as are above mentioned, whether as holding Offices, as Tenants, or as Debtors, must at least *appear* to be against a large Addition; because, if they do not, they must sensibly feel their present Interest hurt. And besides these, there are, doubtless, many well-meaning Gentlemen and Others, who, without any immediate private Interest of their own in View, are against making such an Addition, thro' an Opinion they may have of the Honesty and sound Judgment of some of their Friends that oppose it (perhaps for the Ends aforesaid), without having given it any thorough Consideration themselves. And thus it is no Wonder if there is a *powerful* Party on that Side.

On the other Hand, those who are Lovers of Trade, and delight to see Manufactures encouraged, will be for having a large Addition to our Currency: For they very well know, that People will have little Heart to advance Money in Trade, when what they can get is scarce sufficient to purchase Necessaries, and supply their Families with Provisions. Much less will they lay it out in advancing new Manufactures; nor is it possible new Manufactures should turn to any Account, where there is not Money to pay the Workmen, who are discouraged by being paid in Goods, because it is a great Disadvantage to them.

Again. Those, who are truly for the Proprietor's Interest (and have no separate Views of their own that are predominant), will be heartily for a large Addition: Because, as I have shewn above, Plenty of Money will for several Reasons make Land rise in Value exceedingly: And I appeal to those immediately concerned for the Proprietor in the Sale of his Lands, whether Land has not risen very much since the first Emission of what Paper Currency we now have, and even by its Means. Now we all know the Proprietary has great Quantities to sell.

And since a Plentiful Currency will be so great a Cause of advancing this Province in Trade and Riches, and increasing the Number of its People; which, tho' it will not sensibly lessen the Inhabitants of *Great Britain,* will occasion a much greater Vent and Demand for their Commodities here; and allowing that the Crown is the more powerful for its Subjects increasing in Wealth and Number, I cannot think it the Interest of *England* to oppose us in making as great a Sum of Paper Money here, as we, who are the best Judges of our own Necessities, find convenient. And if I were not sensible that the Gentlemen of Trade in *England,* to whom we have already parted with our Silver and Gold, are misinformed of our Circumstances, and therefore endeavour to have our Currency stinted to what it now is, I should think the Government at Home had some Reasons for discouraging and impoverishing this Province, which we are not acquainted with.

It remains now that we enquire, *Whether a large Addition to our Paper Currency will not make it sink in Value very much.* And here it will be requisite that we first form just Notions of the Nature and Value of Money in general.

As Providence has so ordered it, that not only different Countries, but even different Parts of the same Country, have their peculiar most suitable Productions; and likewise that different Men have Geniuses adapted to Variety of different Arts and Manufactures, Therefore *Commerce,* or the Exchange of one Commodity or Manufacture for another, is highly convenient and beneficial to Mankind. As for Instance, A may be skilful in the Art of making Cloth, and B understand the raising of Corn; A wants Corn, and B Cloth; upon which they make an Exchange with each other for as much as each has Occasion, to the mutual Advantage and Satisfaction of both.

But as it would be very tedious, if there were no other Way of general Dealing, but by an immediate Exchange of Commodities; because a Man that had Corn to dispose of, and wanted Cloth for it, might perhaps, in his Search for a Chapman to deal with, meet with twenty People that had Cloth to dispose of, but wanted no Corn; and with twenty others that wanted his Corn, but had no Cloth to suit him with; to remedy such Inconveniences, and facilitate Exchange, Men have invented MONEY, properly called a *Medium of Exchange,* because through or by its Means Labour is exchanged for Labour, or one Commodity for another. And whatever particular Thing Men have agreed to make this Medium of, whether Gold, Silver, Copper, or Tobacco, it is, to those who possess it (if they want any Thing), that very Thing which they want, because it will immediately procure it for them. It is Cloth to him that wants Cloth, and Corn to those that want Corn; and so of all other Necessaries, it *is* whatsoever it will procure. Thus he who had Corn to dispose of, and wanted to purchase Cloth with it, might sell his Corn, for its Value in this general Medium, to one who wanted Corn but had no Cloth; and with this Medium he might purchase Cloth of him that wanted no Corn, but perhaps some other Thing, as Iron it may be, which this medium will immediately procure, and so he may be said to have exchanged his Cloth for Iron; and thus the general Exchange is soon performed, to the Satisfaction of all Parties, with abundance of Facility.

For many Ages, those Parts of the World which are engaged in Commerce, have fixed upon Gold and Silver as the chief and most proper Materials for this Medium; they being in themselves valuable Metals for their Fineness, Beauty, and Scarcity. By these, particularly by Silver, it has been usual to value all Things else. But as Silver itself is of no certain permanent Value, being worth more or less according to its Scarcity or Plenty, therefore it seems requisite to fix upon Something else, more proper to be made a *Measure of Values,* and this I take to be *Labour.*

By Labour may the Value of Silver be measured as well as other Things. As, Suppose one Man employed to raise Corn, while another is digging and refining Silver; at the Year's End, or at any other Period of Time, the compleat Produce of Corn, and that of Silver, are the natural Price of each other; and if one be twenty Bushels, and the other twenty Ounces, then an Ounce of that Silver is worth the Labour of raising a Bushel of that Corn. Now if by the Discovery of some nearer, more easy or plentiful Mines, a man may get Forty Ounces of Silver as easily as formerly he did Twenty, and the same Labour is still required to raise Twenty Bushels of Corn, then Two Ounces of Silver will be worth no more than the same Labour of raising one Bushel of Corn, and that Bushel of Corn will be as cheap at two Ounces, as it was before at one, *cæteris paribus*.

Thus the Riches of a Country are to be valued by the Quantity of Labour its Inhabitants are able to purchase, and not by the Quantity of Silver and Gold they possess; which will purchase more or less Labour, and therefore is more or less valuable, as is said before, according to its Scarcity or Plenty. As those Metals have grown much more plentiful in *Europe* since the discovery of *America*, so they have sunk in Value exceedingly; for, to instance in *England*, formerly one Penny of Silver was worth a Days Labour, but now it is hardly worth the sixth Part of a Days Labour; because not less than Sixpence will purchase the Labour of a Man for a Day in any Part of that Kingdom; which is wholly to be attributed to the much greater Plenty of Money now in *England* than formerly. And yet perhaps *England* is in Effect no richer now than at that Time; because as much Labour might be purchas'd, or Work got done of almost any kind, for 100 l. then, as will now require or is now worth 600 l.

In the next Place let us consider the Nature of *Banks* emitting *Bills of Credit*, as they are at this Time used in *Hamburgh, Amsterdam, London,* and *Venice*.

Those Places being Seats of vast Trade, and the Payment of great Sums being for that Reason frequent, *Bills of Credit* are found very convenient in Business; because a great Sum is more easily counted in Them, lighter in Carriage, concealed in less Room, and therefore safer in Travelling or Laying up, and on many other Accounts they are very much valued. The Banks are the general Cashiers of all Gentlemen, Merchants, and great Traders in and about those Cities; there they deposit their Money, and may take out Bills to the Value, for which they can be certain to have Money again at the Bank at any Time. This gives the Bills a Credit; so that in *England* they are never less valuable than Money, and in *Venice* and *Amsterdam* they are generally worth more. And the Bankers, always reserving Money in hand to answer more than the common Run of Demands (and some People constantly putting in while others are taking out), are able besides to lend large Sums, on good Security, to the Government or others, for a reasonable Interest, by which they are paid for their Care and Trouble; and the Money, which otherwise would have lain dead in their Hands, is made to circulate again thereby among the People. And thus the Running Cash of the nation is, as it were, doubled; for all great Payments being made in Bills, Money in lower Trade becomes much more plentiful; And this is an exceeding great Advantage to a Trading Country, that is not overstocked with Gold and Silver.

As those, who take Bills out of the Banks in Europe, put in Money for Security; so here, and in some of the neighbouring Provinces, we engage our Land. Which of these Methods will most effectually secure the Bills from actually sinking in Value, comes next to be considered.

Trade in general being nothing else but the Exchange of Labour for Labour, the Value of all Things is, as I have said before, most justly measured by Labour. Now suppose I put my Money into a Bank, and take out a Bill for the Value; if this Bill at the Time of my receiving it, would purchase me the Labour of one hundred Men for twenty Days, but some time after will only purchase the Labour of the same Number of Men for fifteen Days, it is plain the Bill has sunk in Value one fourth Part. Now, Silver and Gold being of no permanent Value, and as this Bill is founded on Money, and therefore to be esteemed as such, it may be that the Occasion of this Fall is the increasing Plenty of Gold and Silver, by which Money is one fourth Part less valuable than before, and therefore one fourth more is given of it for the same Quantity of Labour; and if Land is not become more plentiful by some proportionate Decrease of the People, one fourth Part more of Money is given for the same Quantity of Land; whereby it appears, that it would have been more profitable to me to have laid that Money out in Land which I put into the Bank, than to place it there and take a Bill for it. And it is certain that the Value of Money has been continually sinking in *England* for several Ages past, because it has been continually increasing in Quantity. But if Bills could be taken out of a Bank in *Europe* on a Land Security, it is probable the Value of such Bills would be more certain and steady, because the Number of Inhabitants continues to be near the same in those Countries from age to age.

For, as Bills issued upon Money Security are Money, so Bills issued upon Land, are in effect *Coined Land*.

Therefore, (to apply the Above to our own Circumstances) if Land in this Province was falling, or any way likely to fall, it would behove the Legislature most carefully to contrive how to prevent the Bills issued upon Land from falling with it. But, as our People increase exceedingly, and will be further increased, as I have before shewn, by the Help of a large Addition to our Currency, and as Land in consequence is continually rising, So, in case no Bills are emitted but what are upon Land Security, the Money-Acts in every Part punctually enforced and executed, the Payments of Principal and Interest being duly and strictly required, and the Principal *bonâ fide* sunk according to Law, it is absolutely impossible such Bills should ever sink below their first Value, or below the Value of the Land, on which they are founded. In short, there is so little Danger of their sinking, that they would certainly rise as the Land rises, if they were not emitted in a proper Manner for preventing it. That is, by providing in the Act, *That Payment may be made, either in those Bills, or in any other Bills made current by any Act of the Legislature of this Province;* and that the Interest, as it is received, may be again emitted in Discharge of Publick

Debts; whereby circulating, it returns again into the Hands of the Borrowers, and becomes Part of their future Payments; and thus, as it is likely there will not be any Difficulty for want of Bills to pay the Office, they are hereby kept from rising above their first Value. For else, supposing there should be emitted upon mortgaged Land its full present Value in Bills; as in the Banks in *Europe* the full Value of the Money deposited is given out in Bills; and supposing the Office would take nothing but the same Sum in those Bills in Discharge of the Land; as in the Banks aforesaid the same Sum in their Bills must be brought in, in order to receive out the Money; in such Case the Bills would most surely rise in Value as the Land rises; as certainly as the Bank Bills founded on Money would fall, if that Money was falling. Thus if I were to mortgage to a Loan-Office, or Bank, a Parcel of Land now valued at 100 l. in Silver, and receive for it the like Sum in Bills, to be paid in again at the Expiration of a certain Term of Years; before which my Land rising in Value, becomes worth 150 l. in Silver; 'Tis plain, that if I have not these Bills in Possession, and the Office will take nothing but these Bills, or else what it is now become worth in Silver, in Discharge of my Land; I say it appears plain, that those Bills will now be worth 150 l. in Silver to the Possessor, and if I can purchase them for less, in order to redeem my Land, I shall by so much be a Gainer.

I need not say any Thing to convince the Judicious that our Bills have not yet sunk, tho' there is and has been some Difference between them and Silver; because it is evident that that Difference is occasioned by the Scarcity of the latter, which is now become a Merchandize, rising and falling, like other Commodities as there is a greater or less Demand for it, or as it is more or less Plenty.

Yet farther, in order to make a true Estimate of the Value of Money, we must distinguish between Money as it is Bullion, which is Merchandise, and as by being coin'd it is made a Currency: For its Value as a Merchandise, and its Value as a Currency, are two distinct Things; and each may possibly rise and fall in some Degree independent of the other. Thus, if the Quantity of Bullion increases in a Country, it will proportionably decrease in Value; but if at the same Time the Quantity of current coin should decrease, (supposing Payments may not be made in Bullion) what Coin there is will rise in Value as a Currency, *i.e.* People will give more Labour in Manufactures for a certain Sum of ready Money.

In the same Manner must we consider a *Paper Currency* founded on Land; as it is Land, and as it is a Currency.

Money as Bullion, or as Land, is valuable by so much labour as it costs to procure that Bullion or Land.

Money as a Currency has an Additional Value by so much Time and Labour as it saves in the Exchange of Commodities.

If, as a Currency, it saves one Fourth Part of the Time and Labour of a Country; it has, on that Account, one Fourth added to its original Value.

When there is no Money in a Country, all Commerce must be by Exchange. Now, if it takes one fourth Part of the Time and Labour of a Country, to exchange or get their Commodities exchanged; then, in computing their Value, that Labour of Exchanging must be added to the Labour of manufacturing those Commodities. But if that Time or Labour is saved by introducing Money sufficient, then the additional Value on Account of the Labour or Exchanging may be abated, and Things sold for only the Value of the Labour in making them; because the People may now in the same Time make one Fourth more in Quantity of Manufactures than they could before.

From these Considerations it may be gathered, that in all the Degrees between having no Money in a Country, and Money sufficient for the trade, it will rise and fall in Value as a Currency, in Proportion to the Decrease or Increase of its Quantity: And if there may be at some Time more than enough, the Overplus will have no Effect towards making the Currency as a Currency of less Value than when there was but enough; because such Overplus will not be used in Trade, but be some other way disposed of.

If we enquire, *How much per cent Interest ought to be required upon the Loan of these Bills,* we must consider what is the Natural Standard of Usury: And this appears to be, where the Security is undoubted, at least the Rent of so much Land as the Money lent will buy: For it cannot be expected, that any Man will lend his Money for less than it would fetch him in as Rent if he laid it out in Land, which is the most secure Property in the World. But if the Security is casual, then a kind of Ensurance must be enterwoven with the simple natural Interest, which may advance the Usury very conscionably to any height below the Principal itself. Now among us, if the Value of Land is twenty Years Purchase, Five *per cent* is the just Rate of Interest for Money lent on undoubted Security. Yet if Money grows scarce in a Country it becomes more difficult for People to make punctual Payments of what they borrow, Money being hard to be raised; likewise Trade being discouraged and Business impeded for want of a Currency, abundance of People must be in declining Circumstances, and by these Means Security is more precarious than where Money is plenty. On such Accounts it is no wonder if People ask a greater interest for their Money than the natural Interest; and what is above is to be look'd upon as a kind of *Premium* for the Ensurance of those Uncertainties, as they are greater or less. Thus we always see, that where Money is scarce, Interest is high, and low where it is plenty. Now it is certainly the Advantage of a Country to make Interest as low as possible, as I have already shewn; and this can be done no other way than by making Money plentiful. And since, in Emitting Paper Money among us, the Office has the best of Security, the Titles to the Land being all skilfully and strictly examined and ascertained; and as it is only permitting the People by Law to coin their own Land, which costs the Government nothing, the Interest being more than enough to pay the Charges of Printing, Officers' Fees, &c., I cannot see any good Reason why Four *per cent* to the Loan-Office should not be thoughtfully sufficient. As a low Interest may incline more to take Money out, it will become more plentiful in Trade; and this may bring down the common Usury, in which Security is more dubious, to the pitch it is determined at by law.

If it should be objected, *that Emitting it at so low an Interest, and on such easy Terms, will occasion more to be taken out than the Trade of the Country really requires:* It may be answered, That, as has already been shewn, there can never be so much of it emitted as to make it fall below the Land it is founded on; because no Man in his Senses will mortgage his Estate for what is of no more Value to him than That he has mortgaged, especially if the Possession of what he receives is more precarious than of what he mortgages, as that of Paper Money is when compared to Land: And if it should ever become so plenty by indiscreet Persons continuing to take out a large Overplus, above what is necessary in Trade, so as to make People imagine it would become by that Means of less Value than their mortgaged Lands, they would immediately of Course begin to pay it in again to the Office to redeem their Land, and continue to do so till there was no more left in Trade than was absolutely necessary. And thus the Proportion would find itself (tho' there were a Million too much in the Office to be let out), without giving any one the Trouble of Calculation.

It may, perhaps, be objected to what I have written concerning the Advantages of a large Addition to our Currency, *That if the People of this Province increase, and Husbandry is more followed we shall overstock the Markets with our Produce of Flower, &c.* To this it may be answered, that we can never have too many People (nor too much Money.) For when one Branch of Trade or Business is overstocked with Hands there are the more to spare to be employed in another. So if raising Wheat proves dull, more may (if there is Money to support and carry on new Manufactures) proceed to the raising and manufacturing of Hemp, Silk, Iron, and many other Things the Country is very capable of, for which we only want People to work, and Money to pay them with.

Upon the Whole it may be observed, That it is the highest Interest of a Trading Country in general to make Money plentiful; and that it can be a Disadvantage to none that have honest Designs. It cannot hurt even the Usurers, though it should sink what they receive as Interest; because they will be proportionably more secure in what they lend; or they will have an Opportunity of employing their Money to greater Advantage to themselves as well as to the Country. Neither can it hurt those Merchants, who have great Sums outstanding in Debts in the Country, and seem on that Account to have the most plausible Reason to fear it; *to wit,* because a large Addition being made to our Currency will increase the Demand of our Exporting Produce, and by that Means raise the Price of it, so that they will not be able to purchase so much Bread or Flower with 100 l. when they shall receive it after such an Addition, as they now can, and may if there is no Addition. I say it cannot hurt even such, because they will get in their Debts just in exact Proportion so much the easier and sooner as the Money becomes plentier; and therefore, considering the Interest and Trouble saved, they will not be Losers; because it only sinks in Value as a Currency, proportionally as it becomes more plenty. It cannot hurt the Interest of *Great Britain,* as has been shewn; and it will greatly advance the Interest of the Proprietor. It will be an Advantage to every industrious Tradesman, &c., because his Business will be carried on more freely, and Trade be universally enlivened by it. And as more Business in all Manufactures will be done, by so much as the Labour and Time spent in Exchange is saved, the Country in general will grow so much the richer.

It is nothing to the Purpose to object the wretched Fall of the Bills in *New England* and *South Carolina,* unless it might be made evident that their Currency was emitted with the same Prudence and on such good Security, as ours is; and it certainly was not.

As this Essay is wrote and published in Haste, and the Subject in itself intricate, I hope I shall be censured with Candour, if, for want of Time carefully to revise what I have written, in some Places I should appear to have express'd myself too obscurely, and in others am liable to Objections I did not foresee.

I sincerely desire to be acquainted with the Truth, and on that
Account shall think myself obliged to any one who will take
the Pains to shew me or the Publick, where I am mistaken in
my Conclusions. And as we all know there are among us several
Gentlemen of acute Parts and profound Learning, who are very
much against any Addition to our Money, it were to be wished
that they would favour the Country with their Sentiments on
this Head in Print; which, supported with Truth and good
Reasoning, may probably be very convincing. And this is to be
desired the rather because many People, knowing the Abilities
of those Gentlemen to manage a good Cause, are apt to construe
their Silence in This, as an Argument of a bad One. Had any
Thing of that Kind ever yet appeared, perhaps I should not have
given the Publick this Trouble. But as those ingenious Gentlemen have not yet (and I doubt never will) think it worth their
concern to enlighten the Minds of their erring Countrymen in
this Particular, I think it would be highly commendable in every
one of us, more fully to bend our Minds to the Study of *What
is the true Interest of Pennsylvania;* whereby we may be enabled,
not only to reason pertinently with one another; but, if Occasion requires, to transmit Home such clear Representations, as
must inevitably convince our Superiors of the Reasonableness
and Integrity of our Designs.

Philadelphia, April (sic) 3, 1729.

A PROPOSAL FOR PROMOTING USEFUL KNOWLEDGE AMONG THE BRITISH PLANTATIONS IN AMERICA

[Philadelphia, May 14, 1743]

The English are possessed of a long tract of continent, from
Nova Scotia to Georgia, extending north and south through

different climates, having different soils, producing different plants, mines, and minerals, and capable of different improvements, manufactures, etc.

The first drudgery of settling new colonies, which confines the attention of people to mere necessaries, is now pretty well over; and there are many in every province in circumstances that set them at ease, and afford leisure to cultivate the finer arts and improve the common stock of knowledge. To such of these who are men of speculation, many hints must from time to time arise, many observations occur, which, if well examined, pursued, and improved, might produce discoveries to the advantage of some or all of the British plantations, or to the benefit of mankind in general.

But as from the extent of the country such persons are widely separated, and seldom can see and converse or be acquainted with each other, so that many useful particulars remain uncommunicated, die with the discoverers, and are lost to mankind; it is, to remedy this inconvenience for the future, proposed,

That one society be formed of *virtuosi* or ingenious men, residing in the several colonies to be called *The American Philosophical Society,* who are to maintain a constant correspondence.

That Philadelphia, being the city nearest the center of the continent colonies, communicating with all of them northward and southward by post, and with all the islands by sea, and having the advantage of a good growing library, be the center of the society.

That at Philadelphia there be always at least seven members, viz., a physician, a botanist, a mathematician, a chemist, a mechanician, a geographer, and a general natural philosopher, besides a president, treasurer, and secretary.

That these members meet once a month, or oftener, at their own expense, to communicate to each other their observations and experiments, to receive, read, and consider such letters, communications, or queries as shall be sent from distance members; to direct the dispersing of copies of such communications as are valuable, to other distant members, in order to procure their sentiments thereupon.

That the subjects of the correspondence be: all new-discovered plants, herbs, trees, roots, their virtues, uses, etc.; methods of propagating them, and making such as are useful, but particular to some plantations, more general; improvements of vegetables juices, as ciders, wines, etc.; new methods of curing or preventing diseases; all new-discovered fossils in different countries, as mines, minerals, and quarries; new and useful improvements in any branch of mathematics; new discoveries in chemistry, such as improvements in distillation, brewing, and assaying of ores; new mechanical inventions for saving labour, as mills and carriages, and for raising and conveying of water, draining of meadows, etc.; all new arts trades, and manufactures, that may be proposed or thought of; surveys, maps, and charts of particular parts of the seacoasts or inland countries; course and junction of rivers and great roads, situation of lakes and mountains, nature of the soil and productions; new methods of improving the breed of useful animals; introducing other sorts from foreign countries; new improvements in planting, gardening, and clearing land; and all philosophical experiments that let light into the nature of things, tend to increase the power of man over matter, and multiply the conveniences or pleasures of life.

That a correspondence, already begun by some intended members, shall be kept up by this society with the Royal Society of London and with the Dublin Society.

That every member shall have abstracts sent him quarterly, of everything valuable communicated to the society's secretary at Philadelphia; free of all charge except the yearly payment hereafter mentioned.

That, by permission of the postmaster-general, such communications pass between the secretary of the society and the members, postage-free.

That, for defraying the expense of such experiments as the

society shall judge proper to cause to be made, and other contingent charges for the common good, every member send a piece of eight per annum to the treasurer, at Philadelphia, to form a common stock, to be disbursed by the order of the president with the consent of the majority of the members that can conveniently be consulted thereupon, to such persons and places where and by whom the experiments are to be made, and otherwise as there shall be occasion; of which disbursements an exact account shall be kept, and communicated yearly to every member.

That, at the first meetings of the members at Philadelphia, such rules be formed for regulating their meetings and transactions for the general benefit, as shall be convenient and necessary; to be afterward changed and improved as there shall be occasion, wherein due regard is to be had to the advice of distant members.

That, at the end of every year, collections be made and printed, of such experiments, discoveries, and improvements, as may be thought of public advantage; and that every member have a copy sent him.

That the business and duty of the secretary be to receive all letters intended for the society, and lay them before the president and members at their meetings; to abstract, correct, and methodize such papers as require it, and as he shall be directed to do by the president, after they have been considered, debated, and digested in the society; to enter copies thereof in the society's books, and make out copies for distant members; to answer their letters by direction of the president, and keep records of all material transactions of the society.

Benjamin Franklin, the writer of this proposal, offers himself to serve the society as their secretary, till they shall be provided with one more capable.

PROPOSALS RELATING TO THE EDUCATION OF YOUTH IN PENNSYLVANIA

[Philadelphia, 1749]

ADVERTISEMENT TO THE READER

It has long been regretted as a misfortune to the youth of this province that we have no *academy*, in which they might receive the accomplishments of a regular education. The following paper of hints toward forming a plan for that purpose is so far approved by some public-spirited gentlemen, to whom it has been privately communicated, that they have directed a number of copies to be made by the press, and properly distributed, in order to obtain the sentiments and advice of men of learning, understanding, and experience in these matters; and have determined to use their interest and best endeavors to have the scheme, when completed, carried gradually into execution; in which they have reason to believe they shall have the hearty concurrence and assistance of many who are wellwishers to their country. Those who incline to favour the design with their advice, either as to the parts of learning to be taught, the order of study, the method of teaching, the economy of the school, or any other matter of importance to the success of the undertaking, are desired to communicate their sentiments as soon as may be, by letter directed to B. FRANKLIN, *Printer,* in PHILA-DELPHIA.

PROPOSALS

The good education of youth has been esteemed by wise men in all ages as the surest foundation of the happiness both of private families and of commonwealths. Almost all governments have therefore made it a principal object of their attention to establish and endow with proper revenues such seminaries of learning, as might supply the succeeding age with men qualified to serve the public with honor to themselves and to their country.

Many of the first settlers of these provinces were men who had received a good education in Europe, and to their wisdom and good management we owe much of our present prosperity. But their hands were full, and they could not do all things. The present race are not thought to be generally of equal ability: For though the American youth are allowed not to want capacity; yet the best capacities require cultivation, it being truly with them, as with the best ground, which, unless well tilled and sowed with profitable seed, produces only ranker weeds.

That we may obtain the advantages arising from an increase of knowledge, and prevent as much as may be the mischievous consequences that would attend a general ignorance among us, the following hints are offered toward forming a plan for the education of the youth of Pennsylvania, viz.:

It is proposed,

That some persons of leisure and public spirit apply for a charter, by which they may be incorporated, with power to erect an *academy* for the education of youth, to govern the same, provide masters, make rules, receive donations, purchase lands, etc., and to add to their number, from time to time, such other persons as they shall judge suitable.

That the members of the corporation make it their pleasure, and in some degree their business, to visit the academy often, encourage and countenance the youth, countenance and assist the masters, and by all means in their power advance the usefulness and reputation of the design; that they look on the students as in some sort their children, treat them with familiarity and affection, and, when they have behaved well, and gone through their studies, and are to enter the world, zealously unite, and make all the interest that can be made to establish them, whether in business, offices, marriages, or any other thing for their advantage, preferably to all other persons whatsoever even of equal merit.

And if men may, and frequently do, catch such a taste for cultivating flowers, for planting, grafting, inoculating, and the like, as to despise all other amusements for their sake, why may not we expect they should acquire a relish for that more useful culture of young minds. Thompson says,

> 'Tis Joy to see the human Blossoms blow,
> When infant Reason grows apace, and calls
> For the kind Hand of an assiduous Care.
> Delightful Task! to rear the tender Thought,
> To teach the young Idea how to shoot;
> To pour the fresh Instruction o'er the Mind,
> To breathe th' enliv'ning Spirit, and to fix
> The generous Purpose in the glowing Breast.

That a house be provided for the academy, if not in the town, not many miles from it; the situation high and dry, and if it may be, not far from a river, having a garden, orchard, meadow, and a field or two.

That the house be furnished with a library (if in the country; if in the town, the town Libraries may serve) with maps of all countries, globes, some mathematical instruments, an apparatus for experiments in natural philosophy, and for mechanics; prints, of all kinds, prospects, buildings, machines, etc.

That the rector be a man of good understanding, good morals, diligent and patient, learned in the languages and sciences, and a correct pure speaker and writer of the English tongue; to have such tutors under him as shall be necessary.

That the boarding scholars diet together, plainly, temperately, and frugally.

That, to keep them in health, and to strengthen and render active their bodies, they be frequently exercised in running, leaping, wrestling, and swimming, etc.

That they have peculiar habits to distinguish them from other youth, if the academy be in or near the town; for this, among other reasons, that their behavior may be the better observed.

As to their *studies*, it would be well if they could be taught everything that is useful, and everything that is ornamental. But art is long, and their time is short. It is therefore proposed that they learn those things that are likely to be most useful and most ornamental, regard being had to the several professions for which they are intended.

All should be taught to *write* a fair hand, and swift, as that is useful to all. And with it may be learnt something of *drawing*, by imitation of prints, and some of the first principles of perspective.

Arithmetic, accounts, and some of the first principles of *geometry* and *astronomy.*

The English language might be taught by *grammar;* in which some of our best writers, as Tillotson, Addison, Pope, Algernoon Sidney, Cato's Letters, etc., should be classics: the styles principally to be cultivated, being the clear and the concise. Reading should also be taught, and pronouncing, properly, distinctly, emphatically; not with an even tone, which under-does, nor a theatrical, which over-does nature.

To form their style they should be put on writing letters to each other, making abstracts of what they read; or writing the same things in their own words; telling or writing stories lately read, in their own expressions. All to be revised and corrected by the tutor, who should give his reasons, and explain the force and import of words, etc.

To form their pronunciation, they may be put on making declamations, repeating speeches, delivering orations, etc.; the tutor assisting at the rehearsals, teaching, advising, correcting their accent, etc.

But if *history* be made a constant part of their reading, such as the translations of the Greek and Roman historians, and the modern histories of ancient Greece and Rome, etc., may not almost all kinds of useful knowledge be that way introduced to advantage, and with pleasure to the student? As:

Geography, by reading with maps and being required to point out the places where the greatest actions were done, to give their old and new names, with the bounds, situation, extent of the countries concerned, etc.

Chronology, by the help of Helvicus or some other writer of the kind, who will enable them to tell when those events happened; what princes were contemporaries, what states or famous men flourished about that time, etc. The several principal epochs to be first well fixed in their memories.

Ancient Customs, religious and civil, being frequently mentioned in history, will give occasion for explaining them; in which the prints of medals, bas-reliefs, and ancient monuments will greatly exist.

Morality, by descanting and making continual observations on the causes of the rise or fall of any man's character, fortune, power, etc., mentioned in history; the advantages of temperance, order, frugality, industry, perseverance, etc., etc. Indeed, the general natural tendency of reading good history must be to fix in the minds of youth deep impressions of the beauty and usefulness of virtue of all kinds, public spirit, fortitude, etc.

History will show the wonderful effects of *oratory,* in governing, turning and leading great bodies of mankind, armies, cities, nations. When the minds of youth are struck with admiration at this, then is the time to give them the principles of that art, which they will study with taste and application. Then they may be made acquainted with the best models among the ancients, their beauties being particularly pointed out to them. Modern political oratory being chiefly performed by the pen and press, its advantages over the ancient in some respects are to be shown; as that its effects are more extensive, more lasting, etc.

History will also afford frequent opportunities of showing the necessity of a public religion, from its usefulness to the public; the advantage of a religious character among private persons; the mischiefs of superstition, etc., and the excellency of the *Christian religion* above all others ancient or modern.

History will also give occasion to expatiate on the advantage of civil orders and constitutions; how men and their properties are protected by joining in societies and establishing government; their industry encouraged and rewarded, arts invented, and life made more comfortable: The advantages of liberty, mischiefs of licentiousness, benefits arising from good laws and a due execution of justice, etc. Thus may the first principles of sound politics be fixed in the minds of youth.

On historical occasions, questions of right and wrong, justice and injustice, will naturally arise, and may be put to youth, which they may debate in conversation and in writing. When they ardently desire victory, for the sake of the praise attending it, they will begin to feel the want, and be sensible of the use of *logic,* or the art of reasoning to discover truth, and of arguing to defend it, and convince adversaries. This would be the time to acquaint them with the principles of that art. Grotius, Puffendorff, and some other writers of the same kind, may be used on these occasions to decide their disputes. Public disputes warm the imagination, whet the industry, and strengthen the natural abilities.

When youth are told that the great men whose lives and actions they read in history spoke two of the best *languages* that ever were, the most expressive, copious, beautiful; and that the finest writings, the most correct compositions, the most perfect productions of human wit and wisdom, are in those languages, which have endured ages, and will endure while there are men; that no translation can do them justice, or give the pleasure found in reading the originals; that those languages contain all science; that one of them is become almost universal, being the language of learned men in all countries; that to understand them is a distinguishing ornament, etc., they may be thereby made desirous of learning those languages, and their industry sharpened in the acquistion of them. All intended for divinity should be taught the Latin and Greek; for physick, the Latin, Greek, and French; for law, the Latin and French; merchants, the French, German, and Spanish: And though all should not be compelled to learn Latin, Greek, or the modern foreign languages; yet none that have an ardent desire to learn them should be refused; their English, arithmetic and other studies absolutely necessary, being at the same time not neglected.

If the new *universal history* were also read, it would give a connected idea of human affairs, so far as it goes, which should be followed by the best modern histories, particularly of our mother country; then of these colonies; which should be accompanied with observations on their rise, increase, use to Great Britain, encouragements, discouragements, etc., the means to make them flourish, secure their liberties, etc.

With the history of men, times, and nations, should be read at proper hours or days, some of the best *histories of nature,* which would not only be delightful to youth, and furnish them with matter for their letters, etc., as well as other history; but afterwards of great use to them, whether they are merchants, handicrafts, or divines; enabling the first the better to understand many commodities, drugs, etc., the second to improve his trade or handicraft by new mixtures, materials, etc., and the last to adorn his discourses by beautiful comparisons and strengthen them by new proofs of Divine Providence. The conversation of all will be improved by it, as occasions frequently occur of making natural observations, which are instructive, agreeable, and entertaining in almost all companies. Natural history will also afford opportunities of introducing many observations relating to the preservation of health, which may be afterwards of great use. Arbuthnot on Air and Aliment, Sanctorius on perspiration, Lemery on foods, and some others, may now be read, and a very little explanation will make them sufficiently intelligible to youth.

While they are reading natural history, might not a little gardening, planting, grafting, inoculating, etc., be taught and practiced; and now and then excursions made to the neighboring plantations of the best farmers, their methods observed and reasoned upon for the information of youth? The improvement of agriculture being useful to all, and skill in it no disparagement to any.

The *history of commerce,* of the invention of arts, rise of manufactures, progress of trade, change of its seats, with the reasons, causes, etc., may also be made entertaining to youth and will be useful to all. And this, with the accounts in other history of the prodigious force and effect of engines and machines used in war, will naturally introduce a desire to be instructed in *mechanics,* and to be informed of the principles of that art by which weak men perform such wonders, labor is saved, manufactures expedited, etc. This will be the time to show them prints of ancient and modern machines, to explain them, to let them be copied, and to give lectures in mechanical philosophy.

With the whole should be constantly inculcated and cultivated that *benignity of mind* which shows itself in searching for and seizing every opportunity to serve and to oblige; and is the foundation of what is called *good breeding,* highly useful to the possessor, and most agreeable to all.

The idea of what is *true merit* should also be often presented to youth, explained and impressed on their minds, as consisting in an inclination joined with an ability to serve mankind, one's country, friends, and family; which ability is (with the blessing of God) to be acquired or greatly increased by true learning; and should indeed be the great aim and end of all learning.